On Photography

What is photography? Is it a source of knowledge or an art? Many have said the former because it records the world automatically, others the latter because it expresses human subjectivity. Can photography be both or must we choose?

In *On Photography: A Philosophical Inquiry*, Diarmuid Costello examines these fascinating questions and more, drawing on images by Alfred Stieglitz, Berenice Abbott, Paul Strand, Lee Friedlander, James Welling, and Wolfgang Tillmans, among others, and the writings of Elizabeth Eastlake, Peter Henry Emerson, Edward Weston, Siegfried Kracauer, André Bazin, and Stanley Cavell. This sets the scene for the contemporary stand-off between "sceptical" and "non-sceptical" Orthodoxy in the work of Roger Scruton and Kendall Walton, and a New Theory of Photography taking its cue from László Moholy-Nagy and Patrick Maynard.

Written in a clear and engaging style, *On Photography* is essential reading for anyone interested in the philosophy of photography, aesthetics, art, and visual studies.

Diarmuid Costello is an Associate Professor of Philosophy and Co-Director of the Centre for Research in Philosophy, Literature and the Arts at the University of Warwick, UK.

Diarmuid Costello

On Photography

A Philosophical Inquiry

Routledge
Taylor & Francis Group
LONDON AND NEW YORK

First published 2018
by Routledge
2 Park Square, Milton Park, Abingdon, Oxon OX14 4RN

and by Routledge
711 Third Avenue, New York, NY 10017

Routledge is an imprint of the Taylor & Francis Group, an informa business

British Library Cataloguing-in-Publication Data
A catalogue record for this book is available from the British Library

Library of Congress Cataloging-in-Publication Data
Names: Costello, Diarmuid, author.
Title: On photography : a philosophical inquiry / by Diarmuid Costello.
Description: 1 [edition]. | New York : Routledge, 2017. |
Series: Thinking in action | Includes bibliographical references and index.
Identifiers: LCCN 2017021112 | ISBN 9780415684705 (hardback : alk. paper) | ISBN 9780415684491 (paperack : alk. paper) | ISBN 9781315266688 (e-book)
Subjects: LCSH: Photography–Philosophy.
Classification: LCC TR183 .C675 2017 | DDC 770.1–dc23
LC record available at https://lccn.loc.gov/2017021112

ISBN: 978-0-415-68470-5 (hbk)
ISBN: 978-0-415-68449-1 (pbk)
ISBN: 978-1-315-26668-8 (ebk)

Typeset in Joanna MT and Din
by Out of House Publishing

for three generations of photographers

Contents

List of plates ix

List of figures xi

Acknowledgements xiv

Introduction
On photography, then and now **1**
Photography's values: epistemic and/or aesthetic? 2
Philosophy of photography, old and new 5

One
Foundational intuitions and folk theory **9**
Nineteenth-century origins 10
Pictorial and pure photography 15
Modernism and the limits of photography 24
The emergence of mind-independence 37

Two
Aesthetic scepticism and its critics **52**
Aesthetic scepticism and its limitations 52
Photography and fictional competence 67
Origins of the New Theory 74
New Theory, restrictive and permissive 84

Three
Transparency and its critics **102**
Seeing directly and indirectly 103
Conceptual analysis and theory construction 107
Transparency and mind-independence 113
Photography and epistemic value 121

Conclusion
The unity of photography **141**
Autographic and allographic 141
Photographic art, agency, and exemplarity 145

Bibliography **153**

Index **161**

Plates

1 Gerhard Richter, *Lesende*, 1994. Oil on canvas, $20\frac{1}{8} \times 28$ in. (72×102 cm). Image © Gerhard Richter. Reproduced with permission of the artist.

2 Gerhard Richter, *Betty*, 1988. Oil on canvas, $40\frac{1}{8} \times 28\frac{3}{8}$ in. (102×72 cm). Image © Gerhard Richter. Reproduced with permission of the artist.

3 Édouard Manet, *Roses mousseuses dans un vase* [Moss roses in a vase], 1882. Oil on canvas, $22 \times 13\frac{5}{8}$ in. (55.9×34.6 cm). Credit: Sterling and Francine Clark Art Institute, Williamstown, Massachusetts, USA/Bridgeman Images.

4 Wolfgang Tillmans, *Freischwimmer 16*, 2003. Chromogenic print, on paper on board, $943 \times 707\frac{1}{2}$ in. ($2{,}395 \times 1{,}797$ cm). © Wolfgang Tillmanns. Image courtesy the artist and Maureen Paley, London.

5 Jeff Wall, *Dead Troops Talk (A Vision after an Ambush of a Red Army Patrol, near Moqor, Afghanistan, Winter 1986)*, 1992. Transparency in lightbox, $90\frac{1}{8} \times 164\frac{1}{8}$ in. (228.92×416.88 cm). The Broad Art Foundation.

6 Richard Mosse, *Ruby Tuesday*, 2011. Digital c-print, dimensions variable (48×60 in.; 121.9×152.4 cm). © Richard Mosse. Courtesy the artist and Jack Shainman Gallery, New York.

7 Minos Linea, Jupiter's moon Europa from the Galileo spacecraft. Image courtesy of NASA/Jet Propulsion Laboratory-Caltech.

8 James Welling, *Cascade*, 1980. Gelatin silver contact print, 4¾ × 3¾ in. (12 × 9.5 cm). Courtesy the artist and David Zwirner, New York/London.

9 James Welling, 9818, 2009. Inkjet print on rag paper, 33⅔ × 50½ in. (85.5 × 128.3 cm). Courtesy the artist and David Zwirner, New York/London. Philip Johnson Glass House is a site of the National Trust for Historic Preservation.

10 James Welling, 024, 2006. Chromogenic print, 46 × 37 in. (116.8 × 94 cm). Courtesy the artist and David Zwirner, New York/London.

11 James Welling, *FDB9*, 2009–2012. Inkjet print on rag paper, 48 × 40 in. (101.5 × 122 cm). Courtesy the artist and David Zwirner, New York/London.

12 James Welling, 0371, 2015. Inkjet print on rag paper, 42 × 63 in. (106.7 × 160 cm). Courtesy the artist, David Zwirner, New York/London, and Peter Freeman Inc., Paris.

Figures

Frontispiece Albert Renger-Patzsch, *Töpferhände*, 1925. Gelatin silver print, 7 1/16 × 9 1/16 in. (18 × 23 cm). Archiv Ann and Jürgen Wilde. xvi

0.1 Walker Evans, *Factory and Smokestacks, New York City*, 1928–1930. Film negative dimensions 1 5/8 × 2 1/2 in. (4.13 × 6.35 cm). The Metropolitan Museum of Art, Walker Evans Archive, 1994 (1994.251.102). © Walker Evans Archive, The Metropolitan Museum of Art. 3

1.1 Peter Henry Emerson, *A Rushy Shore*, 1886. Platinum print, 7 3/16 × 11 7/16 in. (18.3 × 29.1 cm). Image: The Horace W. Goldsmith Foundation, The Metropolitan Museum of Art. 16

1.2 Alfred Stieglitz, *The Hand of Man*, 1902, printed 1910. Photogravure, 9 1/2 × 12 9/16 in. (24.2 × 31.9 cm). Alfred Stieglitz Collection, 1949. 20

1.3 Paul Strand, *Railroad Sidings, New York*, 1914. Photogravure, 12 1/2 × 9 1/2 in. (31.7 × 24.1 cm). © Aperture Foundation Inc., Paul Strand Archive. Reproduced with kind permission. 28

1.4 Paul Strand, *Iris, Georgetown, Maine*, 1928. Gelatin silver print, 9 9/16 × 7 5/8 in. (24.3 × 19.3 cm). © Aperture Foundation Inc., Paul Strand Archive. Reproduced with kind permission. 29

1.5 László Moholy-Nagy, *Untitled*, FGM.226, lost, Dessau, 1925–1928. Photogram on developing paper, (presumed) 9½ × 7⅙ in. (24 × 18 cm). © Hattula Moholy-Nagy/DACS 2016. 34

1.6 László Moholy-Nagy, *Untitled*, FGM.345, Chicago, 1939. Photogram on developing paper, 15¾ × 18 13/16 in. (40 × 47.8 cm). © Hattula Moholy-Nagy/DACS 2016. 35

2.1 Lee Friedlander, *Texas*, 2006, from the series America by Car, 1995–2009. Gelatin silver print, 15 × 15 in. (38.1 × 38.1 cm). Collection of the artist. © Lee Friedlander, courtesy Fraenkel Gallery, San Francisco. 62

2.2 Lee Friedlander, *Montana*, 2008, from the series America by Car, 1995–2009. Gelatin silver print, 15 × 15 in. (38.1 × 38.1 cm). Collection of the artist. © Lee Friedlander, courtesy Fraenkel Gallery, San Francisco. 63

2.3 Robert Frank, *U.S. 90, En Route to Del Rio, Texas*, 1955. New York, Metropolitan Museum of Art. Gelatin silver print, image 12⅝ × 8 7/16 in. (32.1 × 21.4 cm). Gift of Joyce F. Menschel, 2014 (2014.209.1). © 2016. Image copyright The Metropolitan Museum of Art/Art Resource/ Scala, Florence. 65

2.4 *King Kong*, 1933. Directed by Merian C. Cooper and Ernest B. Schoedsack. Film still. Licensed by: Warner Bros. Entertainment Inc. All Rights Reserved. 70

2.5 Frank Hurley, *An Episode after the Battle of Zonnebeke*, 1918, printed c. 1919. National Gallery of Victoria, Melbourne. Gelatin silver photograph, 14⅛ × 19⅛ in. (35.8 × 48.5 cm) irreg. (image); 14⅛ × 19¼ in. (36 × 48.8 cm) irreg. (sheet). Purchased NGV Foundation, 2008 (2008.366). 82

2.6 Garry Winogrand, *Los Angeles*, c. 1980–1983. Gelatin silver print, dimensions unspecified. Garry Winogrand Archive, Center for Creative Photography, University of Arizona. © The Estate of Garry Winogrand, courtesy Fraenkel Gallery, San Francisco. 91

3.1 Lee Friedlander, *Stems 1*, 1999. Gelatin silver print, paper dimensions 20 × 16 in. (50.8 × 40.64 cm). Collection of the artist. © Lee Friedlander, courtesy Fraenkel Gallery, San Francisco. 118
3.2 Lee Friedlander, *Stems 2*, 1999. Gelatin silver print, paper dimensions 20 × 16 in. (50.8 × 40.64 cm). Collection of the artist. © Lee Friedlander, courtesy Fraenkel Gallery, San Francisco. 119
3.3 Bill Brandt, *Nude, Campden Hill, London*, 1949. Gelatin silver print, 9½ × 7¾ in. (24.1 × 19.7 cm). © Bill Brandt Archive. 131

Endpiece Berenice Abbott, *Hands of Jean Cocteau*, 1927. Gelatin silver print, 6⅞ × 9¼ in. (17.5 × 23.5 cm). © 2017 Berenice Abbott/Commerce Graphics. Image: Getty Images. All rights reserved. 152

Acknowledgements

This book concerns a relatively small corner of my interests in photography: recent debates about the aesthetic and epistemic values of photography, and their roots in a particular way of thinking about its nature. Even so, I have amassed a large number of debts in its composition.

I would like to thank the Arts and Humanities Research Council for funding the "Aesthetics after Photography" research project (2007–2011), co-directed with Margaret Iversen of the University of Essex, and ably supported by our two research fellows, Dawn Wilson (née Phillips) and Wolfgang Brückle. This turned out to be a model of good collaboration, and I would like to acknowledge my co-editors on the resulting special journal issues: Iversen on "Photography after Conceptual Art" (*Art History* 32:5, 2009); Iversen and Joel Snyder on "Agency and Automatism: Photography as Art since the 1960s" (*Critical Inquiry* 38:4, 2012); and Dominic McIver Lopes on "The Media of Photography" (*Journal of Aesthetics and Art Criticism* 70:1, 2012). In 2011, Sarah Shalgovsky, Director of the Mead Gallery at the University of Warwick, invited me to curate what became "29 Pictures," the first mid-career retrospective of Hannah Starkey, thereby alerting me to a need I did not previously know I had. The Shpilman Institute of Photography, in Tel Aviv, supported early work on this book with one of its first "Philosophy and Photography" research fellowships.

During its writing I have benefited from great colleagues, both in the Department of Philosophy and the Centre for Research in Philosophy, Literature and the Arts at the University of Warwick, and the students on my "Philosophy of Photography" and "Aesthetics and Photography" courses over the years. The book benefited enormously from my presenting draft material at a number of seminars and workshops. I would like to single out Martin Seel's Kolloquium, at the Goethe Universität, Frankfurt, during my tenure as an Alexander von Humboldt research fellow, the Aesthetics Research Group at the University of Kent, with whom I have a longstanding connection, and "The New Philosophy of Photography" workshop at the Institute of Philosophy, University of London in 2015, funded by the British Society of Aesthetics. The audiences at all three helped me to tighten up the material that follows. I have also benefited from conversations over the years with a number of critics, historians, theorists, and philosophers working on photography, including Paloma Atencia-Linares, Wolfgang Brückle, David Campany, James Elkins, Jonathan Friday, Michael Fried, Gordon Hughes, Margaret Iversen, Karen Lang, Hans Maes, Patrick Maynard, Aaron Meskin, Bence Nanay, Charles Palermo, Martin Seel, Murray Smith, Joel Snyder, Scott Walden, Kendall Walton, Dawn Wilson, and especially Dom Lopes, with whom I have crossed and re-crossed paths over the last five years—most recently as a respondent to his *The Four Arts of Photography* and as co-author of a paper on James Welling. As anyone who knows Dom will know: he's a class act, and a tough one to follow.

Though many theorists seem to find it curiously hard to admit, I actually enjoy looking at photographs; indeed I far prefer doing so to theorizing about photography. But sometimes one needs to work something out of one's system. In my looking I have benefited from discussions with a number of photographic artists, including James Coleman, Silke Helmerdig, Melanie Manchot, Hannah Starkey, Jeff Wall, and especially James Welling. It will be obvious that Jim's work has proved a substantial spur to thought. When I first started working on photography, I recall thinking: either this is not photography and first-order critical practice is wrong; or it is photography front and centre, and philosophy needs to put its house in order. That it was the latter seemed obvious, at least to me.

Dom Lopes and Dawn Wilson read the manuscript in full, Murray Smith and Phillip Schink read it in part, and Paloma Atencia-Linares read it for the press. Katrin Flikschuh continues to put up with me. What more could one want?

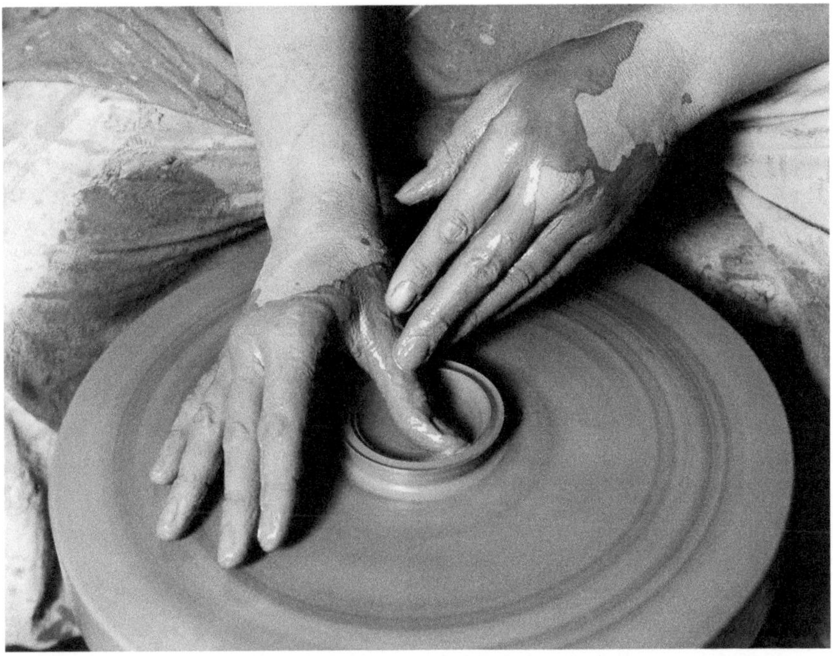

Frontispiece Albert Renger-Patzsch, *Töpferhände*, 1925. Gelatin silver print, 7 1/16 × 9 1/16 in. (18 × 23 cm). Archiv Ann and Jürgen Wilde.

Introduction

On photography, then and now

Forty years ago Susan Sontag published a book with the same title as this one. The chapters of Sontag's book first appeared as a series of essays in the *New York Review of Books*, and their content and style reflect this.[1] Comprising broad cultural, sociological, and psychological observations about the nature of photography, her remarks are often acute, sometimes tendentious, and typically asserted rather than argued. And though she cites Walter Benjamin, among other philosophers, her frame of reference is more cultural criticism than philosophy.

Since the publication of Sontag's book, photography has become an object of sustained philosophical attention for the first time. It is surprising that it took so long: philosophy of film has been a staple of aesthetics for some time, even though its invention succeeded that of photography by more than half a century. Yet, despite photography's historical priority, almost all influential theories of photography that pre-date Sontag's book—whether by philosophers, cultural critics, or film theorists—were conceived as propaedeutics to more developed theories of film. This is true, for example, of Walter Benjamin, Siegfried Kracauer, André Bazin, and Stanley Cavell. Today, by contrast, philosophy of photography is a recognizable field of aesthetics in its own right, with its own foundational texts, canonical authors, and topics of debate. This book reflects these transformations in how photography has been conceived and written about since Sontag's day. It is not an exercise in cultural criticism. It aspires to treat photography philosophically, rather than sociologically, psychologically, or what is sometimes generically called "theoretically." But to do so without being insensitive, as so much philosophy is, to either history or artistic uses of the medium.

Photography's values: epistemic and/or aesthetic?

So what is it to treat photography philosophically? To date, philosophy of photography has primarily concerned aesthetic and epistemic questions, and their implications for one another. That is, broadly speaking, questions concerning the artistic value of photography, and questions concerning its value as a means of gaining knowledge about the world.[2] Of course, this is not all that philosophy of photography could, or indeed should, encompass: it might equally address questions about the politics of certain kinds of photography or the morality of depicting certain kinds of subject-matter, metaphysical questions about the identity of photographic works of art, or ontological questions about the unity of photography. With the exception of the latter, however—prompted largely by the shift from analogue to digital photography—such questions have yet to be seriously debated by philosophers. This is not to say that they should not be more widely debated than they are: it is hard to deny that mainstream philosophy of photography has been hobbled by its limited scope to date.

Be that as it may, it is notable that the standard answers to those epistemic and aesthetic questions that have held sway to date seem incompatible. On the one hand, photography is standardly portrayed as epistemically privileged vis-à-vis other forms of imagery: we typically, although not exclusively, rely on photographic rather than "manugraphic" (hand-drawn) images for evidence and information.[3] Legal, forensic, archival, medical, and scientific contexts all make extensive use of photography, on the basis of which we make what we take to be justified inferences about the world. On the other hand, photography is now regarded by all but the most unapologetic sceptic as an art: we appreciate it aesthetically, savouring the stylistic and other differences between the work of various photographers and schools. In the hands of such a master as Walker Evans, even the most straight, seemingly documentary image can feel as meant, articulate, and expressive as anything in painting.

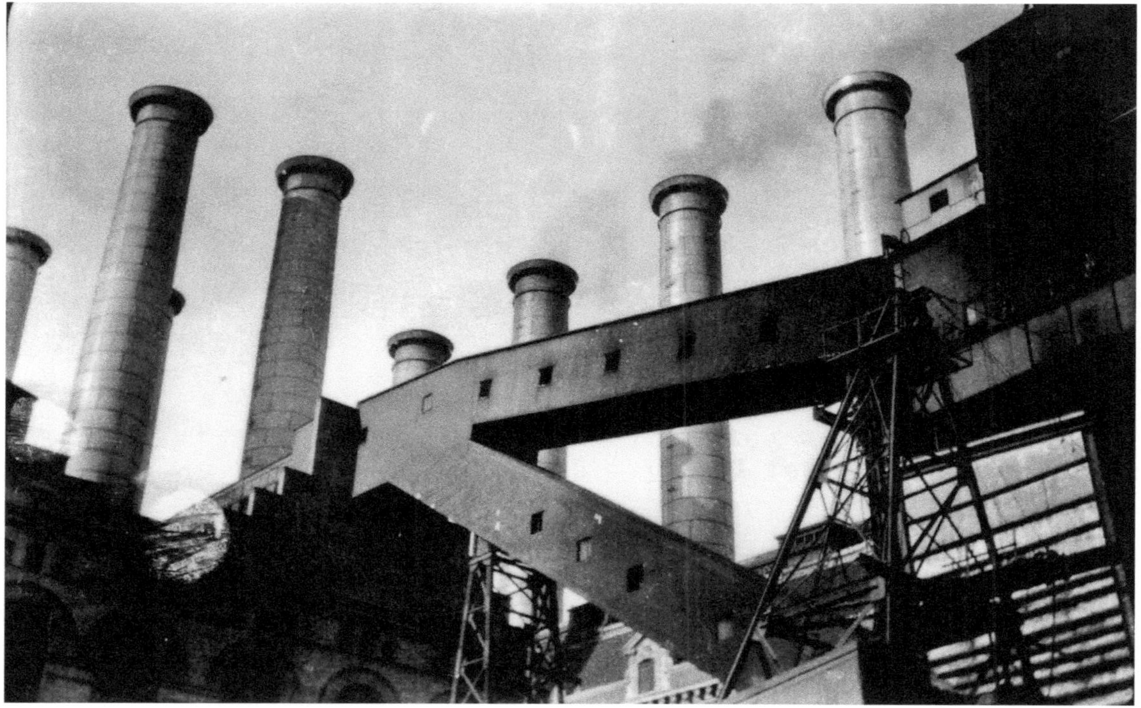

Figure 0.1 Walker Evans, *Factory and Smokestacks, New York City*, 1928–1930. Film negative dimensions 1⅝ × 2½ in. (4.13 × 6.35 cm). The Metropolitan Museum of Art, Walker Evans Archive, 1994 (1994.251.102). © Walker Evans Archive, The Metropolitan Museum of Art.

It is not hard to see that these two natural thoughts about photography are in tension. Photographs are taken to be accurate sources of information about the world because a machine rather than a human being does the recording, and machines do not lie, have subjective preferences or opinions, or suffer from false beliefs or selective attention. When they are selective or partial in what they reproduce, they are selective systematically, in ways that can be isolated and accounted for: black-and-white films reproduce tonal but not colour values; different aperture and shutter settings generate legible images within specific tolerances of depth of field and speed of movement, and so on. Anyone who understands the variables applied will know what one can and cannot legitimately infer on the basis of the resulting images. Photography is objective, in other words, precisely because it mechanically brackets the kind of subjectivity that differentiates one artist's work from another's. By contrast, images made by hand are often selective in non-systematic ways that cannot be isolated or easily accounted for. Imagine a painting that depicts a real cluster of farm buildings among fields, in which three isolated oaks dot the landscape. Do we have good warrant to infer, solely on the basis of viewing the painting, that there were just that number and kind of trees, of just that size, just so disposed? Perhaps it merely suited the painter's sense of composition to so arrange them.

If you believe that this is the sort of thing that painting typically permits but photography—or at least "pure" photography—typically rules out, in virtue of the way in which photographic images are generated, you will have difficulty accounting for, and perhaps even fully accepting the possibility of, photographic art. Because in that case, your conception of photography will significantly constrict the space of photographic agency. Conversely, if you believe that to deny the possibility of photographic art flies in the face of the evidence, and that there is no reason to believe that what holds for art in general does not also hold for photographic art in particular, you will have difficulty accounting for widespread intuitions about photographic objectivity. For we look to the work of particular artists for just those traces of subjectivity that their decisions about what to thematize and what to suppress, and how to go about doing so, reveal; but such choices will almost always compromise an image's neutrality and reliability as an information carrier. So photography's epistemic and aesthetic claims certainly appear to be in tension. Despite this, both have much to recommend them. Can both be true?

One response is to deny that this is a problem. Perhaps it is true that we can either have information-preserving pure photography or non-information-preserving impure photographic art. If so, photography can either be objective or artistic, but not both. So what? The problem with this response is that it unwittingly abets scepticism about photographic art. Saving the possibility of photographic art, but only at the cost of denying its purity, is to concede that whatever it is that makes photography art, it is not that it is photographic. Even when an artwork is a photograph, it is not art (at least in part) *because* it is a photograph; it is art *despite* being a photograph. What makes it art must lie elsewhere: were this not true, pure photography could be art. But is this the only response available?

Philosophy of photography, old and new

To find out, we need a better grip on how philosophers have understood the nature of photography. That is what I set out to provide in this book. Chapter 1 traces the historical and conceptual roots of what I call "Orthodox Theory" (or "Orthodoxy") back to photography's invention in the 1830s. Beginning with photography's pioneers, it moves through Victorian debates about photography's standing as art, turn-of-the-century skirmishes between pictorialists and advocates of the straight print, varieties of twentieth-century modernism, right up to post-war cultural criticism, which forms the immediate historical backdrop to the emergence of Orthodoxy proper. Throughout I focus on the competing conceptions of photography at stake in these debates, rather than particular movements, styles or oeuvres. My goal is to show how deep the roots of Orthodoxy run, and the extent to which the intuitions that underwrite it continue to inform not just what philosophers call "folk theory" (everyday wisdom), but criticism, theory, and philosophy of photography alike.

Chapters 2 and 3 track the philosophical fruition of such thought through the work of Roger Scruton and Kendall Walton, respectively, and the responses to which each has given rise. I divide these between "sceptical" and "non-sceptical" Orthodoxy, where whether a theory is sceptical or not turns on its implications for photography's standing as art. The former, in particular, has generated an impetus to what I call "New Theory." This takes its cue from the quite different starting point of Patrick Maynard's understanding of photography as a diverse family of technologies for marking surfaces with light and other radiations. Taken together, however, it is the work of Scruton and Walton and their commentators who remain, for better or worse, responsible for most of the more influential recent analytic philosophy of photography, writing that I believe often boils down to a formalization of folk wisdom that can be traced all the way back to photography's pioneers. Alfred Stieglitz summed up the outlook well in 1899:

> In the infancy of photography … it was generally supposed that after the selection of the subjects, the posing, lighting, exposure and development, every succeeding step was purely mechanical, requiring little or no thought. The result of this was the inevitable one of stamping on every picture thus produced the brand of mechanism.[4]

Note the reference to photography's infancy. Stieglitz clearly believed that enlightened opinion had moved beyond this caricature by the end of the nineteenth century. Sadly, much philosophical reflection on photography over the last 40 years has failed to rise to even this level. That said, there are significant differences among Orthodox commentators, not least concerning Orthodoxy's implications for photography's standing as art, and these differences need to be acknowledged. For this reason, distinguishing sceptical from non-sceptical variants of philosophical Orthodoxy, and their respective merits, is central to this book. Nonetheless, subtending these differences is a widely shared set of intuitions concerning the mechanical or automatic nature of the photographic apparatus, the natural or "mind-independent" causality of the photographic process, and the objectivity or epistemic privilege of the images resulting from this apparatus and process. Sometimes this whole cluster of ideas is bundled together in the idea of photography's "automaticity."

There is no denying that Orthodoxy presents a powerful, intuitively appealing picture of photography's epistemic advantage over other forms of depiction, one that continues to hold many philosophers in its grip. But it has its weaknesses, as well as its strengths: in particular, the difficulties it often faces doing justice to photographic art have motivated a new generation of philosophers to try to fashion a new theory. From the perspective of these "New Theorists" the Orthodox account is committed to a set of background beliefs about the nature of photography, taken over largely unreflectively from folk theory, that prevent its straightforward application to much photographic art. So either photographic art is a special case, in which case we are owed an explanation as to why that does not presuppose the truth of the Orthodox account—since that is precisely what is in question—or the difficulties that both Orthodoxy and folk theory alike face in accommodating the agency of photographic artists suggest that they may be based on a partial conception of the field in need of revision.

My goal, in addition to introducing readers to debates in these fields, is to assemble the resources for such a revision. These have in fact been available for some time, going back to Patrick Maynard's attempt to redirect philosophers' attention from the photographic product to the process underlying that product, but they are only now being built upon by a wider group of philosophers. The revisionist account is rooted in a new way of distinguishing between photographic and non-photographic processes, one that no longer turns on the contrast between machine and hand-made images. On the New Theory, these distinctions cut across one another. As a result, the New Theory has significant implications for Orthodox views of photographic agency, which have dovetailed neatly with folk theory to date. Because the New Theory rules in much that the old ruled out, it has no difficulty accommodating photographic art. But it does have a different burden to discharge. If the old theory explained photography's epistemic capacities, but fell down with respect to its artistic uses, the challenge for the new is to provide an alternative explanation of photography's epistemic capabilities. If it is to be taken seriously, it cannot secure photography's artistic standing on grounds that render its epistemic capacities inexplicable.

A good way to flush out one's own intuitions about such questions is to ask oneself two seemingly simple questions at the outset. What is a photograph? What is photography? Once you have an answer, however sketchy, to both in mind consider the relation between them. Chances are that you will have defined one or other term entirely passively. By this I mean that you will have either conceived photography as a means for delivering *photographs* (defined in such and such a way), or conceived photographs as the product of a process called *photography* (understood in such and such terms). Which you have done is a good indicator of which side of one of the main fault-lines in the philosophy of photography you fall on. If photography is the silent partner, and your answer biases towards getting clear about what a photograph is—especially if it focuses on what is special about the relationship between a photograph and what it is a photograph of—your intuitions align with philosophical Orthodoxy; if photographs are the silent partner, and your definition biases towards understanding photography—especially if it focuses on what is distinctive about the photographic process—your intuitions align you with the new kids on the block. In fact, there are pros and cons of starting either with the nature of photographs or with the nature of photography, and the risks are not dissimilar. For the former, the risk is unwittingly distorting the data by mistaking a sub-section of the field for the whole, perhaps by privileging a particular kind of example or use; for the latter, the risk is unwittingly distorting the data by mistaking a part of the process for the whole. Either way, one has to be wary of generalizing over insufficient cases or from partial conceptions.

Notes

1 Susan Sontag, *On Photography* (New York: Farrar, Straus and Giroux, 1977). More recently, a collection of Benjamin's essays on photography, edited by Esther Leslie, has appeared under the same title: Walter Benjamin, *On Photography* (London: Reaktion Books, 2015); but that has even less overlap with the aims of the current book.

2 I set aside questions about the relation between aesthetic and artistic values and qualities here.

3 Jonathan Friday, *Aesthetics and Photography* (Aldershot: Ashgate, 2002), pp. 38–42.

4 Alfred Stieglitz, "Pictorial Photography," in Beaumont Newhall (ed.) *Photography: Essays and Images* (London: Secker & Warburg, 1981), p. 164.

One

Foundational intuitions and folk theory

> How can we trace the nature of the photographic medium? … Historical movements cannot be grasped with the aid of concepts formed, so to speak, in a vacuum. Rather, analysis must build from the views held of photography in the course of its evolution—views which in some way or other must reflect actually existing trends and practices. It would therefore seem advisable first to study the historically given ideas and concepts. … [T]he principles and ideas instrumental in the rise of a new historical entity do not just fade away once the period of inception is over; on the contrary, it is as if, in the process of growing and spreading, that entity were destined to bring out all their implications.
>
> Siegfried Kracauer
> "Photography," from *Theory of Film: The Redemption of Reality*

What is perhaps most striking about the Orthodox account is just how close it is to folk theory of photography. But this is not surprising: for what I am calling "Orthodoxy" is essentially a philosophical formalization of intuitions about photography that can be traced all the way back to photography's inventors, early pioneers, and commentators. In their early form, these intuitions were typically expressed in terms of giving nature the means to depict herself, without the aid of a human draughtsman. So conceived, photography consists of self-generated "natural" images. Today, the same underlying thought is likely to be couched in terms of the "causal," "mechanical," or "automatic" aspect of photographic recording. It varies by author, but in each case seems intended as a contrast term to some perceived characteristic of humanly mediated depiction, perhaps "intentional," "hand-made," and "agential," respectively. Whatever its precise formulation, the emphasis on the *non-human* dimension of photography runs like a leitmotif through the writings of photographers, critics, art theorists, and philosophers alike.[1]

This chapter traces this pattern of thought from its origins in the 1830s, through nineteenth-century debates about straight versus pictorial photography and their inheritance by twentieth-Century skirmishes about "pure" photography, via mid-twentieth-century cultural criticism, up to the immediate pre-history of its formalization in recent analytic philosophical accounts. By its end, the depths of Orthodoxy's historical roots should be apparent, and we will be better placed to assess its strengths and weaknesses. Given how widespread the intuitions underpinning it are, it is hardly surprising that it has proved resilient. The question is whether these intuitions should command the assent that they do, and what explains their hold if not.

Nineteenth-century origins

It is generally held that photography was invented in the 1820s and 1830s, though whether this is true depends on what one means by "photography." The principles of the *camera obscura* (literally, dark room), the precursor to the modern camera, were documented as early as Leonardo; and Vermeer among others is widely believed to have employed one to make his paintings. So if photography is understood to mean the formation of detailed and life-like light images, it is at least three centuries older. This is not how photography is typically understood, because the images formed in a *camera obscura* are not static; they continue to change in accordance with changes in the scene projected. The problem faced by photography's nineteenth-century pioneers was not how to produce such images, but how to produce a light-sensitive surface that would record passing states of these images and, having done so, how to "fix" (render permanent or at least relatively stable) the images so recorded.

In the first half of the nineteenth century various sensitized surfaces were tried. Joseph Nicéphore Niépce is credited with fixing the first photograph on sensitized pewter plate in 1826, but the all-day exposure required rendered "heliography" (literally, sun-writing or drawing) impractical. Louis-Jacques Mandé Daguerre and William Henry Fox-Talbot, working independently of one another in France and Britain in the 1830s, solved this problem. The French Academy of Sciences and the Royal Society in London were notified of their respective inventions within a few weeks of each other in January 1839. Each secured one important aspect of modern photography: daguerreotypes, direct positives on silver-coated copper plate, were detailed but non-reproducible; calotypes, made on paper sensitized with silver and salt, were softer, but produced a paper negative from which multiple positives could be printed. These virtues were combined by Frederick Scott Archer's collodion wet plate process, in 1851, though the process was cumbersome, especially outside the studio, and would be superseded by various, easier to use, "dry" processes such as silver gelatin in the 1870s and 1880s.

My interest here is not primarily in the history of photography's technical evolution, however, but in how photography has (in part as a result) been conceived over the years. What stands out in reflection on photography from the first half of the nineteenth century is twofold: on the one hand, an emphasis on the "self-generated" aspect of photographic images; on the other, a stress on photography's accuracy, speed and labour-saving potential. The former comes out clearly in statements by its inventors, the latter in statements by its commentators. Niépce, in his "Memoire on the Heliograph," describes photography as an "automatic reproduction by the action of light … of the images obtained in the camera obscura."[2] Daguerre describes his eponymous process, in similar terms, as "spontaneous reproduction of the images of nature received in the camera obscura."[3] When he does so, it is clear that he intends "spontaneous" in its more philosophical sense as active and self-generating: "The Daguerreotype is not merely an instrument which serves to draw Nature; on the contrary it is a chemical and physical process that gives her the power to reproduce herself."[4] This shared concern was formalized in 1829, when Niépce and Daguerre jointly contracted to "fix the images which nature offers, without the assistance of a draughtsman."[5]

Meanwhile in England, Fox-Talbot conceived of "photogenic drawing" as a way of harnessing the "pencil of nature." As though to remove any doubt as to who or what was responsible for the resulting images, he subtitled his 1839 account, "The Process by Which Natural Objects May be Made to Delineate Themselves Without the Aid of the Artist's Pencil."[6] So understood, photogenic drawing is not to be attributed to human beings; it is a way of capturing, "by optical and chemical means alone," the images "impressed by nature's hand."[7] When Fox-Talbot succeeded in taking pictures of his country estate with a primitive camera in 1835, he described the achievement, entirely consistently, as "the first [house] that was ever known *to have drawn its own picture*."[8]

It is clear that all three took themselves to be inventing a process that allows nature to depict itself through the action of light. Elizabeth Eastlake neatly sums up Niépce's "heliography," Daguerre's "spontaneous" self-depiction, and Fox-Talbot's "pencil of nature" in her coinage, the "solar pencil."[9] The focus of photography's commentators tends to be somewhat different. When François Arago commends Daguerre's invention to the Chamber of Deputies, he extols the instrumental value of its speed and accuracy for archaeology, art, and science. What is crucial are the labour-saving benefits it offers a range of artistic, scientific, and documentary purposes by mechanizing out the technical training and manual skill required to depict the world.[10] Taken together with the claims of photography's pioneers, the value of mechanization turns out to be not merely speed and economies of scale—though both are important—but that by removing the human agent from the depictive process, nature is allowed to produce a more accurate image of herself than any artist could achieve. Essentially the same thought, but with the weight on machine rendering rather than self-made images, recurs as a central tenet of contemporary philosophical Orthodoxy.

The view comes to fruition in *sceptical* form for the first time in Eastlake's "Photography" (1857). The photographers' tendency to attribute their images to the sun is singled out when Eastlake asks "how far the sun can be considered an artist," and whether photography may be considered a "picturesque agent."[11] In answering, she distinguishes between the manual and intellectual aspects of making art. This is not new: Eastlake is consolidating a trope of contemporaneous writing. Nathaniel Parker Willis and Timothy O. Porter, writing just after photography's public announcement, in April 1839, acknowledge that while art's "merely imitative" functions are sure to be "nearly annihilated" by photography, the new technology cannot touch the "poetry of the mind," art's higher, imaginative capacities.[12] The Belgian painter Antoine-Joseph Wiertz, writing in 1855, divides the art of painting into the material and intellectual; daguerreotypy does not touch the latter, it merely removes the drudgery of the former: "Let it not be thought that the daguerreotype kills art. No, it only kills the work of patience and pays homage to the work of thought."[13] So construed, what photography actually does is liberate painting, by freeing conception ("architecture") from the drudgery of execution ("masonry"), which photography now takes over. A similar thought recurs a century later when the film theorist André Bazin, a key precursor of Orthodox theory, claims that photography frees the plastic arts, notably painting, to pursue their proper aesthetic function of representing spiritual reality ("true realism") by liberating them from our psychological need for *trompe l'oeil* illusion ("pseudo-realism"), the burden of which photography henceforth takes over.[14]

Eastlake entrenches the same distinction. Where true art *transforms* matter by suffusing it with mind, photography is only able to (literally) *re-present* it in raw form. Indeed, the more it perfects the recording of appearances celebrated by Arago, the more it surrenders the terrain of art proper: photography's conquest of appearances relegates it to replacing the manual facility that subtends (and thereby serves) art, but is not itself art. For in doing so photography only replaces artistic labour, not the work of imagination, conception, or vision. Because the camera records *unthinkingly*, impartially and non-selectively documenting whatever is put before it, photography provides a wealth of detail, but is incapable of unifying thought or articulating vision. Roger Scruton will say essentially the same thing 125 years later, in a foundational text of mainstream philosophy of photography—*pace* Stieglitz's confidence in conceptual progress. This inability to distinguish what is significant from what is not, and thereby guide the viewer's attention, precludes photography rising to the status of art proper:

> The power of selection and rejection … the marriage of his own mind with the object before him, and the offspring, half

> stamped with his own features, half with those of Nature, which is born of the union—whatever appertains to the free-will of the intelligent being, as opposed to the obedience of the machine—this … constitutes that mystery called Art, in the elucidation of which photography can give valuable help simply by showing what it is not.[15]

Eastlake brings together all those elements that photography's previous commentators celebrated—the speed and accuracy of photographic representation, the replacement of skill, and the removal of manual drudgery—combines these with the photographers' enthusiasm for images that appear to render themselves, and uses this as the ground to deny photography the status of art. It is a bravura performance, but the grounds of Eastlake's conclusion bear remarking: at bottom, the assumption seems to be that this *could not* be art, because this is not pictorial art as it has been hitherto understood.[16]

This response is the template for what has become a depressingly familiar reaction during the course of photography's brief history, and it leaves those who want to defend photography's artistic credentials with two options: to take issue with the Idealist assumption that what is valuable in art can only be what it expresses of human spirit, which Eastlake assumes, or the conception of photography according to which it fails to meet such an assumption.[17] The former is a live option, and one that has proved popular with many defenders of photography, especially in art theory and criticism.[18] I take the latter route here for two reasons. First, it allows me to remain neutral about theories of art; I want to show, contrary to what Eastlake and others believed, that photography can be a significant vehicle for human self-understanding, but without committing myself to this or any other general theory of art; I merely want to show that we have as yet seen no reason to think photography incapable of meeting Eastlake's own. Second, and perhaps more importantly, since it is internal to Eastlake's own starting point and assumptions, the demonstration is one that Eastlake & Co. could be expected to recognize the force of. It does not fault Eastlake anachronistically merely for holding a theory of art that expresses—as all theories, our own included, are wont to do—the doxa of its age.

Pictorial and pure photography

It is remarkable how many recurrent tropes of later thinking about photography's standing as art are set in play by these debates from photography's first two decades. The half-century or so after Eastlake's article, through to the clamour for a "pure" photography by century's end, was dominated by pictorialism, itself a response to the kind of worries about photography's artistic credentials that Eastlake entrenches. As a result, theoretical reflection on photography during these years often concurs with Eastlake's conception of what art requires, even as it tries to argue that photography does indeed provide it.

Henry Peach Robinson is a case in point. It is precisely because Robinson, an allegorical Victorian painter turned photographer, concurs with Eastlake's view of the ideation and subjectivity that art requires that he champions "combination printing."[19] Robinson inveighs against a purely mechanical realism that copies the disjointed facts of reality, untransformed by the intelligence and personal vision that art supplies, in terms of which Eastlake would have wholeheartedly approved: "A pure, unadulterated machine-made … photograph … is the most perfect specimen of realism the world could produce; useful in a thousand ways, it would not be art any more than a minute catalogue of the facts of nature, however full of insight is a poem."[20] The belief that photography has a special claim on realism runs right through to Walton. For good measure Robinson dresses his critique of it up, like Eastlake, with a bit of flummery about the "mystery" of art.

Peter Henry Emerson, naturalism's great advocate from the next generation, was having none of this. He took issue with Robinson's use of combination printing and artificial studio construction to inject the ideation supposedly required to redeem photography. Emerson argued that photographers should abandon studio construction and work outdoors, directly from nature: "Pictorial Art is man's expression by means of pictures of that which he considers beautiful in nature."[21] This should not be taken to imply that the photographer is constrained simply to record nature, however, as that would be to fall back into Eastlake's position: "[t]here is ample room for selection, judgement, and positing, and, in a

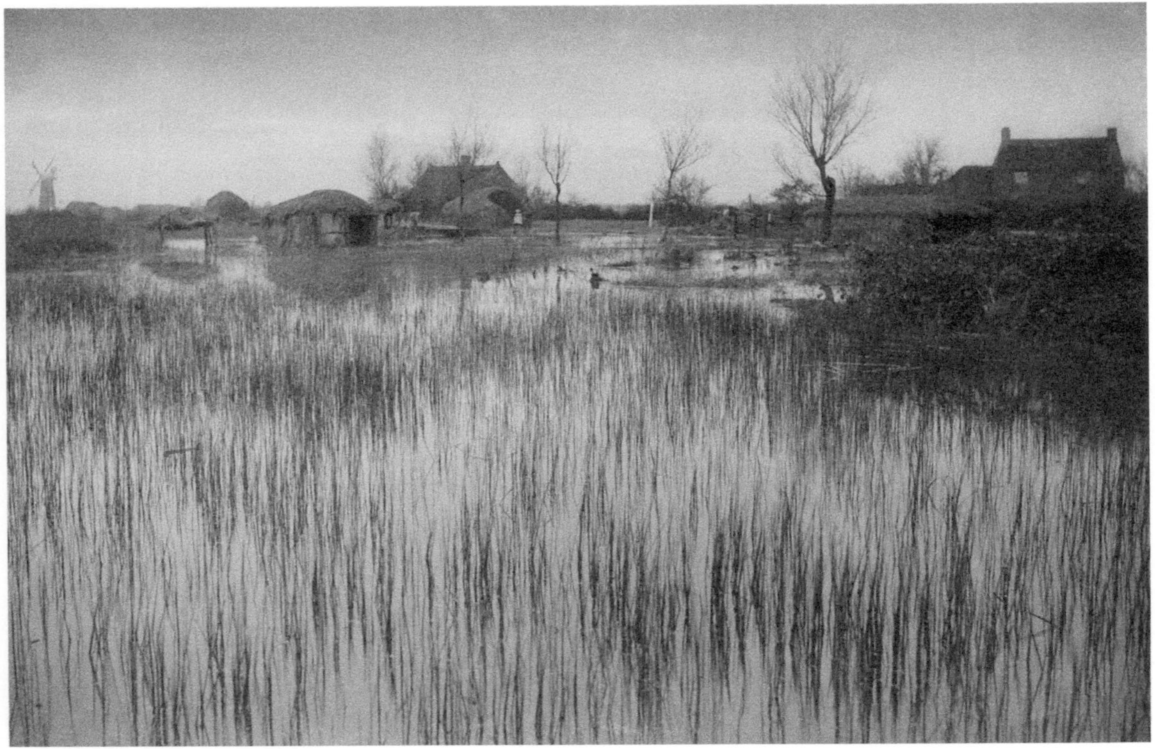

Figure 1.1 Peter Henry Emerson, *A Rushy Shore*, 1886. Platinum print, $7\frac{3}{16} \times 11\frac{7}{16}$ in. (18.3 × 29.1 cm). Image: The Horace W. Goldsmith Foundation, The Metropolitan Museum of Art.

word, in capable hands, a finished photograph is a work of art."[22] Focusing is one of the ways in which photographers may demonstrate this; photographers should dispense with the all-over focus that characterizes images combined from separately shot, discretely focused elements, so as to emulate natural vision, which is heavily weighted towards a central focus of attention. This affords the eye a natural resting place within the scene.[23] The challenge was to show—without resorting to Robinson's methods—that photography leaves room for artistic control. From Emerson's perspective, far from demonstrating that photography can be art, combination printing is an admission of defeat; it abandons the terrain of photography altogether.

Despite this, Emerson agrees with Robinson and Eastlake about the need for mystery and poetry in art: unlike Eastlake, however, he maintains that photography can provide it; and, unlike Robinson, he argues that it can be achieved by adhering to the principles of naturalistic photography, so need not be artificially introduced by studio artifice and combination printing. Emerson would later famously retract this view, on learning from the experiments of the chemists Ferdinand Hurter and Vero C. Driffield that photographers can exert no control over the relative density of tonal values during development. This meant photographers had far less control over the final image than Emerson had initially supposed:

> The limitations of photography are so great that … the medium must always rank … *lower* than any graphic art, for the individuality of the artist is cramped. … Control of the picture is possible to a *slight* degree, by varied focusing, by varying the exposure … by a certain choice in printing methods.
>
> But the all-vital powers of selection and rejection are *fatally* limited, bound by fixed and narrow barriers. No differential analysis can be made, no subduing of parts, save by dodging—no emphasis—save by dodging, and that is not pure photography, impure photography is merely a confession of limitations.[24]

Emerson's "renunciation" now aligns him, surprisingly, with Eastlake not only as to what art requires, but as to whether photography provides it. What remains unique to Emerson, however, is his emphasis on "pure" photography. Emerson is arguably the first to advance normative claims about what photography should and should not do, as opposed to descriptive claims about what it does or does not do, or modal claims about what it can or cannot do, given the nature of its medium, in a systematic way.[25] The standard difficulty such claims face is justifying their own authority: *why*, for example, are "dodging" and "burning"—selectively under- or over-exposing areas of a print during printing, often to compensate for under- or over-exposure in the plate or negative—not pure photography? Emerson declines to say. By contrast, controlling relative density of tonal values through development—had this been possible—would have been fine. Such claims, together with worries as to whether they are defensible, on principled grounds, recur throughout the history of photography.

They come to a head for the first time in turn-of-the-century debates between pictorialists and purists over the legitimacy of new methods such as the "gum print." Gum bichromate gave photographers the kind of control that Emerson craved, albeit in a manner that Emerson himself could never have sanctioned. By brushing emulsion tinted with pigments or dyes onto a heavy sheet of a paper, an image could be built up in layers, by recoating, re-exposing, and redeveloping the same print multiple times. To its champions, the gum print represented the final flowering of photography as art, offering the photographer-printmaker an unprecedented level of control over the final image. To its detractors, particularly advocates of the "straight" print, it was an unholy admixture of painting and photography: it was not always clear, when looking at the work of leading exponents, such as Edward Steichen or Robert Demachy, whether one was looking at a photograph, a hand-rendered print, or even a watercolour. Because the method allowed areas to be worked up or taken back locally, more or less painterly effects could be achieved, and because none of this need respect initial exposure, the result was neither "straight," nor "pure."

In 1899 Alfred Stieglitz, at this point still an advocate of the new methods, celebrated the "plastic nature" of plate development and printing that such processes engendered: "the photographer of today enters practically every field that the painter treads, barring that of colour."[26] Stieglitz recognized that as photographers' processes approximated those of painters, they would increasingly need a painter's aptitudes and abilities; like the painter's, the photographer's handwork needs to be underpinned by poetic conception, a sense of composition, a knowledge of and feeling for tonality in nature. Notice the remarkable reversal from only half a century earlier: for the first time, the very aspects of painting as an intellectual activity ("poetry of mind," imagination, conception, and so on) that Wiertz and Eastlake believed photography—conceived mechanically—had liberated in painting, now re-emerge as the preserve of photography itself. Nonetheless, the reversal is consistent with that earlier reasoning: photography, as pursued by artists such as Steichen and Demachy, effectively just *is* painting to Stieglitz's mind. Note that exactly the same logic underpins the more recent reception of digital photography as "painting with pixels." What one learns, when one looks into the history, is just how little debates about photography have changed.

Advocates of the "straight print" refused to accept such work as photography. A year after Stieglitz's article appeared, the architectural photographer Frederick H. Evans, a champion of "pure" photography, rejected excessive handwork as alien to photography. Beyond limited retouching to remove flaws and technical blemishes, the print should respect the original exposure, and be otherwise free of both retouching and dodging: "too much time is spent in trying to make bad negatives yield good prints, and they will not. Plain prints from plain negatives is … pure photography."[27] Here Evans is ventriloquizing Emerson, who famously quipped: "retouching is the process by which a good, bad, or indifferent photograph is converted into a bad drawing or painting."[28] Good work in bichromate is, by contrast, a testament to painterly rather than photographic abilities, as the work of the painter-photographer Steichen demonstrated. For Evans, as for Emerson, initial exposure is everything. The true art in photography resides in getting the initial exposure, and with it the plate or negative, right.

Emerson and Evans did not, however, have things all their own way. In his 1907 broadside, Robert Demachy, a fellow-traveller of Steichen and Stieglitz, sets out the case for the defence. Demachy's goal is to show that only a hand-worked print can be art, and he bases his argument on a familiar contrast between the objectivity of

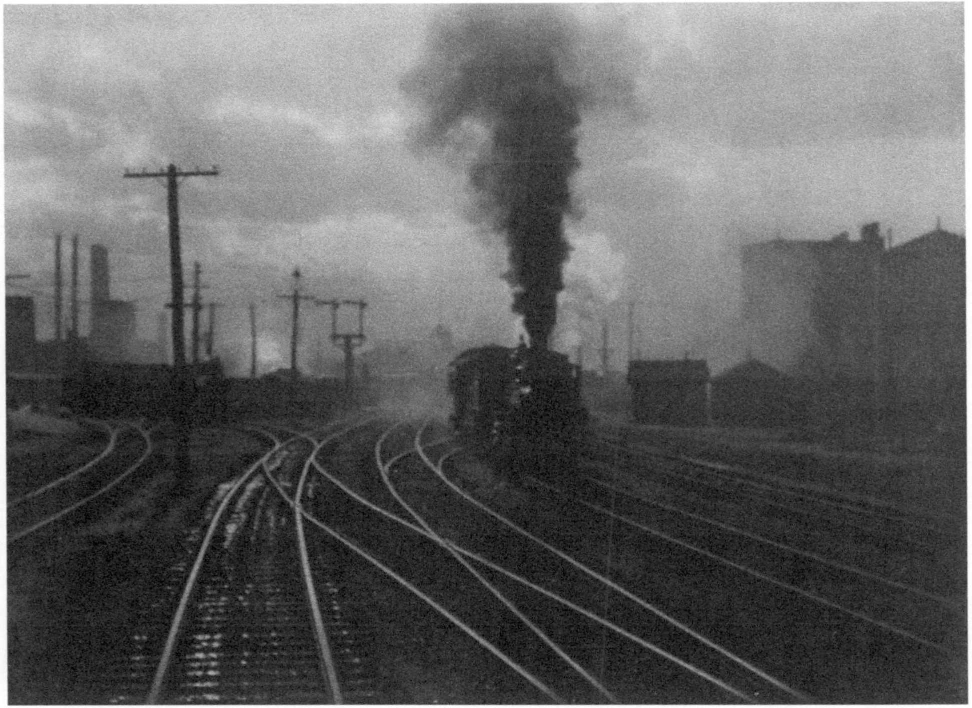

Figure 1.2 Alfred Stieglitz, *The Hand of Man*, 1902, printed 1910. Photogravure, $9\frac{1}{2} \times 12\frac{9}{16}$ in. (24.2×31.9 cm). Alfred Stieglitz Collection, 1949.

the camera and the subjectivity of the artist. The camera itself, being a copying machine, can only relay what nature provides. But

> [a] work of art must be a transcription, not a copy, of nature. The beauty of the motive in nature has nothing to do with the quality that makes a work of art. This special quality is given by the artist's way of expressing himself. … [T]here is not a particle of art in the most beautiful scene of nature. The art is man's alone, it is subjective not objective.[29]

Both Demachy's reasoning, and his idealist assumptions about art, will be familiar from Eastlake and Robinson; if there is to be art, there must be subjective expression, and this requires a perceptible intervention by the artist: "this mysterious something, this thumb-mark of the living, thinking, and feeling artist."[30] But this is precisely what printing straight from a straight negative or plate precludes. The result can only be a copy, and a copy cannot be art.

Taking a leaf out of the philosopher's playbook, Demachy asks his readers to imagine two photographers, one an inept bungler, the other consummately skilled: give them exactly the same materials; set their cameras up in exactly the same way, under exactly the same conditions, in front of exactly the same scene—to the point that the bungler places his tripod legs in the dents left by the master's. Of necessity, they will return with the same results. The results would only be distinguishable were the two photographers to work on their plates, thereby forfeiting the straight print. Only then would artistically relevant differences arise, because only then "*the man* has intervened in both cases."[31] Demachy draws two lessons from this thought experiment: "It shows that a beautiful straight print may be made by a man incapable of producing a work of art, and that a straight print cannot possibly be a work of art even when its author is an artist, since it may be identical to that made by a man who is no artist."[32]

Though Demachy delivers this argument with considerable brio, examined closely, it smuggles in everything required to generate his preferred conclusion at the outset. The goal is to demonstrate that the straight print cannot be art, and the thought experiment claims to establish this by showing that when everything is held constant there can be no difference in results between a bungler and an artist. And this is true. But the relevant question—if everything is held constant to the point of telling the bungler exhaustively what to do—is *who* makes the prints in question? Knowing how to set up the camera, which lens to use, how to frame the scene, and the best moment to expose the plate—given the conditions, point of view, and intended result—are all part of taking the picture. Indeed to know all this, and be able to put it into practice, just is to photograph like a master. As such it is *internal* to making the photograph; it does not precede it. Granted: Demachy's thought experiment reminds us that feeding the same inputs into the same mechanism under the same conditions will generate the same outputs. But this is hardly news: given a mechanism designed, like the camera, to deliver standardized results (and assuming that it is functioning correctly) how could it not? What the thought experiment does not give us reason to think, however, is that the second print is made by the bungler; instead it suggests that it is made by the master, who uses the bungler as a closely supervised pair of external hands to execute the print remotely. For the same reasons, it does not show that a straight print cannot be art because it can be identical to the work of a bungler: what it actually suggests is that, when everything is held constant, two works by the master will be identical.

As for Demachy's claims about the hand-worked print: were the thought experiment framed consistently, the master would also have to guide the bungler's hand to the point of executing the hand-work remotely, as this is what he does in the case of exposure. But of course this would not generate the desired conclusion. Under these conditions the bungler's interventions would again mimic the master's; indeed, as before, they would just *be* the master's. In his reply, Evans notes that Demachy's conception of the straight print is a caricature: no actual straight print would count as such by the criteria that he employs. Calling a print "straight" merely requires that the image's photographic nature be respected: "the photographic aspect should never be injured … it must suggest what it really is, a something due to the camera and lens and printing paper, plus an artist controlling every stage of the work." As to what such control amounts to, Evans lists the numerous ways in which photographers may control subject-matter, lighting, time and nature of exposure, filtering, developing, printing, spotting, even mounting and display, asking in conclusion: "Where are the mechanics of photography in all this?"[33]

By insisting on the degree of control that even pure photography permits, Evans is responding to a prevailing worry about the possibility of photographic art, and at the same time anticipating twentieth-century debates. One assumption of nineteenth-century debates, from Eastlake on, is that genuine art requires the artist to intervene in a way that can be tracked in their work. If this is true, and it is also true that pure photography precludes such intervention, then the straight print cannot be art. This is Demachy's reasoning: if the photograph is to be pure, the photographer must refrain from intervention. But if the photographer refrains from intervention there can be no subjective expression, and where there is no subjective expression there can be no art. Conversely, if the photographer does intervene and in so doing expresses himself, the result may be art, but it can no longer be (pure) photography. In sum: purity precludes intervention, but art requires it. The argument is intended to present advocates of pure photography with a dilemma: accept that transgressing the constraints of the medium, narrowly construed, is the price to pay for making art; or give up one's pretensions to making art as the cost of maintaining one's purity.

Is the reasoning that generates the dilemma compelling? It depends on what is meant by "intervention." To see this, one needs to grasp that Demachy and Evans are addressing different questions. Demachy is concerned with what is art and what is not. His question is: what does a photographer have to do to make art? Evans is concerned with what is photography and what is not. His question is: what does a photographer have to do to make (pure) photographs? Demachy's answer is: demonstrate his artistry in the photographic process. Evan's answer is: respect the photographic nature of that process. Need these two answers be in conflict? Is it inconceivable that one could demonstrate one's artistry in *how* one respects the photographic process? Because Demachy takes that process to be entirely mechanical, there is no "how" to examine. Intervention is something extra-photographic that one does on or to the photographic materials, which are merely the support for that activity. Evans, by contrast, takes how one handles those materials to permit considerable artistry. As a result, he does not share Demachy's views about what artistic expression requires of photographers. For Evans, artists can express themselves in how they handle the materials and processes proper to photography. This is intervention enough. Purity only precludes certain forms of "extra-photographic" intervention, but there are other kinds of control and these may be sufficient to track what the artist has done, and thereby understand what he or she is trying to express.

Modernism and the limits of photography

Precisely what counts as photographic and extra-photographic—and hence "proper" or "improper" to photography—is the defining question of twentieth-century photographic modernism. Though the roots of the latter can be traced back, via turn-of-the-century debates about pure photography and the straight print, to Emerson's normative claims about what photographers should and should not do, the art critic Carl Sadakichi Hartmann is the first, in 1904, to frame the question in its characteristic modernist form: "every medium of artistic expression has its limitations. We expect an etching to look like an etching, and a lithograph to look like a lithograph, why then should not a photographic print look like a photographic print?"[34] By borrowing freely from the other arts, rather than establishing its own credentials, photography only succeeds in diminishing itself as a medium for expression in its own right. Instead of inflating the expressive capacity of photography artificially, by means of handwork, authentic photographic expression can only be achieved photographically, by means of what the medium allows: "Why do they [advocates of the gum, glycerine, and photo-etching processes associated with the Photo-Succession] obstinately insist on carrying mediums farther than they go?"[35] Hartmann's advice, like Emerson's and Evans's before him, is to focus one's energies instead on getting the negative right, so that it requires no manipulation. Only this will make photography more rather than less artistic, which is to say artistic in a manner *fitting* to photography. This is the archetypal modernist solution: photography is at its best when it is most itself, and what is "most itself" is whatever differentiates it from, rather than what it has in common with, other artistic media. What this might be is the question that modernist critics and photographers now seek to answer.

Given the basic animus of modernism—that the arts have distinct media, and the best modern art tends to thematize what is unique to those media—the answers of modernists are unified by a strong antipathy for anything perceived to muddy the waters between the arts. Disputes along such obvious, and potentially porous, borders as photography/painting and photography/printmaking tend to generate the most heat. Very little anxiety is expressed, by comparison, about photography's relation to music or sculpture, presumably on the assumption that these are borders that do not need policing. Leading the charge, in 1917, is Paul Strand: "the full potential power of every medium is dependent upon the purity of its use," by which measure, "the introduction of hand work and manipulation is merely the expression of an impotent desire to paint."[36] Edward Weston, his fellow American, is still pursuing the theme a quarter of a century later: "each medium of expression imposes its own limitations on the artist—limitations inherent in the tools, materials, or processes he employs."[37] Properly grasped, such limitations are spurs to artistic creativity, not constraints to be avoided; this is what the painter-photographers of the nineteenth century failed to realize. Like (Frederick) Evans, Weston recognizes that the turn to handwork was a defensive reaction to the worry that "the straight photograph was purely the product of a machine and therefore not art," a worry that led photographers to "taking a camera to make a painting" even though this was "incompatible with the logic of the medium."[38]

Though the negative accounts of modernists converge on rejecting anything that does not respect the (alleged) constraints of its medium, their positive accounts have slightly different emphases. The two most worked out are those of Strand and Weston.[39] For Strand, the "very essence of photography" is "an absolute unqualified objectivity."[40] Strand's commitment to "objectivity" is just a pugnacious expression, delivered in the characteristically strident tones of the modern period, of a view that runs from Arago to Walton, according to which photography is an objective record of how things stood in the world at a particular moment of time. But if this is really photography's essence, what distinguishes it from mere recording? Here Strand comes into his own:

> It is in the *organization* of this objectivity that the photographer's point of view toward Life enters in, and where a formal conception born of the emotions, the intellect, or of both, is as inevitably necessary for him, before an exposure is made, as for the painter before he puts brush to canvas.[41]

This emphasis on a particular organization of objectivity, reflective of the photographer's particular outlook on life, and required of the photographer *prior to* exposure, anticipates the notion of pre-visualization standardly attributed to Edward Weston. "Absolute, unqualified objectivity," so understood, is anything but bare recording. In Strand's own work it is the vehicle of a powerful personal vision: his early cityscapes are characterized by striking compositions, strong lighting, stark shadows, and bold, bordering on abstract, design. For just this reason, however, it is hard to regard "unqualified, absolute objectivity," given that this implies the kind of neutrality to which scientific, forensic or medical imaging might aspire, as adequate to what he was about. Both his work and his conception of photography are much more passionate than impartial. The goal is always to put the camera, that "very wonderful machine," at the service of a particular photographer's expressive goals.[42] This comes out clearly in the terms in which he celebrates other photographers: David Octavius Hill's photographs are "the most extraordinary assertion of the possibility of the utterly personal control of a machine"; late Stieglitz is the "crystallization of the photographic principle, the unqualified subjugation of a machine to the single purpose of expression."[43] Strand regrets that so few photographers have grasped this:

> Without the slightest realization that in this machine, the camera, a new and unique instrument had been placed in their hands, photographers have in almost every instance been trying to use it as a short cut to an accepted medium, painting. … We find all through the work done … a singular lack of perception and respect for the basic nature of the photographic machine. At every turn the attempt is made to turn the camera into a brush, to make a photograph look like a painting, an etching, a charcoal drawing, or whatnot, like anything but a photograph.[44]

The worry driving this flight from camera's true nature is misplaced, given that the machine itself is "a passive and innocent party." "The control of its mechanism and materials, the fineness and sensitivity of its accomplishment are those of man."[45] We are back in the company of Emerson and Evans: photographs are "products of an intelligence and spirit channelled through a machine."[46] Just what Eastlake sanctioned photography for precluding, Strand now celebrates it for achieving, but the underlying logic remains unchanged: 65 years after Eastlake, it continues to run along tracks laid down in its first two decades.

Weston's "Seeing Photographically," from 1943, provides the other signal account of photographic specificity from its modernist heyday—though the basic idea behind it was already in place some 20 years earlier. In the lecture "Random Notes on Photography," given in June 1922 to the Southern Californian Camera Club, Weston's account of "pre-visualization" is already substantially worked out: "I see my platinum print in the ground glass in all its desired qualities, before my exposure—and the only excuse I make for after manipulation, shading, dodging, retouching is the possibility of losing a different position of expression by the delay in correcting some minor fault."[47] Gratuitous handwork, by contrast, is "devitalizing—texture-destroying—prostituting. ... Photography is a medium destroyed in value through manual interference."[48]

Weston's pre-visualization thesis does, however, add something new to the debate or, if not strictly new, it makes concrete and explicit what remained implicit in Strand. We are familiar, from Emerson and Evans, with the importance of getting the negative right. Pre-visualization, like Ansel Adams's more technical zonal system of exposure, is one way of explaining how this is to be achieved, by taking a step back, *prior to* the point at which defenders of the Orthodox account assume the photographic process begins.[49] But the argument Weston gives for its necessity is interesting in its own right. It rests on two observations, one about the photographic process, the other about its products. Rather than stressing the mechanical nature of the photographic apparatus, as almost everyone else had done, Weston instead draws attention to its speed—the fact that it is too quick to allow for corrections once under way. This is significant because the mechanical nature of the photographic apparatus,

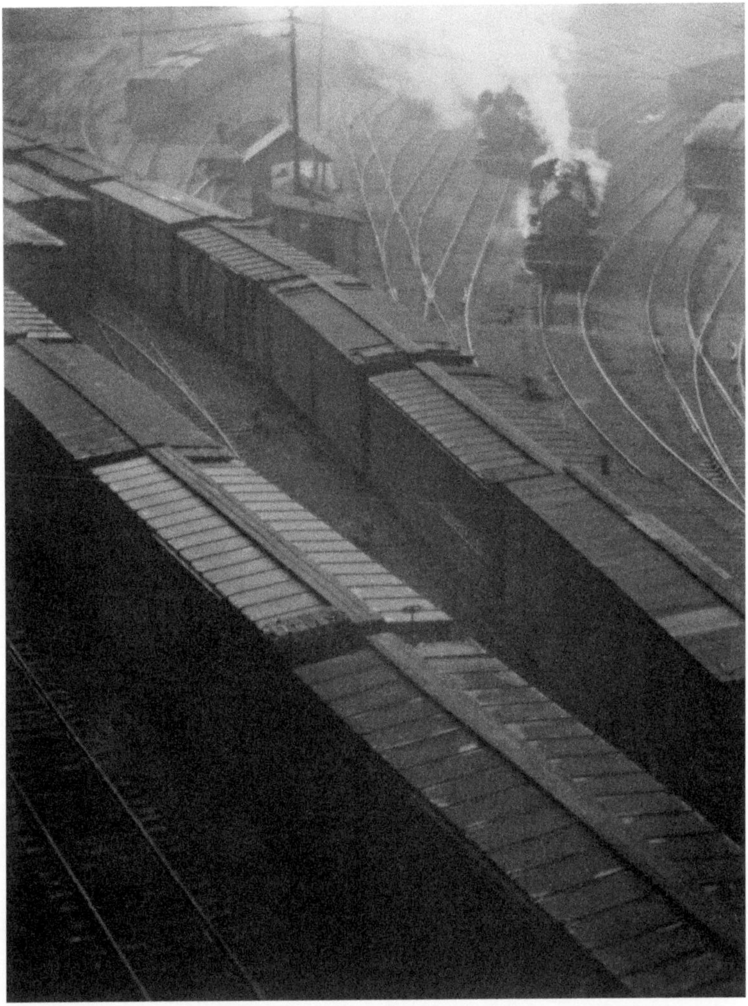

Figure 1.3 Paul Strand, *Railroad Sidings, New York*, 1914. Photogravure, 12½ × 9½ in. (31.7 × 24.1 cm). © Aperture Foundation Inc., Paul Strand Archive. Reproduced with kind permission.

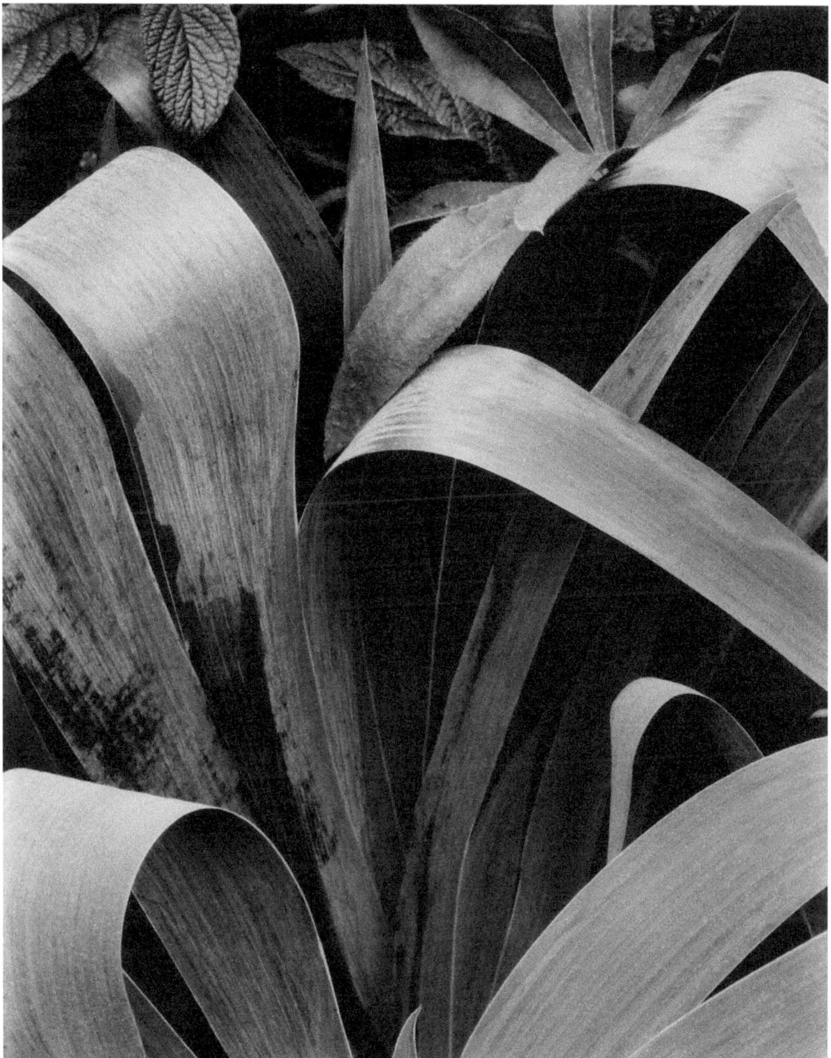

Figure 1.4 Paul Strand, *Iris, Georgetown, Maine*, 1928. Gelatin silver print, $9\frac{9}{16} \times 7\frac{5}{8}$ in. (24.3 × 19.3 cm).

as Orthodoxy understands it, rules out intervention in principle; the implication of Weston's account is that Orthodoxy confuses mechanism with speed. But a quick process only rules out intervention contingently: should we speed up, or it slow down, the difficulty lapses?[50] About the photographic image he emphasizes its precision, detail, and tonal variation, but again alights on something original: that the analogue photographic image is made up entirely of grain, rather than lines or masses. Indeed, it is this fineness of grain that is responsible for the precision, detail, and tonal gradation that are so valued in silver gelatin prints.

Taken together, the two observations explain the need for pre-visualization: if the recording process is too quick to allow corrections to be made once initiated, and corrections made after the fact, by painting on the negative or print, destroy the grain that gives photographs their distinctive quality and value, successful pre-visualization removes the need for both. In Weston's famous formulation: "*the finished print must be created in full before the film is exposed.*"[51] Because the constraints of the medium require that any photograph that is not an accident be visualized in advance, it is to the print that we turn to assess whether a photographer has succeeded. If you want to know what the photographer intended, or was trying to express, look to the print; if they have succeeded (and you are a competent judge), it will be apparent.

This is arguably the first response in the history of photographic theorizing to meet the worries of the sceptic head on, by indicating both the direction in which to look for a theory of photographic appreciation, and why. Given the importance that pre-visualization plays in Weston's response to the sceptic, the most important skill that photographers must cultivate is the ability to "see photographically": that is, "to see his subject-matter in terms of the capacities of his tools and processes, so that he can instantaneously translate the elements and values in a scene before him into the photograph he wants to make."[52] Thus, from the persistent worry that photography's mechanical substrate allows insufficient control to be art, Weston draws a pleasingly novel conclusion: rather than concluding that the pictorialists were simply wrong, he concedes that they were right in their diagnosis, but wrong in their prognosis. What aesthetic scepticism shows is not that photographers need to resort to handwork to dignify their productions as art but, rather, that control needs to be exercised *upstream* of the exposure that gets the mechanical process under way. The pictorialists' mistake was not to worry about mechanism, but to address this worry too late. Weston does not actually say this, but it is the logic of his position vis-à-vis earlier debates nonetheless.

This also explains why Weston, like his compatriot at Group f.64, Ansel Adams, is so relaxed about dodging and burning, unlike proto-modernists such as Emerson and Evans.[53] So long as this takes place "within the limits of his medium, without resorting to any method of control that is not photographic (i.e., of an optical or chemical nature), the photographer can depart from literal recording to whatever extent he chooses."[54] Because, undertaken according to these constraints it will not—unlike brushwork—overwrite the grain that gives silver gelatin prints their distinctive quality and appeal. Pre-visualization thereby liberates Weston from the tyranny of the right exposure and the perfect negative. Rather than make a fetish of exposure, as embodied by the negative, the photographer should instead cultivate an appreciation of her process as a whole so that, working backwards from the desired result, she can do whatever is necessary to realize it—until doing so becomes second nature.

In these respects, Weston can be claimed as an unexpected harbinger of the New Theory. For rather than focusing on the photograph, or what is special about the photograph's relationship to what it is of, he focuses instead on what is special about the *activity* of taking photographs, given the nature of the process (taken in its entirety) that generates them. And he understands that process as starting well before exposure.

Siegfried Kracauer takes up where Strand and Weston leave off: his "basic aesthetic principle" is that "achievements within a particular medium are all the more satisfying aesthetically if they build from the specific properties of that medium … a product that, somehow, goes against the grain of its medium—say by imitating effects more 'natural' to another medium—will hardly prove acceptable."[55] This is as pure an expression of modernist doctrine as one could want, and Kracauer sets out to locate these properties "specific" to the medium of photography in the opening chapter of his *Theory of Film* (1960).

What Kracauer adds to modernist medium-specificity are his observations about the new perception of the world that photography affords. The photographic record is capable of expanding our vision and conception of the world, whether by showing it to us from strange and surprising new points of view, or by exploiting the capacities of photography to show us what is either too fast or too small for natural vision to make out.[56] Think of microphotography, aerial reconnaissance images, high-speed photography of atomic bomb blasts, or images of the earth as seen from space. All show the world in a way that it had never been seen before, and with an impact that only something with photography's presumed objectivity and epistemic privilege could secure. By shaking up past certainties—both visual and ideological—Kracauer claims, such images help us "acclimatize" to the technological age in which we now live. This is close to Walter Benjamin's claim that the primary cultural significance of photography and especially film is its function as a means of "adapting" or "training" perception for the challenges of urban modernity.[57]

Perhaps for this reason, Kracauer, like Benjamin, is attentive to other (non-realist) modernisms, such as the "experimental" modernism of László Moholy-Nagy and Man Ray. Unlike Benjamin, although he acknowledges that abstract and camera-less photography, and even photomontage, dispense with handwork in the pictorialist sense, Kracauer nonetheless rejects them as latter-day pictorialists for whom realistic recording is insufficient for art: "they are clearly the descendants of the nineteenth-century artist-photographers … they still aim at achieving art in the traditional sense [and] exactly like the early champions of pictorialism, they tend to neglect the specific properties of the medium."[58] This is a deeply uncharitable assessment of Moholy-Nagy, whose art can hardly be dismissed without qualification as "traditional," and whose thematization of light seems to be as well placed as anything might be to qualify as a property "specific" to the medium of photography. It is certainly more plausible than Kracauer's own stress on realism and recording: realism is a genre of which many arts partake, rather than a property specific to any, and even realistic recording generalizes across photography, film, and music, requiring light to sort between the photographic and non-photographic varieties of such recording.[59] Prima facie, Moholy-Nagy is on much firmer ground.

Kracauer's account of the difference between "experimental" and "realist" modernists—or what he calls the "formative impulse" as opposed to "recording and revealing"—replays turn-of-the-century debates between artist-photographers and advocates of the straight print. Of the experimental modernists, Kracauer remarks: "it is as if they suffered from their obligations toward nature in the raw, as if they felt that, to be artists, they would have to work the given raw material into creations of an expressive rather than reproductive order."[60] Having done so, at least they no longer need worry about whether they are making art—even if it may not be pure photography. By contrast, it is less clear, even for many realists themselves, whether selection and organization suffice for art. Nonetheless, there can be no doubt as to where Kracauer's own sympathies lie:

> The photographer's approach may be called "photographic" if it conforms to the basic aesthetic principle. In an aesthetic interest [*sic*], that is, he must follow the realistic tendency under all circumstances. This is of course a minimum requirement. Yet in meeting it, he will at least have produced prints in keeping with the photographic approach. Which means an impersonal completely artless camera record is aesthetically irreproachable, whereas an otherwise beautiful and perhaps significant composition may lack photographic quality.[61]

Set to one side Kracauer's conflation of medium and art form—which cannot simply be equated because most arts partake of more than one medium, and most media serve more than one art. This identification pervades modernist theorizing. Set aside also the assumption that there *are* properties "specific" to media in some non-trivial (materially reductive) sense, and that whatever these properties are that distinguish one medium from others, they are its most essential properties. Focus instead on Kracauer's final claim. Even setting aside the standard tropes of modernist theorizing, we are left with

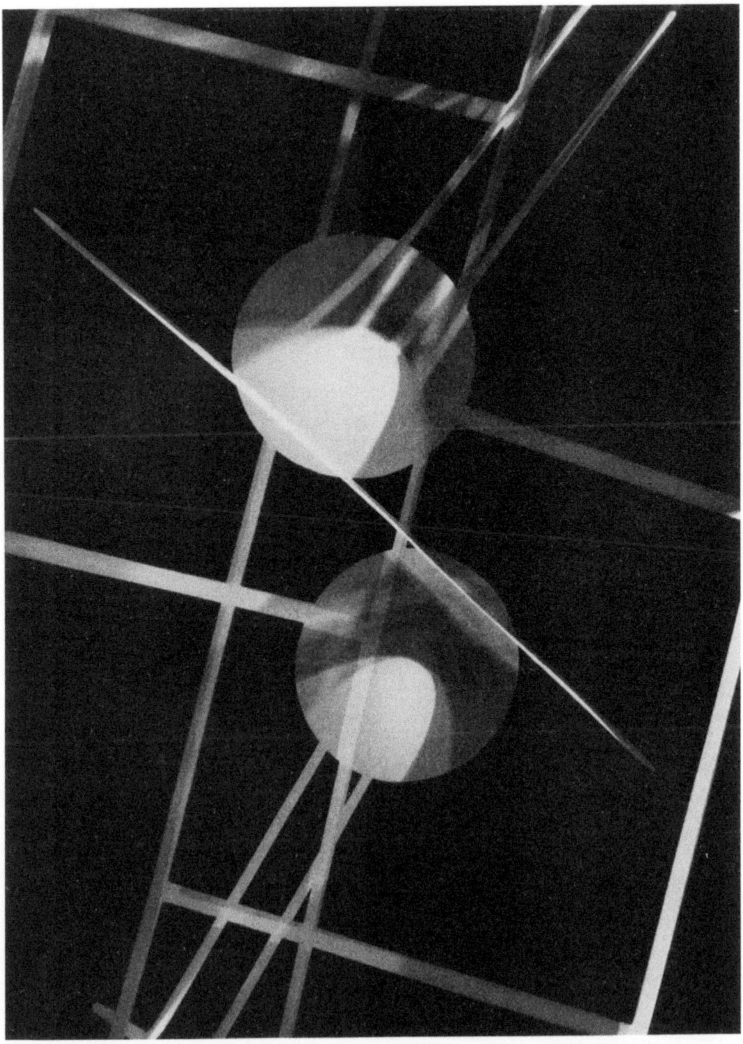

Figure 1.5 László Moholy-Nagy, *Untitled*, FGM.226, lost, Dessau, 1925–1928. Photogram on developing paper, (presumed) 9 ½ × 7 ⅙ in. (24 × 18 cm). © Hattula Moholy-Nagy/DACS 2016.

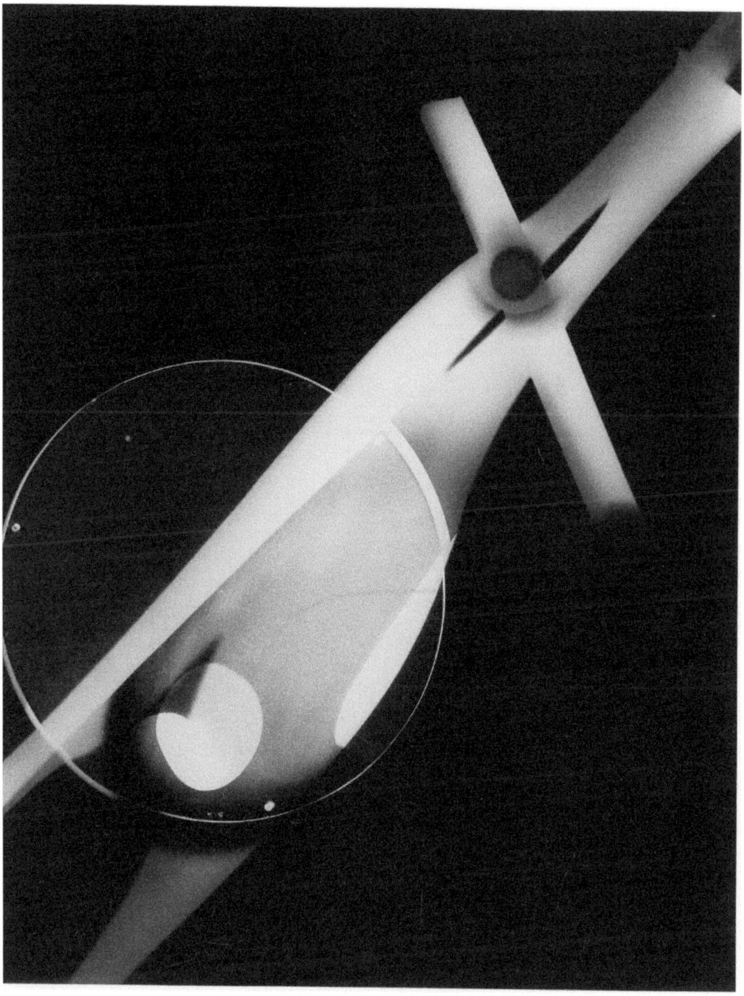

Figure 1.6 László Moholy-Nagy, *Untitled*, FGM.345, Chicago, 1939. Photogram on developing paper, 15¾ × 18$^{13}/_{16}$ in. (40 × 47.8 cm). © Hattula Moholy-Nagy/DACS 2016.

the assertion, motivated by Kracauer's "basic aesthetic principle," that photographers should pursue the realist route irrespective of whether it is most artistically rewarding. What could possibly justify such a demand? It is not for theorists to tell artists what they can and cannot do in order to produce compelling art: the proof of the pudding is in the eating. Theorists have to wait and see—just like the rest of us.[62]

Note that, were Kracauer's claim true, an entirely white photograph of an entirely white wall would be as "aesthetically irreproachable" as a completely black photograph of an entirely dark room—so long as both were produced solely through "realistic recording." But given that this exhausts the possibility space of images in black-and-white photography, it deprives the notion of "aesthetic irreproachability" of all meaning: aesthetically irreproachable as opposed to what other way that a black-and-white photograph might look? It would be less tendentious to describe such photographs as theoretically rather than aesthetically irreproachable (as a matter of modernist credo) but as having no a priori aesthetic significance either way. This is for aesthetic judgement to decide; it cannot be extrapolated from the fulfilment of a set of a priori theoretical requirements.

Though Kracauer intermittently seems to want to row back from this extreme position to recommend a middle way between realist recording and artistic formation, in the last analysis it comes down to those properties specific to the medium that the experimental photographers allegedly fail to respect. These consist of the tendencies to: (i) render nature in the raw as it exists independently of human beings; (ii) depict the fortuitous accident, adventitious or random event rather than the elaborately staged; (iii) excerpt fragments from a greater whole in such a way as to suggest potentially endless extension beyond the frame; and (iv) a certain indeterminacy of meaning and intention, given the isolated nature of the excerpted moment.[63] The price to be paid for ignoring these properties is abandoning the terrain of photography proper. As Kracauer puts it, quite beautifully: the photographer's "peculiar and truly formative effort to represent significant aspects of physical reality" must not "overwhelm that reality."[64] This is the mistake made by experimentalists, and for this reason "the free compositions of the experimental photographers … lie outside the province of photography proper [and thereby] divert attention from what is really characteristic of the medium."[65] Such work is best understood as "a special genre of the graphic arts rather than photography proper."[66] Though "affiliated to" photography, it is actually "remote from it."[67] This is Orthodoxy in a nutshell: Kracauer's evident feeling for photography notwithstanding, there is no theoretical light between himself and Scruton on this point. Critically, of course, they remain poles apart.

The emergence of mind-independence

The influential mid-century film theorist and critic André Bazin shares Kracauer's commitment to realism. Together with the philosopher Stanley Cavell, Bazin's work constitutes the immediate pre-history to Orthodox theory proper. Both anticipate the "mind-independence thesis" that underwrites Orthodox accounts in their mature form, and both introduce substantive new claims into the debate. In "The Ontology of the Photographic Image," Bazin suggests that the history of Western art can be viewed aesthetically or psychologically, and that there is a form of realism that correlates with each: "true realism" and "pseudo-realism." As these terms suggest, the opposition is normatively coded from the outset. The former concerns the expression of "spiritual realities" that, Bazin claims, was art's (entirely proper) function from the Egyptians through to the Renaissance. Photography, by contrast, represents the final culmination of naturalistic depiction that overtook painting during the Renaissance. Although Bazin regards this as an aberration, he also believes that, by satisfying our psychological need for a "pseudo-realism" that fools the eye, photography potentially frees the plastic arts from their aesthetically corrupting obsession with imitating appearance. So liberated, they may revert to their true vocation of representing spiritual realities. The structure of this argument will be familiar: it is a recapitulation of Wiertz, also writing in French a century before. My goal here is not to interrogate Bazin's substantive claims; the issue for us is what Bazin thinks enables photography to achieve this.

> No matter how skilful the painter, his work was always in fee to an inescapable subjectivity. The fact that a human hand

> intervened cast a shadow of doubt over the image. [T]he essential factor in the transition from the baroque to photography … [lies] … in completely satisfying our appetite for illusion by a mechanical reproduction in the making of which man plays no part. The solution is not to be found in the result but in the way of achieving it. …
>
> For the first time, between the originating object and its reproduction there intervenes only the instrumentality of a non-living agent. For the first time an image of the world is formed automatically, without the creative intervention of man.[68]

This is the first expression of the mind-independence thesis in its modern form: because no "living agent" is internal to the creation of the image, it has an authority, credibility, and presumed objectivity that it would otherwise lack. The idea of an image formed automatically, free from the vagaries of subjectivity, will prove central to later debates; but it is important to grasp that the automatism thesis, on its own, guarantees nothing about how a photograph will look. Thus Bazin grants that hand-made images may give us more accurate information about their objects than photographs, without this compromising the advantage of automatically generated images: "No matter how fuzzy, distorted, or discoloured, no matter how lacking in documentary value the image may be, it shares by virtue of the very process of becoming, the being of the model of which it is the reproduction: it is the model."[69]

The former point, about the power of individual photographic images to survive the degradation of their informational value, is important, and worth dwelling on more carefully than Bazin does; the latter is something that he clearly should not say. Taken literally, it is a nonsense: how could an image composed of silver salts suspended in a photographic emulsion partake of the being of, or even be, say, the Giza Pyramids in any sense that Bazin might credibly intend? Let's rule out, in the absence of evidence to the contrary, that he has in mind some metaphysical thesis about the basic fabric of the universe. Of course, commentators who rush to condemn Bazin on this point have to ignore or explain away Bazin's remark a few pages earlier that flatly contradicts the view typically then attributed to him. "No one," Bazin writes, "believes any longer in the ontological identity of model and image, but all are agreed that the image helps us to remember the subject and to preserve him from a second, spiritual death."[70]

Either Bazin is suffering an attack of enthusiasm, or he is not making the identity claim standardly attributed to him. It seems obvious that Bazin is speaking figuratively, in some sense, but in what sense exactly? What it might mean for the image to share a "common being" with the model becomes clearer when Bazin likens photographs to fingerprints. A fingerprint is neither the finger itself, and nor is it solely the finger's appearance, an image of the finger's surface; it is also a direct imprint of that surface preserved in some medium. Hence the analogies Bazin typically invokes, including moulds, impressions, death masks, and relics. He even likens the "transference of reality from thing to its reproduction" to the relation between the body of Christ and the Turin Shroud: "Only a photographic lens [*objectif*] can give us the kind of image of the object that is capable of satisfying the deep need man has to substitute for it something more than a mere approximation, a kind of decal or transfer."[71] Like the Shroud, photographs are often thought to preserve the direct impression of their object. Objects do not literally impress themselves into photographic surfaces, of course, but their reflected or emitted light does physically impact a light-sensitive surface, causing silver salts to darken or capacitors in a CCD sensor to emit electrical charges.

Why is this important? Here one needs to keep in mind the psychological framework within which all of Bazin's claims about photography are couched.[72] It is because we know that photographs are formed through "imprinting"—of their object's reflected or emitted light, if not of their object itself—that, Bazin implies, *we invest* the photograph with the being of the model.[73] Vernacular photographic images of loved ones, in particular, fulfil our desire for identity substitutes better than any other kind of image for this reason. Seen in this light, the "identity thesis" reduces to a psychological thesis about how we treat photographs in virtue of what we know, or think we know, about how they come into existence. The direct causal dependence of photographs on what they are of leads us to invest them with the "being of the model." Not only is this account unusually explicit about folk theory of photography, it folds that theory back into the argument as an explanation of why we treat photographs in the ways we do.[74]

Whether Bazin is committed to the identity thesis in a more substantive sense remains controversial. But irrespective of whether he is, his account faces difficulties. Since automatism, by his own admission, does not guarantee realistic images, more needs to be said to explain why we treat photographs in the ways that Bazin claims we do. Is it plausible to suppose that this is due wholly to what we believe about how they are generated? Would it continue to hold if photographs did not generally allow us to recognize their subjects so easily? It seems more plausible to think that our continued receptivity to poor individual photographs depends on this being the exception rather than the rule. Perhaps we are responsive to photographs as a class of images because they typically resemble their models so well; reports of early responses to the unprecedented clarity and life-likeness of daguerreotypes suggest this fact is hugely important for how we respond to photographs.[75] What is generally true of photographs might then explain why we continue to respond to degraded examples as we do. It depends not only on how they were made but, implicitly, on what is generally true of how images made this way appear, given the way that cameras have been engineered. Imagine this were to change such that photographs no longer allowed us to recognize people from their images: suppose the surface of camera lenses comprised numerous angled facets, causing them to fragment images like a kaleidoscope. Images obtained in this way would still be automatic. But would we continue to invest the decorative abstract patterns thereby obtained with the "being of the model"? It seems unlikely.

But perhaps this is to misunderstand Bazin's account. After all, he begins by claiming that photography and cinema "are discoveries that satisfy, once and for all … our obsession with realism."[76] This is why they can relieve the plastic arts of the non-aesthetic burden of replicating appearances. It is only because photographs and paintings are realistic that the automatic means of generating the former holds special significance for us. But in that case, automatism cannot explain the psychological efficacy of realism; automatism must presuppose realism to have the psychological efficacy that it does. If it explains anything, automatism explains our investment in a specific kind of realism that meets additional conditions; it explains the psychological efficacy of photographic realism, as opposed to realism *tout court*.[77] Automatism and realism are clearly independent: there are highly informative realistic images (such as technical illustrations) rendered by hand, and automatic images that are so under- or over-exposed, blurred, or empty of incident (correctly exposed photographs of empty skies or clean sheets of paper) as to convey little or no information. Because automatism is neither necessary nor sufficient for realism, explaining realism requires a separate argument, which Bazin does not here provide.

Besides the correlation of automatism and realism, the other aspect of Bazin's account that casts a shadow over later debates is his tendency to conflate imprinting and automatism. These are also independent. Imprinting, in Bazin's examples, is either intentional or non-intentional. Death masks are made intentionally, and while one can leave one's prints intentionally, fingerprints, footprints, and other tracks are typically left unintentionally. Either way, imprinting is in principle a natural process that does not require agency: "The photograph … and the object … share a common being, after the fashion of a fingerprint … photography actually contributes something to the order of natural creation instead of providing a substitute for it."[78] Were this true, photographs would be akin to freckles, paw prints, or the pattern of tracery bleached over time into the paintwork of a wall exposed to sun through a net curtain. But what has any of this got to do with automatism?

Automatism—to the extent that Bazin characterizes it at all—seems to be an optical process for projecting light from a three-dimensional scene via a lens onto a two-dimensional surface, so as to mark it. Photographers can determine many things about what shows up in photographs, but it is camera designers, lens manufacturers, and (more recently) software engineers who determine how scenes are mapped by cameras. Automatism is thus perhaps best understood as a way of standardizing, and thereby mechanizing out, individual control of the mapping process. Nonetheless, because it is designed to replace human transcription, automatism always presupposes human ends. Natural processes such as imprinting, by contrast, need not. In sum, a process can be both natural and causal (sunburn, freckles) or both causal and automatic (photography), but one and the same process cannot be both natural and automatic—if "natural" is taken, as it is by Bazin, to contrast with "human." Yet this conjunction is just what Bazin's conception of photography as "automatic imprinting" requires. *Pace* Bazin, as soon as light's causal efficacy is harnessed by camera and lens design, it no longer "contributes something to the order of natural creation," but is indeed a substitute for it.

Like Bazin, Cavell is interested both in what is distinctive about the relation between a photograph and what it is of, and why this relation has a special significance for us. Cavell takes the fact that photographs are of "reality" to be non-contentious; the question is how this should be understood. According to Cavell, a photograph of *x*, unlike a painting of *x*, neither represents nor resembles *x*, but transcribes or records it. This leads Cavell to assert that a photograph presents us not with a "likeness," but with the "thing itself." We are back in Bazinian terrain, but Cavell is much more sensitive to the difficulties of cashing this thought out in a philosophically respectable way.

Cavell's first pass, building on the differences between visual and auditory transcriptions, is to point out that, despite presenting a likeness, photographs do not put us in the presence of the object itself. This is what perplexes us: we are not familiar with seeing things, as opposed to representations of things, when those things are not themselves present. So, despite maintaining that we see *x* (and not a representation of *x*) by seeing *y*, when *y* is a photograph of *x*, Cavell does not claim that photographs reproduce what they record.

Cavell's second pass, building on these differences between seeing things through photographs and seeing things face to face, is to suggest that photographs not only present us with a world to which we are ourselves not present, but mechanically ensure our absence from the world presented:

> Photographs are not *hand*-made; they are manufactured. And what is manufactured is an image of the world. The inescapable fact of mechanism or automatism in the making of these images is the feature Bazin points to as "[satisfying] once and for all and in its very essence, our obsession with realism."[79]

Cavell thinks Bazin right to stress automatism, but that he fails to plumb its depths sufficiently. For Cavell, this concerns photography's relation to scepticism. Rather than manifesting our desire for "identity substitutes," photography reveals our susceptibility to the sceptical fantasy that transcending our subjectivity is the only way to secure an objective world: "So far as photography satisfied a wish, it satisfied a wish … to escape subjectivity and metaphysical isolation—a wish for the power to reach this world, having for so long tried, at last hopelessly, to manifest fidelity to another."[80] If photography reflects the sceptical desire to escape the constraints of subjectivity for unmediated access to the world, unearthing the sceptical substrate of its fascination for us is to get to the "right depth" of the question concerning its automatism.[81]

This is why Cavell homes in on the automatic, *non-subjectively* mediated, relation between a photograph and what it is of. Where Bazin sees photography as furnishing identity-substitutes that derive their power from our wish to defeat time, Cavell views photography, not unrelatedly, as the expression of a sceptical wish to escape the limits of human finitude. What they share, and what distinguishes them from more analytic thinkers on photography, is the depth of their claims on behalf of photography. For Cavell, automatism does not enable photography to do something that painting once did, only better; it allows it to achieve something unprecedented in the history of representational art: it

> overcame subjectivity in a way undreamed of by painting, a way that could not satisfy painting, one which does not so much defeat the act of painting as escape it altogether: by *automatism*, by removing the human agent from the task of reproduction.[82]

But this is an achievement that cuts both ways: automatically recording reality may produce a world from which the exclusion of subjectivity, with all the associated vagaries and infelicities, is mechanically guaranteed; but for precisely that reason, it is a world that we cannot acknowledge as our own.[83] By achieving what the sceptic desires—by granting us access to a world unmediated by subjectivity—photography does not restore our connection to the world so much as exacerbate our separation from it. Viewers of photographs share neither a space nor a time with the objects perceived. So construed, photography partakes of scepticism's paradox: by removing the human agent (and so too subjectivity) from the reproduction of reality, photography facilitates its perfection, but the price to be paid for such perfection is a world from which our absence is mechanically guaranteed.

This account, though highly suggestive, is hardly non-contentious. The focus on scepticism arguably tells us much more about Cavell's project than it does about photography, so I set this to one side here. But Cavell's account remains controversial even so. In particular, it involves a number of questionable claims about the nature of photography per se.[84] Are these supposed to apply throughout photography's diverse uses? What about speed cameras, photo-finish technology, diagnostic medical imaging, microphotography, astrophotography, time-lapse nature photography, or infrared and other non-visible-spectrum forms of photography? These do not typically show us something that we could have seen with our own eyes, so presumably cannot satisfy our senses of the presence of the world in anything like the way natural vision can.[85] At the very least, the scope of Cavell's account needs clarifying, and once that is done we will be owed an explanation as to why the particular sub-set of photographic practices to which it does apply is being held up as a model for photography per se.[86]

Though further worries as to whether Cavell's account picks out all and only photographs can be pressed, it is Bazin and Cavell's shared stress on photography's mechanical, non-agential substrate, rather than the significance either attributes to it, that is their enduring legacy for Orthodox theory.[87] Of all Cavell's critics, Joel Snyder is most sensitive to this. His critique of Cavell on this score can be read as a critique of Orthodoxy *avant la lettre*. In "What Happens by Itself in Photography?" Snyder grants both the intuitive force of describing photography as automatic, and that Cavell offers the most robust characterization of this notion to date.[88] For all that, it remains unclear precisely what is supposed to happen by itself in photography. After all, objects do not depict themselves and photographs do not make themselves—except in the limit case of natural, "self-generated" photographs. And even automatism's proponents accept that there are numerous non-automatic aspects of the medium. Once all the elements of operator control, selection, and intention to which Evans and Emerson draw attention are acknowledged, just what is it that is supposed to "happen by itself"?

This is hard to pin down. Is the worry that the photographer does not draw the image? That seems an odd thing to say, since the camera does not draw it either. There just is no drawing (in that sense) in photography. By comparison to painting there is no gradual building up of a surface. As a result, the activities of the photographer are not reflected in the same way in the final image. In photography, almost everything that expresses comparable choices happens *off* the support—the choice of lens, distance, lighting, moment of exposure, point of view, etc. This is why any adequate aesthetics of photography needs to pay as much attention to what happens off the support as on it. The mark of such actions often cannot be found on the support—if one looks for it in the same way that one might look for it in a painting—though their effects surely can. This can give those who have no idea where to look the impression that the photographer has done very little, or that the mechanism is responsible. But this is plain ignorance. The fact that so many of the acts take place prior to the image appearing "all at once" does not negate the photographer's responsibility for what then appears. Merely noting depth of field markers in an image already tells us much about what the photographer was after. One needs to be a competent judge in photography as in any other domain; and this requires a basic grasp of the internal relations between focus, depth of field, and exposure that most Orthodox theorists fail to evince.

It is equally illegitimate to assume that photographs must be automatically generated from the mere fact that they are not made by hand. This does not suffice for automaticity. There are many things not made by hand (sparks, fossils, high-water marks) that are not, just in virtue of that fact, automatically generated. For something to count as "automatic" requires the mechanizing out of human (or animal) labour in the service of human ends. If photographs are generated automatically, as opposed to merely causally, it should be possible to specify the labour that the machine cuts out. Washing-machines and car washes replace scrubbing by hand; trains, planes, and automobiles replace self-propulsion; and cameras replace rendering scenes by hand. Photography requires both human agency and natural processes, while resisting exhaustive explanation in terms of either.

Photographs are made, but not hand-made. Yet this does not suffice to make them automatic. In some standard uses, automatic seems to reduce to mechanical. Cavell talks interchangeably about the "fact of mechanism or automatism." But this does not explain automatism either. "Automatic," as standardly used, seems to mean little more than "not made by hand." But in that case, the automatism thesis is a redescription of the problem, and not a solution. That the problem will endure so long as philosophers insist on understanding photography through a conceptual framework more appropriate to painting is demonstrated by Orthodoxy proper. It is to this that I now turn.

Notes

1 The tensions between these terms standardly used to characterize photography bear noting: a causal process may be natural (the tide) or automatic (a washing-machine), but not both natural and automatic. Because automated processes are designed to reduce human labour, they cannot be understood without reference to human ends. So they cannot be entirely "natural," if that is taken to imply a contrast with the human.

2 Joseph Nicéphore Niépce, "Memoire on the Heliograph," in Alan Trachtenberg (ed.) *Classic Essays on Photography* (New Haven, CT: Leete's Island Books, 1980), p. 6.

3 Louis-Jacques Mandé Daguerre, "Daguerreotype," in Trachtenberg, *Classic Essays*, p. 9.

4 Ibid., p. 13.

5 Cited in Mary Warner Marien, *Photography: A Cultural History of Photography* (London: Lawrence King, 2002), p. 23.

6 Henry Fox-Talbot, "Some Account of the Art of Photogenic Drawing," in Newhall, *Photography: Essays and Images*, p. 23

7 Fox-Talbot, "Introductory Remarks," in *The Pencil of Nature* (London: Longman, Brown, Green & Longmans, 1844), p. 2.

8 Fox-Talbot, "Some Account of the Art of Photogenic Drawing," p. 28 (Talbot's italics).

9 Lady Elizabeth Eastlake, "Photography," in Trachtenberg, *Classic Essays*, p. 43.

10 Dominique-François Jean Arago, "Report," in Trachtenberg *Classic Essays*, p. 17ff.

11 Eastlake, "Photography," p. 43, p. 58.

12 Nathaniel Parker Willis and Timothy O. Porter, "The Pencil of Nature: A New Discovery," in Andrew Hershberger (ed.) *Photographic Theory: An Historical Anthology* (Oxford: Wiley-Blackwell, 2014), p. 60.

13 Antoine-Joseph Wiertz, "La Photographie," in Hershberger, *Photographic Theory*, p. 60.

14 André Bazin, "Ontology of the Photographic Image," repr. in *What is Cinema?*, vol. 1 (Berkeley: University of California Press, 1967), p. 12.

15 Eastlake, "Photography," p. 66. Note that non-selectivity is celebrated by more sympathetic commentators: "This distinctness of the lesser details of a building or a landscape often gives us incidental truths which interest us more than the central object of the picture. . . . The very things which an artist would leave out, or render imperfectly, the photograph takes infinite care with." Oliver Wendell Holmes, "The Stereoscope and the Stereograph," in Trachtenberg, *Classic Essays*, pp. 78–79.

16 "Is Photography a New Art?" published anonymously in *Camera Work* 21 (1908) and collected in Trachtenberg's *Classic Essays* makes the interesting claim that two questions about photography are widely conflated: the right question is whether photography is a *fine* art; the wrong question is whether it is a *graphic* art. The former is the one posed, the latter the one typically answered by sceptics in the negative. Against this, the author argues that photography is an art, but not one well understood on the model of graphic art: like architecture it expresses the "personal touch" we expect of art, but does so by composing rather than corporeally.

17 Walter Benjamin recognized this early on: "They undertook nothing less than to legitimize the photographer before the very [artistic] tribunal it was in the process of overturning." See "A Little History of Photography," in Michael W. Jennings, Howard Eiland, and Gary Smith (eds.) *Walter Benjamin Selected Writings*, vol. 2.ii, 1931–1934 (Cambridge, MA: Harvard University Press, 1999), p. 508.

18 Benjamin's impatience with idealist bridling at photography, read through Roland Barthes's and Michel Foucault's influential critique of authorship, served as a template for the equally pervasive anti-authorial tenet of postmodern theory and criticism of photography associated with Douglas Crimp, Craig Owens, and Abigail Solomon-Godeau, among others, from the late 1970s onwards.

19 Henry Peach Robinson, *Pictorial Effect in Photography: Being Hints on Composition and Chiaroscuro for Photographers. To Which is Added a Chapter on Combination Printing* (London: Piper & Carter; Marion & Co., 1869).

20 Henry Peach Robinson, *Elements of a Pictorial Photograph* (London: Percy Lund & Co., 1896), p. 70

21 Peter Henry Emerson, "Photography, a Pictorial Art," in Newhall, *Photography: Essays and Images*, p. 160.

22 Ibid., p. 162.

23 Peter Henry Emerson, *Naturalistic Photography for Students of the Art*, 2nd, rev. edn. (London: Samson Low, Marston, Searle & Rivington, 1890), pp. 148–153.

24 Peter Henry Emerson, "The Death of Naturalistic Photography," in Hershberger, *Photography Theory*, p. 89 (Emerson's italics). This exemplifies the slippage between *fine* and *graphic* art diagnosed in "Is Photography a New Art?".

25 "Keep rigidly within the limits of your medium, do not strive for the impossible, and so miss the possible." Emerson, *Naturalistic Photography*, p. 256.

26 Stieglitz, "Pictorial Photography," p. 165.

27 Frederick H. Evans, "On Pure Photography," in Newhall, *Photography: Essays and Images*, p. 180. Little has changed. In 1989, in the face of worries generated by digital technologies, the National Press Photographers Association marked the 150th anniversary of photography's invention by formally outlawing non-blemish-removing image manipulation by its members. This spirit continues to pervade its code of ethics, and photographers discovered to have broken it are expelled. See https://nppa.org/code_of_ethics.

28 Emerson, *Naturalistic Photography*, p. 184.

29 Robert Demachy, "On the Straight Print," in Hershberger, *Photographic Theory*, p. 115.

30 Ibid., p. 117.

31 Ibid., p. 116 (Demachy's italics).

32 Ibid.

33 Frederick H. Evans, "What is a 'Straight' Print?" in Hershberger, *Photographic Theory*, p. 119.

34 Carl Sadakichi Hartmann, "A Plea for Straight Photography," in Newhall, *Photography: Essays and Images*, p. 186.

35 Ibid., p. 187.

36 Paul Strand, "Photography," in Trachtenberg, *Classic Essays*, p. 142.

37 Edward Weston, "Seeing Photographically," in Trachtenberg, *Classic Essays*, p. 170.

38 Ibid., p. 171. Even Walker Evans, least given among mid-century modernists to theoretical pronouncements, ridiculed late nineteenth-century pictorialists as "unsuccessful painter[s] with a bag of mysterious tricks." Walker Evans, "The Reappearance of Photography," in Trachtenberg, *Classic Essays*, p. 185.

39 For a critique of Strand and Weston, and medium-specificity claims in photography, see Noël Carroll, "Medium Specificity Arguments and the Self-Consciously Invented Arts: Film, Video and Photography," in Carroll, *Theorizing the Moving Image* (Cambridge: Cambridge University Press, 1996).

40 Strand, "Photography," pp. 141–142.

41 Ibid., p. 142, my italics.

42 Paul Strand, "Photography and the New God," in Trachtenberg, *Classic Essays*, p. 148.

43 Ibid.

44 Ibid., pp. 147–148.

45 Ibid., p. 150.

46 Ibid.

47 Edward Weston, "Random Notes on Photography," in Newhall, *Photography: Essays and Images*, p. 225.

48 Ibid.

49 Though they probably did not know it, Strand and Weston were on sound legal footing. In 1884 the Supreme Court ruled, in *Burrow-Giles Lithographic Co. v. Sarony*, that US copyright law extended to photographs. Photographs are "original intellectual conceptions" whenever pre-exposure interventions suffice to render the photographer an original author. See Terry S. Kogan, "The Enigma of Photography, Depiction and Copyright Originality," *Fordham Intellectual Property, Media and Entertainment Law Journal* 25:4 (2015).

50 This is a difference that makes a difference. Gary Schneider's 1990s "durational portraits" involve exposures of up to an hour, during which a torch is used to selectively illuminate a subject in a darkened room. This enables Schneider to exert considerable control over the formation of the light image itself.

51 Weston, "Seeing Photographically," p. 172 (Weston's italics).

52 Ibid., p. 173.

53 Ansel Adams, "A Personal Credo," in Newhall, *Photography: Essays and Images*, p. 260.

54 Weston, "Seeing Photographically," p. 173.

55 Siegfried Kracauer, "Photography," in *Theory of Film: The Redemption of Reality* (Oxford: Oxford University Press, 1960), p. 12.

56 Kracauer is following László Moholy-Nagy and Walter Benjamin here. See, respectively, "Light: A Medium of Plastic Expression," *Broom: An International Magazine of the Arts* 4:4 (March 1923), p. 283, and "A Little History of Photography," p. 510.

57 Walter Benjamin, "The Work of Art in the Age of its Technical Reproducibility," in Michael W. Jennings and Howard Eiland (eds.) *Walter Benjamin Selected Writings*, vol. 3, 1935–1938 (Cambridge, MA: Harvard University Press, 2002). I take issue with the technological determinism of this essay in "Aura, Face, Photography: Re-reading Benjamin Today," in Andrew Benjamin (ed.) *Walter Benjamin and Art* (London: Continuum, 2005).

58 Kracauer, "Photography," p. 10.

59 Moholy-Nagy "Light: A Medium of Plastic Expression," pp. 283–284.

60 Kracauer, "Photography," p. 10.

61 Ibid., p.13.

62 For a critique of medium-specificity claims along these lines, see the essays collected in "Questioning Media," Part I of Noël Carroll, *Theorizing the Moving Image* (Cambridge: Cambridge University Press, 1996). See also "Forget the Medium!" and "Kracauer's *Theory of Film*," in Noël Carroll, *Engaging the Moving Image* (New Haven, CT: Yale University Press, 2003).

63 Six years later John Szarkowski also set out to capture the "characteristics and problems inherent in the medium": the thing itself (actuality or reality); the detail (or isolated fragment); the weight that excerpting a fragment confers on the framing edge; the focus on a particular instant; and the (often unexpected) vantage point. See John Szarkowski, *The Photographer's Eye* (New York: Museum of Modern Art, 2007), pp. 6–11.

64 Kracauer, "Photography," p. 23.
65 Ibid.
66 Ibid., p.18.
67 Ibid.
68 Bazin, "The Ontology of the Photographic Image," p. 13.
69 Ibid., p. 14.
70 Ibid., p. 10. For a critique, see Noël Carroll, *Philosophical Problems of Classical Film Theory* (Princeton: Princeton University Press, 1988) and Gregory Currie, *Image and Mind: Film, Philosophy and Cognitive Science* (Cambridge: Cambridge University Press, 1995).
71 Bazin, "The Ontology of the Photographic Image," p. 14.
72 Jonathan Friday, "André Bazin's Ontology of Photographic and Film Imagery," *Journal of Aesthetics and Art Criticism* 63:4 (2005).
73 Robert Hopkins's defence of Scruton turns on the claim that a certain kind of photography consists essentially of imprinting. See "The Real Challenge of Photography (as a Communicative Representational Art)," *Journal of the American Philosophical Association* 1:2 (Summer 2015).
74 Bazin's acknowledgement of the irreducible role played by background beliefs about the photographic process in our responses to photographs re-emerges as a key marker of what I call "second-generation" Orthodoxy below.
75 Compare the early German daguerrotypist, Karl Dauthendey: "We didn't trust ourselves at first to look long at the first pictures he developed. We were abashed by the distinctness of these images, and believed that the little tiny faces in the picture could see *us*, so powerfully was everyone affected by the unaccustomed clarity and the unaccustomed truth to nature of the first daguerreotypes." Cited in Benjamin, "A Little History of Photography," p. 512.
76 Bazin, "The Ontology of the Photographic Image," p. 12.
77 A host of worries beset Bazin's psychological explanation of our interest in photographs. What might count as evidence for such claims? Are they supposed to bear on *all* photographs, including technical forms of photographs? Are people who claim to feel no need for "identity substitutes" self-deceived or lacking some basic human trait? But I set such worries aside here.
78 Bazin, "The Ontology of the Photographic Image," p. 15.
79 Stanley Cavell, *The World Viewed* (Cambridge, MA: Harvard University Press, 1979), p. 20 (Cavell's italics).
80 Ibid., p. 22.
81 Ibid., p. 21.
82 Ibid., p. 23.
83 I am indebted here to Stephen Mulhall, *Stanley Cavell: Philosophy's Recounting of the Ordinary* (Oxford: Oxford University Press), pp. 227–229.
84 This is ironic given Cavell's commitment to the Wittgensteinian project of "teaching us differences" between things we assume to be similar. See Ludwig Wittgenstein on games, in *Philosophical Investigations*, trans. G.E.M. Anscombe (Oxford: Blackwell, 1953), §66

85 The alignment of photography and natural vision is one of the most threadbare claims in writing about photography. Neil Walsh Allen and Joel Snyder lampoon it in "Photography, Representation and Vision," *Critical Inquiry* 2:1 (Autumn 1975).

86 A similar objection can be levelled at Bazin: will a photograph of a well-executed joint in a carpentry manual have greater psychological resonance for us, in virtue of being a photograph, than a technical drawing?

87 For such criticism see Douglas P. Lackey, "Reflections on Cavell's Ontology of Film," *Journal of Aesthetics and Art Criticism* 32:2 (Winter 1973), and H. Gene Blocker, "Pictures and Photographs," *Journal of Aesthetics and Art Criticism* 36:2 (Winter 1977).

88 Joel Snyder, "What Happens by Itself in Photography," in Ted Cohen, Paul Guyer, and Hilary Putnam (eds.) *Pursuits of Reason: Essays in Honor of Stanley Cavell* (Lubbock: Texas Tech University Press, 1993).

Two

Aesthetic scepticism and its critics

We are now in a position to assess the claims of Orthodoxy proper, focusing on Roger Scruton and Kendall Walton, authors who have set the terms of debate in mainstream philosophy of photography. Scruton is a sceptic about the possibility of photographic art and Walton is not. Not surprisingly then, New Theory develops out of responses to Scruton in particular. In this chapter and the next I shall consider sceptical and non-sceptical versions of Orthodox theory, as spurs to new theorizing about photography.

Together with Walton's "Transparent Pictures," Scruton's "Photography and Representation" is responsible for galvanizing interest in photography as a stand-alone topic of philosophical enquiry—despite still approaching it from within the framework of film. Scruton's significance for Orthodox theory is largely, though not exclusively, negative, arising from one theorist after another taking issue with his scepticism about the possibility of photographic art. Despite this, it is striking how many of Scruton's philosophical critics share his underlying view of photography as an essentially causal process; they mainly aspire to show that this is compatible with its standing as art. As a result, the general picture of photography underpinning Scruton's scepticism continues to pass largely unchallenged.

Aesthetic scepticism and its limitations

Scruton's aesthetic scepticism stems from his belief that the "ideal photograph" (his term for what earlier writers would have called pure photography or the straight print) is constrained to show us how things stood in a particular place at a particular time: such photographs can make scenes available to perception, but cannot communicate anything about those scenes, which viewers might take as their focus of attention. For if nothing differentiates the appearance of the scene photographed from the appearance of the same scene seen directly, whatever interest we may take in its photograph is an interest we could in principle have taken in the scene itself, and the scene itself cannot be an expression of any artist's thoughts about it.

To take an aesthetic interest in a photograph, by contrast, requires taking an interest in it as a representation: not merely in the weak sense of being aware of one thing standing for another—as one can see *x* in *y*, without believing that *x* is *y*—but in the stronger sense of taking an interest in the thought thereby expressed. Understood in this more demanding way, representational art requires the expression of some attitude towards or thought about whatever is depicted. Only in this way can a work elicit the viewer's aesthetic interest. In aesthetically appreciating a painting, for example, we focus on how the painter depicts a given subject. In so doing, we are taking an interest in the artist's representational activity, and what this reveals about how she views her subject that—according to Scruton—the mechanical nature of photography rules out. But the capacity to elicit and sustain such interest is foundational to our appreciation of representational art:

> Representation in art has a special significance precisely because of the possibility that we can understand it—in the sense of understanding its content—while being indifferent to, or unconcerned with, its literal truth. That is why fictional representation is not merely an important form of representational art but in fact the primary form of it, the form through which the aesthetic understanding finds its principal mode of expression.[1]

The underlying rationale for this claim is clearly Kantian. Scruton even distinguishes painting from photography, in a manner recalling the First Moment of the 'Analytic of Beautiful,' in terms of the aesthetic and practical interests to which they allegedly give rise. To take a properly aesthetic interest in something is to take an interest in it for its own sake, rather than as a means to something else. The latter would include taking an interest in photography for the information it furnishes about the world. Scruton thinks taking this kind of interest in photographs is inevitable, given the causal dependence of photographs on their objects. To take an aesthetic interest in a painting, by contrast, is to take an interest in *how* the painting depicts whatever it depicts, rather than in *what* it depicts; it is to take an interest in the representational properties of the picture itself. It is always the painting, rather than the objects depicted in the painting, that is the focus of genuine aesthetic interest.

Fictional representation is the primary object of such interest because paying attention to the representational properties of a picture directs attention to what the artist is trying to communicate. Since nothing depicted in a work of fiction need ever have existed, we cannot understand what such a work depicts without viewing it as an expression of the artist's thoughts about whatever is depicted. Fictional representation thereby directs our attention to what Scruton takes to be central to aesthetic interest in artistic representation more generally: the primacy of the representation over what is represented as the focus of appreciative attention.

A thought experiment may help bring this out. Imagine a line of cheap plastic crap washed up on a Kent beach by the retreating tide. However much it resembles the contour of England's south coast, it cannot be interpreted as a comment on the demise of the English seaside in an era of cheap foreign travel; indeed it cannot be interpreted as a *comment* on anything. Contrast this to a very similar, perhaps even indiscernible, line of detritus deposited on another Kent beach as part of the Folkstone Triennial. The latter might be making a comment on social deprivation, human desecration of nature, global warming and rising sea levels, or simply celebrating the beauty of the marginal and overlooked. Perhaps attending closely to that line of crap, together with supporting materials and a knowledge of the artist's broader practice, will enable us to say which. By contrast, the line left by the retreating sea (if not the rubbish of which it is made) is a product of natural processes that can be entirely accounted for in non-agential terms. And therein lies the problem: if photography reduces to natural causality in anything like the same way, it will preclude photographers expressing their thoughts about what is depicted by controlling the manner of its depiction.

This reasoning underwrites the basic distinction from which everything else in Scruton's argument follows: the "ideal photograph," which Scruton takes to reveal the essential nature of photography, has a strictly causal relation to what it is of; the "ideal painting," which Scruton takes to capture the essential nature of painting, has a strictly intentional relation to what it is of. Scruton unpacks this difference in terms of transparency: photographs are transparent to their objects; paintings are transparent to their maker's thoughts and intentions. Since all representational art requires the latter, photography cannot be a representational art. Because photographs are transparent to their objects, any aesthetic interest we believe we take in a photograph reduces to an interest in the object or scene it depicts. Scruton thinks we mistake this for an interest in its depiction. The underlying thought is simple: to see an object in a photograph is no different from having one's attention directed to it by means of a frame. Any interest we take in an object viewed through such a frame is an interest in that object, and not the frame through which we see it. Far from being objects of aesthetic interest in their own right, photographs are merely "surrogates" for the interest of what we see through them. Scruton need not (and does not) deny that many actual, "non-ideal" photographs do elicit aesthetic interest; he need only deny that this is ever by means that are strictly photographic.

Because everything that appears in an ideal photograph can be explained in purely causal terms, ideal photographs do not exhibit the intentionality required of art. Rather than being complete expressions of an artist's thoughts about what is depicted, ideal photographs are constrained to record whatever was in frame during the moment of exposure, affording only the "grossest control" of detail. We cannot know whether everything in the photograph is there because intended, and so to be interpreted as contributing to the communication of some thought about what the photograph depicts, or there simply because it was in shot alongside whatever was intended, and so could not be excluded—despite being irrelevant and perhaps even detrimental to the intended meaning. The photographer, Scruton maintains, is a "victim" of such constraints. Lee Friedlander puts it rather more charitably:

> I only wanted Uncle Vern standing by his new car (a Hudson) on a clear day. I got him and the car. I also got a bit of Aunt Mary's laundry, and Beau Jack, the dog, peeing on a fence, and a row of potted tuberous begonias on the porch and 78 trees and a million pebbles in the driveway and more. It's a generous medium, photography.[2]

Because photography is a "generous medium" in Friedlander's sense, photographs cannot—according to Scruton—give viewers sufficient guidance as to where to direct their attention. We cannot take an aesthetic interest in a photograph because we cannot know what precisely the artist means for us to attend to, or why. How could we know, without Friedlander's helpful commentary, that the envisaged photograph was intended as a celebration of Uncle Vern's pride in his new Hudson rather than, say, a comment on suburban life, domestic pets, or 1960s fashions?

Moreover, because photographs are condemned to record how whatever is in frame looks from a particular point of view, at a particular moment, under particular conditions, they must be fictionally incompetent. Photographs may "record fictions" if that means documenting the staging of a play or an actor playing a fictional character, but that staging or actor must be physically present to the camera to be recorded. The fictional entities represented cannot, qua fictional, leave photographic traces in real light-sensitive surfaces. It may look like fairies at the bottom of the garden but, given what you know about fairies and what (you think) you know about photographs, it cannot be:

> The relation between a photograph and its subject is a causal relation. If *a* is the [only] cause of *b*, then the existence of *b* is sufficient for the existence of *a*. The photograph lacks that quality of "intentional inexistence" which is characteristic of painting. The ideal photograph, therefore, is incapable of representing anything unreal; if a photograph is a photograph of a man, then there is some particular man of whom it is a photograph.[3]

If Scruton is right, photography thereby rules out the "primary form" of artistic representation. Like everything else in Scruton's response to photography, this follows from his foundational distinction between the intentional nature of (ideal) paintings and the causal nature of (ideal) photographs. If ideal paintings stand in a purely intentional relation to their subjects, and ideal photographs stand in a purely causal relation to their objects, we already know that photography could not count as a representational art on Scruton's account. It follows straightforwardly from his opening definitions: if taking an aesthetic interest in a photograph as a work of representational art requires seeing it as the complete expression of a thought about what it depicts, but standing in a purely causal relation to what it depicts precludes so seeing it, ideal photographs cannot be objects of genuine aesthetic interest. Photographs necessarily have objects (something they are of), but only paintings can have subjects (something they are about).[4]

Scruton grants that his ideals are "logical fictions": most, and perhaps even all, real-world examples will depart more or less from these ideals.[5] As a result, any actual photograph that might seem to constitute counter-evidence is neutralized in advance as a departure from the relevant ideal and, hence, not a genuine counter-example after all. Nonetheless, Scruton maintains that his ideals do indeed capture the *essential* nature of painting and photography—at least in their pure forms. This is a claim that needs to be true for the argument to go through: should these ideals turn out to be stipulations that distort the true nature of their respective activities, Scruton's argument will be vitiated by its questionable premises.

So is it? The short answer is yes. But to give the answer bite, we need to see how his ideals falsify the true nature of their respective art forms.[6] Start by noting several assumptions built into the account that Scruton seems to think so self-evident as to require no justification. The first is that painting and photography have distinct (non-overlapping) natures. One might think this is to assume a large part of what needs to be demonstrated. Depending on the frame of comparison, photographs and paintings will have more in common than sets them apart. And even restricting one's frame of reference to the arts, both meet the basic pictorial condition of being two-dimensional surfaces in which one can see three-dimensional objects. Does it follow, just in virtue of this being shared, that it cannot be an essential feature of both? It is hard to see why it should. At the very least, we are owed some explanation as to why what distinct art forms share cannot be as essential to their natures as what distinguishes them.

An even more basic assumption that Scruton seems to think requires no justification is that painting and photography have essential natures at all, irrespective of whether these turn out to be distinct or overlapping. Is there really some set of non-disjunctive conditions that all and only paintings or photographs fulfil? Consider the following two lists: (A) face-painting, T-shirt painting, body painting, toenail painting, house-painting, boat painting, custom car painting, toy-soldier and model painting, painting-by-numbers, sign-painting, false marbling, ceiling painting, oil painting; (B) time-lapse photography, infrared photography, astrophotography, aerial photography, cartographic photography, medical and diagnostic photography, forensic photography, traffic enforcement photography, advertising photography, food photography, archival photography, cruise ship photography, school yearbook photography, royal portrait photography, photojournalism, art photography. Do these look like two activities with mutually exclusive essential natures, or a variety of activities within complex patterns of similarity and difference, such that many may have more in common with items on the other list than with other items on their own?[7]

Note that the response to list (A) cannot be that only those activities recognized as art should be on the list, since that would be to assume what the argument purports to establish, namely, that painting is a representational art. Similarly, the response to list (B) cannot be that only those activities that produce easily recognizable images of everyday objects and scenes should be on the list, since that would also be to assume what the argument claims to establish: that photography cannot be a representational art because it reduces to holding up a frame to the world. Once this is recognized, one sees how much gets smuggled into the very ideas of "painting" and "photography," as Scruton employs them. This seems to be what underwrites his conviction that his ideals capture, rather than distort, what is essential to their respective domains. "Painting," as Scruton understands it, is the subset of painting that is art, and "photography" excludes everything other than (roughly) vernacular and reportage. But this is to jerry-rig the data, by populating one's comparison classes in such a way as to secure in advance what the argument is meant to establish—that painting is always art and photography never is.

What about Scruton's assumption that having a strictly causal relation to its objects is sufficient to distinguish photography: does causality parse cleanly between photography and non-photography in the way that Scruton's account requires? Even were it accurate, Scruton's characterization of photography as a strictly causal process would not distinguish it from myriad other such processes that need have nothing to do with making pictures, and if they do pertain to making pictures, need have nothing to do with making photographic ones: the transfer of paint from brush to canvas is no less governed by the laws of physics than the formation of photographic images is by those of optics and chemistry.[8] If the response to this is that painting does not have a *strictly* causal relation to what it depicts, Scruton's critics may concede this point, while noting that the same is almost always true of photographs. It may not be true in the limit case of "self-generated" photographs (that is, images produced naturally by the action of light on a variety of light-sensitive surfaces) but these are clearly not the kind of "photographs" that Scruton has in mind—not least because such images exist independently of the invention of photography as a human practice.

Moreover, despite insisting on causality as the basis of photography, Scruton neglects to mention what is surely the defining causal characteristic of photography if anything is: the action of light in the formation of the image itself. A mechanism for making rubbings or taking impressions in shallow relief would count as photographic by Scruton's definition, despite having nothing to do with photography, as standardly understood, because light would play no role in the formation of the resultant images. What kind of photograph involves no registration of a light array? Absent some reference to the role of light in the formation of the image, we are not even in the ballpark of a viable definition.

Finally, consider the relation between the pair of terms that do the heavy lifting in Scruton's argument: causality and intentionality. Scruton presents these as mutually exclusive, such that a process that is wholly causal must be entirely non-intentional and vice versa. But this is an implausible view, both of photography in particular and of the relation between causality and intentionality in general. At one extreme self-generated and, at the other, accidental photographs might be described as purely causal processes. Think of the negative after-image of a piece of lace bleached over time by the sun onto a light-sensitive surface, or a camera knocked from a windowsill by a billowing curtain so as to trigger its shutter. But photography in general is not accidental and nor, as a whole, does it instantiate the natural causality of the tide eroding a shoreline, even if a natural process (the darkening of silver halides on exposure to light) plays a basic role in the generation of at least analogue photographs. But to boil photography down to this moment of natural causation is to treat it like hair lightening or skin darkening on exposure to the sun. The fact that photography harnesses such processes hardly shows that it can be reduced to them. Despite this, Scruton claims that the "ideal photograph" captures what is essential to photography.

Causality and intentionality in general are not well understood as mutually exclusive. Drawings and paintings are paradigmatically intention-saturated art forms, despite being permeated by processes re-describable in purely causal terms, such as the transfer of paint from brush to canvas. Yet we have no difficulty thinking of the transfer of paint from brush to canvas as expressing a thought or intention. The expression of intention is manifest in the causal process itself, not somewhere prior to or outside it. The application of paint to canvas is not a causal process that happens in addition to a thought; it is partly constitutive of and partly constituted by that thought.

More generally, intentionality, in the sense of intentional action, is manifest in the way in which various causal processes can be harnessed for human ends. One simply needs a sufficiently broad description to show that the causal process in question falls under, or is done in the service of, the fulfilment of some broader intentional goal: not "applying the brush with sufficient force to cause paint of such and such viscosity to be transferred at such and such a rate to a canvas of such and such a weave or resistance," but "painting in the highlights on the rim of the foreground vase."[9] Photography is no different: not "opening the shutter for long enough at such and such an aperture to cause silver halides to react at such-and-such rates to such-and-such intensities of light," but "capturing the fleeting play of light and shadow in the corner of the courtyard."

Scruton underplays the intentionality of photography in two senses that are not always clearly distinguished in his account. He conceives photography in such a way as to preclude it expressing a thought about or attitude towards what is depicted; and he underplays the respects in which photographs are products of intentional action. These are in principle distinct. Expressing a thought or attitude is very often intentional, but it need not be: a royal portrait may betray an attitude towards the sitter that the court artist does not intend to express, and might not even be aware of holding. And there are a great many intentional actions, such as tying one's shoes or cutting one's food, that need not express some attitude towards a mental content. Though distinct, underplaying both is a consequence of conceiving causality and intentionality in zero-sum terms: unlike paintings, photographs can neither express thought contents, nor be understood as the outcome of intentional actions. Why not? Because only photographs are products of a purely causal process. Generalizing this zero-sum picture would make a mystery of our capacity for intentional action altogether.[10]

So much for the questionable nature of Scruton's premises and underlying assumptions; a number of more detailed objections can be and have been pressed to his argument. A common response has been to point out, quite rightly, that he underplays the degree to which photographs can exhibit stylistic features, in virtue of the ways in which photographers exert intentional control over their images. Scruton's contention that photography affords only the grossest stylistic control is manifestly false. One can recognize an image that one has never seen before as a Diane Arbus or Lee Friedlander from a certain period as readily as one can identify a painting as an early Van Gogh or late Cézanne. And once one has seen enough Friedlander cityscapes taken through the open window of a car, one will recognize that the framing provided by the car window and dashboard, the partial reflection of the photographer in the wing mirror, and the off-kilter composition are all intended, and so something to pay attention to when trying to make sense of his images. Appreciation so sharpened, one is more likely to notice the frequency with which

Friedlander's reflection or shadow encroaches on other images, where it might previously have passed unremarked.

Similarly, examining the contact sheets of any major photographer, alongside those images chosen for reproduction, will tell you as much about their intentions as studying the sketches and other preparatory drawings or notes of a painter will tell you about theirs. This is because the best evidence of a photographer's intentions and decision-making, and hence of their thought-processes,

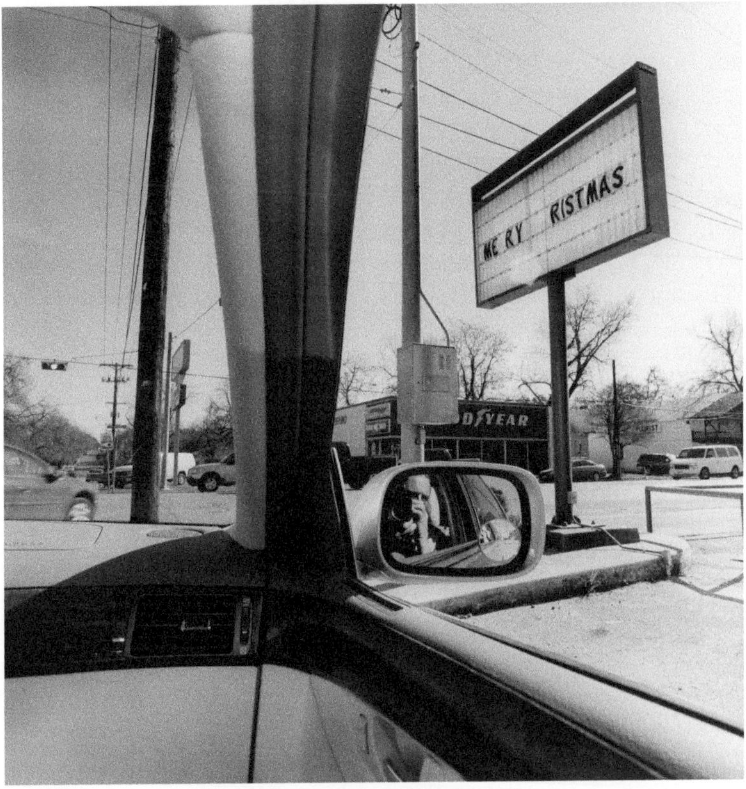

Figure 2.1 Lee Friedlander, *Texas*, 2006, from the series America by Car, 1995–2009. Gelatin silver print, 15 × 15 in. (38.1 × 38.1 cm). Collection of the artist. © Lee Friedlander, courtesy Fraenkel Gallery, San Francisco.

is not always to be sought on the support. Indeed, it very often requires looking elsewhere. Just as an art historian will use X-ray, infrared and ultraviolet to uncover and analyse the stages through which a painting has passed, the photo historian or critic can look to contact sheets, whether analogue or digital: like previous stages of a painting that the painter rejected before affirming the final state of the work, the contact sheet shows the related images that the photographer tried out, only to reject as not fully capturing their

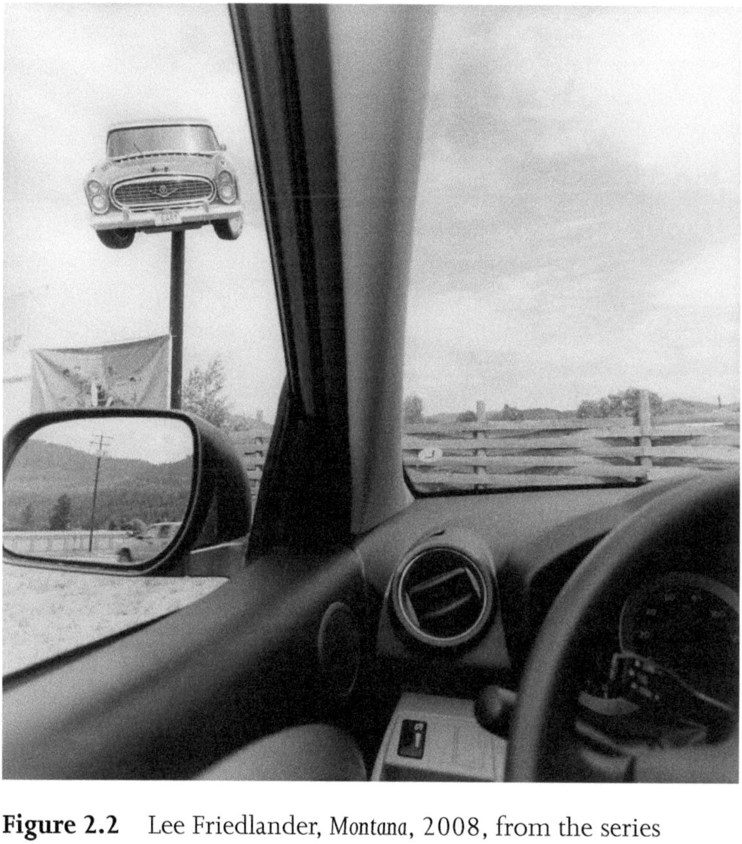

Figure 2.2 Lee Friedlander, *Montana*, 2008, from the series America by Car, 1995–2009. Gelatin silver print, 15 × 15 in. (38.1 × 38.1 cm). Collection of the artist. © Lee Friedlander, courtesy Fraenkel Gallery, San Francisco.

intentions. Anyone who has looked at Diane Arbus's contact sheets will be struck by how often she alights on an image, often anomalous within the sheet, that shows the subject in the most unflattering light—take *Child with Toy Hand Grenade in Central Park* (1962).

Paying attention to both image selection and crop often throws characteristic ways of generating meaning in photography into relief. To the extent that photographs isolate some fragment from the wider world, commending it to our attention (and not all photographs do), framing tends to carry more weight in photography than painting. In particular, placing an object close to a photograph's edge may serve to stress its importance, unlike in painting, where the converse more often holds. For this is where many photographs pointedly crop away the rest of the world, revealing photographic decision-making at work. Given this, placing an object close to, or even cut by, an edge will often serve to draw attention to it.[11] The edges of painting—with the exception of certain paintings that have internalized the lessons of photography—rarely function this way. Once one recognizes this, it is hard not to think that Scruton, in addition to his insensitivity to photography, is guilty of a more basic appreciative failure: judging photographs by inappropriate criteria. The differences between the kinds of photographs and paintings that Scruton has in mind are as stark as those between an art of gradual addition (starting from nothing and building up a surface) and all-at-once subtraction (starting from everything, and cutting away almost all of it in an instant). Why should the fact that photographs fail a test designed for the former—if indeed they do—have any bearing on their standing as photographs?

Such objections are common in the literature.[12] Dominic McIver Lopes calls them the "style argument" and notes that, while true, merely observing that Scruton underestimates photographic style (and with it photographic agency and control) does not suffice to undermine his argument. On Lopes's reconstruction, Scruton's argument turns on what he calls the "equivalence thesis": the view that any interest, aesthetic or otherwise, that we take in a photograph of *x* is an interest that we could (in principle) have taken in *x* seen face to face.[13] The style argument alone cannot refute this thesis, because it leaves what Lopes calls Scruton's "object argument" untouched. This is the claim that photographs are, contrary to what we often believe,

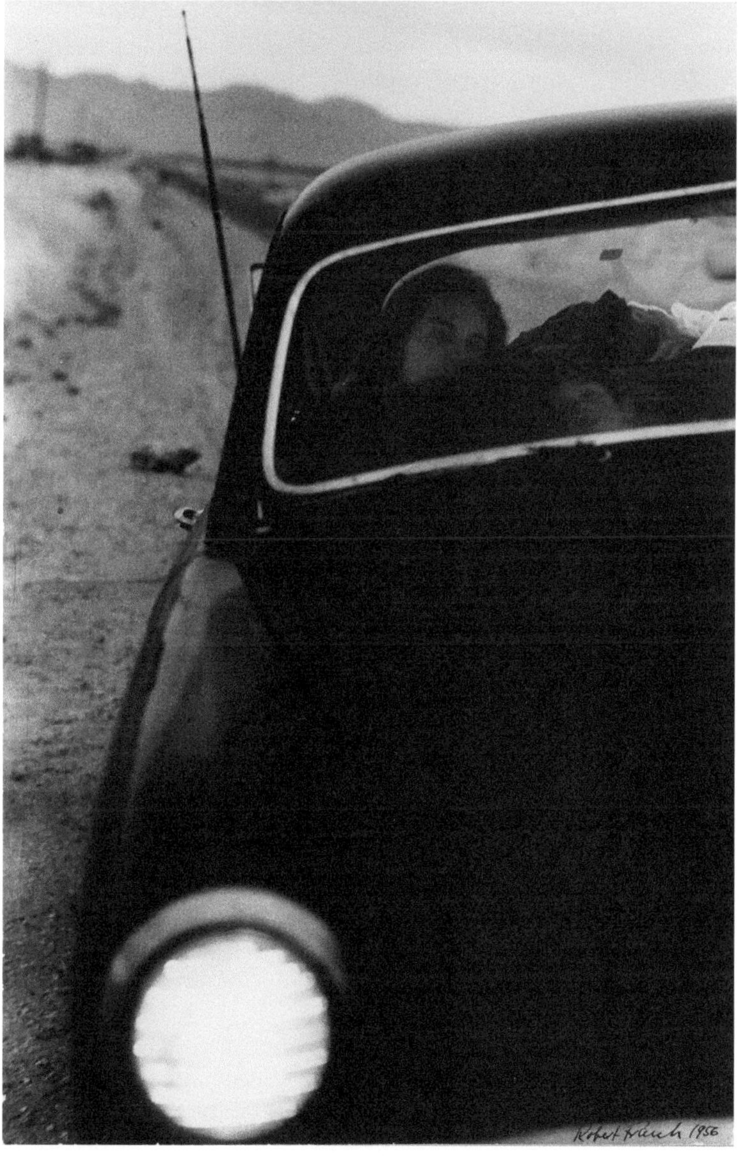

Figure 2.3 Robert Frank, *U.S. 90, En Route to Del Rio, Texas*, 1955. New York, Metropolitan Museum of Art. Gelatin silver print, image $12\frac{5}{8} \times 8\frac{7}{16}$ in. (32.1×21.4 cm). Gift of Joyce F. Menschel, 2014 (2014.209.1). © 2016. Image copyright The Metropolitan Museum of Art/Art Resource/Scala, Florence.

mere conduits for our aesthetic interest in the object depicted. That photographs exhibit stylistic features only shows that the *way* the object is depicted is subject to the photographer's control. But of itself this does not suffice to show that it is not still the object, however depicted by the photographer, rather than the photograph, that is the focus of our aesthetic interest. But if the equivalence thesis is compatible with acknowledging photography's stylistic features, then any argument that satisfies itself with demonstrating the centrality of such features to our appreciation of photography cannot establish that photographs can be works of representational art in Scruton's sense.

It is here that Lopes, drawing on Kendall Walton's notion of "transparency," makes his key move.[14] Seeing objects through photographs is not, contra Scruton, like seeing them through windows or frames. Seeing an object through a window or frame is one way of seeing it *directly*, as are seeing it through eyeglasses, binoculars, or a keyhole. Seeing an object in a photograph, by contrast, is a way of seeing it *indirectly*. We see something indirectly when we see it by means of seeing something else, as we see *x* by seeing *y*, when *y* is a photograph of *x*. Because it is a mode of indirect seeing, transparency does not entail the invisibility of the surface through which the object is seen, as seeing through glasses and/or windows typically does. Indeed, not only is it compatible with seeing that surface, it requires doing so. But if one sees the object only by seeing the photographic surface, then seeing an object through a photograph cannot be like seeing it face to face. Instead, the interest we take in seeing a photograph is an interest we take in seeing an object or scene *as it appears through* its photograph, and this can be different from seeing the same scene face to face in a variety of ways.

But the question is whether any of the interests elicited by the ways in which seeing directly and seeing through photographs differ are aesthetic. Lopes singles out two: photographs can promote "clear seeing," by focusing attention on features that are easily overlooked when seen directly, and transformative, "defamiliarized" seeing, by estranging the appearance of everyday objects or scenes. Lopes sees these as the bases for a documentary and revelatory aesthetics of photography respectively. This defuses aesthetic scepticism because only the scene *as it is seen through* the photograph could afford this. We take an aesthetic interest in a photograph as a photograph when we take an interest in it as a vehicle for seeing through to the photographed scene. Because the photograph no longer falls away in favour of the object photographed, the equivalence thesis is false: not all aesthetic interests we take in photographs are interests that we could have taken in the same scene seen directly; some are possible only in virtue of the indirect means through which we see them.

Photography and fictional competence

This remains one of the best responses to Scruton in the literature.[15] Nonetheless, by focusing on Scruton's account of why photography *cannot* be art, Lopes passes over Scruton's positive account of what would be required to secure its full standing as art. Defusing the former does not suffice to show that photography can achieve the latter: Lopes shows that photography need not fail as representational art in all the ways that Scruton claims it must; but he does not thereby show, having defused what Scruton regards as prima facie impediments to an aesthetic appreciation of photography, that photography elicits aesthetic interests that Scruton would recognize. This requires a further argument.

For Scruton, to demonstrate its credentials as art, photography must be capable minimally of expressing some thought about, or attitude towards, what it depicts rather than merely making it available to perception. According to Scruton, this is something that photography cannot do, because our interest necessarily falls through to the object photographed, rather than remaining with the photograph itself—as would be required to take an aesthetic interest in the thought expressed. Lopes shows this view to be false. But Scruton places the bar on what photography must do to demonstrate full standing as art much higher than this. His positive account makes "fictional competence," the capacity to represent fictional states of affairs, criterial for representational art. Nothing in Lopes's demonstration that, when we take an aesthetic interest in a photograph we are taking an interest in the scene as it appears through the photograph, establishes that photography has this capacity. If anything, it suggests the converse: given that ideal photography has a strictly causal relation to its objects on Scruton's account, and fictional entities cannot leave traces in real light-sensitive media, it follows that strictly photographic representations must be fictionally incompetent, irrespective of whether they are able to elicit our aesthetic interest as vehicles for indirectly seeing through to the scenes depicted. In so far as photographs elicit our interest in this way, this will be as vehicles for seeing through to real, rather than fictional, scenes. So the rejection of aesthetic scepticism remains incomplete. But can an argument that photography is fictionally competent be made? The prospects do not look good, but this is the gauntlet that Scruton throws down to anyone wishing to defeat his argument on its own terms.

In what follows, I trace the origins of what I call "New Theory," as it emerges from various attempts to do just this. Gregory Currie's distinction between "trace" and "testimony," though itself an expression of philosophical Orthodoxy, provides a useful introduction to some of the issues at play. For Currie, photographs belong to a broader class of traces (along with footprints, death masks, thermometers, and seismographs) and paintings belong to a broader class of testimonies (along with diaries, descriptions, chronicles, and drawings). The former are a belief-independent record of how things stood in a particular place at a particular time, the latter a belief-dependent record; they record not how things were, but how somebody believed them to be. While these may often coincide, they need not.[16]

Only testimonies come out as fictionally competent on this division, by virtue of their dependence on the intervening mental states of the artist. Like other forms of testimony, because what a painting depicts need never have existed as depicted, we cannot understand it without understanding it as the expression of beliefs or thoughts about the contents represented. And the same goes for diaries, descriptions, drawings, and the like. Photographs, by contrast, come out as fictionally incompetent. Given that they are constrained—like footprints, fingerprints, and death masks—by their causes, beliefs about what they register ultimately fall away as irrelevant. A photographer may believe, under the influence, that he is photographing pink elephants, but what was in fact in front of the camera is what will be made out, if anything can be, in the pictures that come back from the lab. So far, it seems, so Scrutonian. But Currie does not see this as the only possibility open to photography:

> If photographs represent the fictional, they are not photographs of fictional things. There is a difference between what a photograph is of, and what it is about: a photograph can be about things other than the things it is of. What it is of is just the thing it is a trace of, something we can identify by examining brute causal connections. But if the photograph is part of a fiction, then it may also be about things—fictional things—other than the things it is of.[17]

What we need to know is what it is to be "about" rather than "of" something, and what it means to be "part of" a fiction. Take these in turn. Currie's conception of the former recapitulates a distinction central to the work of Patrick Maynard, between something's being a "photographic picture of" (that is, *about*) *x* and a "photograph of" (that is, *of*) *x*. Only the latter, in Maynard's terms, need depict what it also detects, namely, what it is in fact a photo-chemical trace of; in the former, by contrast, the two may come apart.[18] Take a photograph of Laurence Olivier playing Othello or a film still of King Kong atop the Empire State Building: setting aside the racial politics of blacking up, the former is a photographic depiction (a picture made photographically) of Othello, the latter of King Kong; but, since both depict fictional entities, this cannot be what either detects.[19] The former detects, in addition to incident light and the channel conditions of the equipment used, Olivier got up as Shakespeare's Moor of Venice; and whatever the latter detects—presumably some combination of props, scale models, and special effects such as back projection—it cannot be a 60-foot gorilla, there being no such animals in existence to detect. Contrast these with a publicity shot of Olivier, or a production still of various outsized gorilla parts scattered about the special-effects shop; in both cases these pictures depict what they also detect: Olivier and some props. In Currie's terminology, the former pair of pictures are "about" what they depict, the latter simply "of" them. In Maynard's, the former are "photographic pictures" of their subjects, the latter simply "photographs."

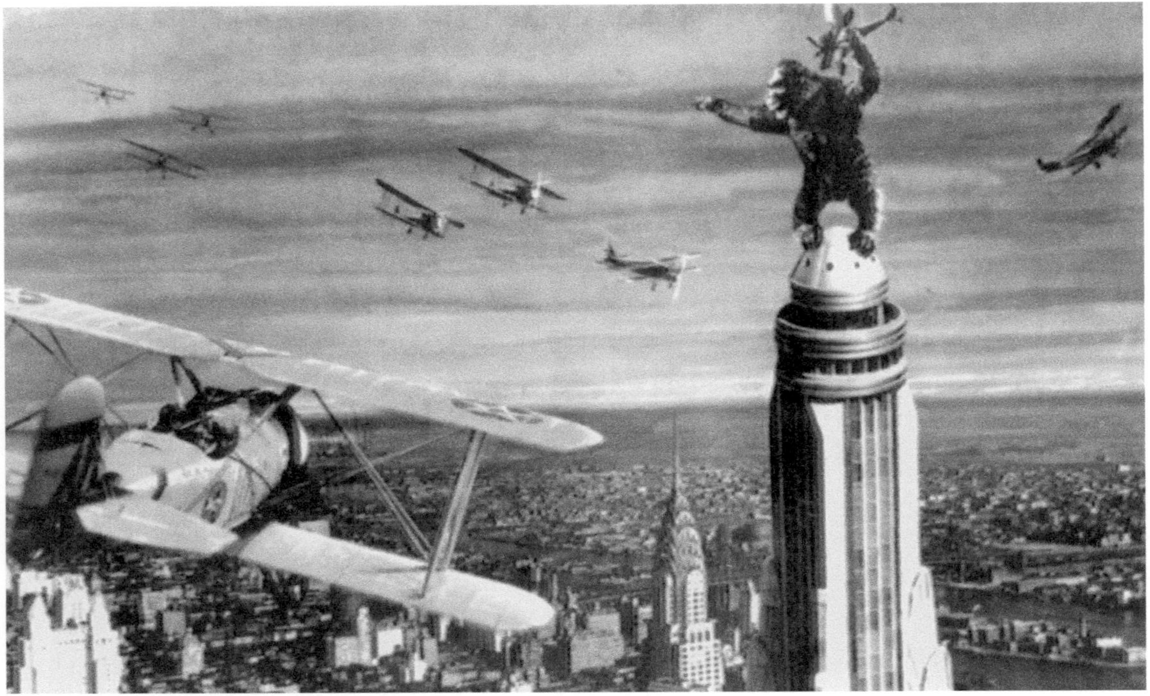

Figure 2.4 *King Kong*, 1933. Directed by Merian C. Cooper and Ernest B. Schoedsack. Film still. Licensed by: Warner Bros. Entertainment Inc.

None of this need trouble Scruton, and nor it is intended to, at least by Currie, since it implies only that photographs may be fictionally competent at one remove.[20] To put it as a slogan: some (but not all) photographs may *represent* ficta, but only by *recording* non-ficta.[21] In the case of Elsie Wright and Frances Griffith's infamous photographs of fairies, they represent fairies by recording painted cardboard props. They are about the fairies that they are photographic pictures of, but they are not plain photographs of them, since that would require recording ficta directly, when ficta cannot leave real traces to record.[22] Nonetheless, they can and do use what they record to represent ficta indirectly. Bringing these resources from Currie and Maynard together, we can say that (sometimes) photographs are "about" the ficta that they depict, but they can only be "of" the non-ficta they detect. As for Maynard, a single photograph can function as both trace and testimony for Currie, though these will remain distinct representational roles: a photograph will be a trace of Olivier and a testimony of Othello if it detects, qua trace, how Olivier actually looked, and depicts, qua testimony, how Othello is thought to have looked:

> A photograph or film image has, potentially, at least two representing functions. It represents in virtue of being a photograph, and in thus representing, it represents the things and events of which it is a trace. But a photograph can also have another representing role: a role imposed on it by its association with some narrative.[23]

This returns us to the second question, left hanging above: what does it mean to be "part of"—or "associated with"—some narrative? Currie addresses this in a later text by distinguishing between "representation by origin" and "representation by use." A photograph represents *by origin* when it depicts what it detects or was caused by; it represents *by use* when it depicts one thing by detecting another, as in the Othello and King Kong examples above.[24] In the case of narrative film, this turns on the relation between the photographs that comprise the film and its narrative: either the images determine narrative content, as in documentary film, or they derive their content from the narrative, as in fictional film. In the former case, representation by origin (what the photographs are of) determines the film's narrative content; in the latter, narrative content determines representation by use (what the photographs are about). Both are genuine possibilities for photography, as used in film, because film only functions as such under conditions of projection, and so cannot be reduced to its bare photographic substrate without loss.

Currie grants that photographs can represent what they are not caused by outside this context, but takes this to be much more difficult. Once photographs no longer serve as the narrative's primary vehicle—as when they function as illustrations to a separate narrative text—photography only flourishes as a trace-recording medium. Thus, according to Currie, Juliet Margaret Cameron's illustrations to Alfred Tennyson's *King Arthur* fail because the photographs' dependence on real sitters (or "sources"), which they are obliged to represent by origin, conflicts with what those sitters are tasked to represent by use. Our awareness of the actual source intrudes on our experience of the picture, and in so doing interferes with our ability to engage imaginatively with the fictional character thereby represented.[25]

Like Scruton, Currie understands photography, fundamentally, by means of a contrast to painting. A painting does not require a sitter: it may have a sitter, whether the actual subject or a model, on the basis of which a real or fictional subject is painted, but it need not have either. This is because what a painting represents by origin is not determined by what the painter worked from while painting it, but by the right kind of intention, embodied in the right kind of way, in the resulting work—such that it can be appreciated by the work's intended audience. With photographs, by contrast, intention is dispensable, as accidental photographs show. A photograph of Durham Cathedral occasioned by dropping a camera is still of Durham Cathedral, no matter how poor the resulting image, simply because it has the right kind of causal relation to the Cathedral. It was reflected light from the Cathedral, rather than something else, that impacted on the camera's light-sensitive surface during exposure. It is in this causal sense that the photograph is of the Cathedral; no intention to depict the Cathedral is required. By contrast, a painting that appears to depict Durham Cathedral, whether generated by an explosion in a paint shop, or unintentionally by painting something that unbeknownst to the painter resembles the Cathedral from that point of view, is not a painting of the Cathedral, no matter how good a likeness, because it does not embody the right kind of intention to make it so. In the first case it would not count as a painting for Currie, in the second, it would not count as a painting of the Cathedral.[26]

In sum: what a painting depicts by origin is constrained by intention, and what a photograph depicts by origin is constrained, causally, by what was in frame during exposure, just as Scruton would have it. Imagine a photograph that appears to depict Durham Cathedral, but was in fact caused by photographing a momentary alignment of objects or buildings seen from a moving train through a telephoto lens. It may be used to represent Durham Cathedral—it may even have been taken for that very purpose—but it does not do so by origin. Photographs represent by origin only what they have the right causal relation to, not whatever they might appear to depict, if this did not in fact cause them. This is what it means to represent by photographic means: it is to use "the ordinary operations of camera and film [to] enable something, the source, to be represented only if it projects light into the camera and onto the film."[27] For Currie, a photograph can represent only its source by such means: "A representation is photographic when it represents by photographic means, and such means confine us to the representation of the source."[28] The obvious inference would be that a picture represents by *strictly* photographic means when it represents its source by origin, and *only* so represents.

Of course, it does not follow from the claim that photographs may represent only their source by photographic means, that they may only represent their source, and nor does Currie take it to—since, even on his own account, photographs are not constrained to represent by photographic means alone. Photographs may also represent by use, as when one person is photographed in order either to represent someone else or even themselves, albeit under other, counterfactual circumstances. In such cases, the photograph represents *x* by recording *y*: that is, it represents another (possibly fictional) state of affairs, but only by recording the actual state of affairs before the camera. Imagine the following case: two brothers who are identical twins are sent to war, but only one returns. The brother who died fathered a child he did not live to see. His widow, distressed by the fact that her husband did not live to see the child he fathered, commissions a rather macabre family portrait in which her brother-in-law stands in for her husband, holding his dead brother's child. To make the representation of the (now fictional) family—the family as it might have been but for the war—as authentic as possible, the surviving brother wears his dead brother's clothes, and has his hair styled in the same way. The resulting photograph represents the fiction that the deceased survived the war to bring up his child by use, but it only represents his widow, child and brother by origin.

For Currie such a photograph represents a fiction, but it does not do so by strictly photographic means. This is the claim that has to be defeated for photography to count as fictionally competent in a strong sense and—to the extent that fictional competence goes proxy for artistic standing in such debates—robustly artistic qua photography. For the same reason, it is the claim that has to be defeated in order to answer the aesthetic sceptic on his own terms. If Currie is right, photographs remain stubbornly constrained by what they are traces of at the first-order level of representation, just as Scruton maintained: they may represent ficta, but only by recording non-ficta; what they cannot do is represent ficta directly, by origin. There is nothing here from which Scruton need demur. Only demonstrating that photographs can be fictionally competent at the first-order level, by strictly photographic means, would secure its fictional competence in the eyes of a committed sceptic like Scruton.

Origins of the New Theory

To find out whether it is possible to make this stronger claim for the fictional competence of photography, it is necessary to examine the conception of photography underlying the Orthodox account more closely. Should it turn out to be incomplete or indefensibly narrow, this would immediately broaden the scope of what photographs can be said to represent by strictly photographic means. Dawn Wilson's (née Phillips) recent presentation of photography as a multi-stage image-rendering process suggests that the photographic process has indeed been seriously under-described by Orthodox theorists, so it is to Wilson that I turn next.

But first a little backfilling is required. Wilson is pushing a central insight of Patrick Maynard's work in a new direction. In *The Engine of Visualization*, Maynard takes aim at the theoretical tendency to ground general claims about photography on what is supposed to be true of how all (and only) photographs relate to their objects. One sees this tendency writ large in Scruton's and Currie's remarks about causality and photochemical traces, respectively, but it also generalizes to foundational accounts in art theory. Rather than starting from this question (which locks in, without argument, a referential relation at the outset), Maynard suggests that we focus instead on the nature of photography as an imaging process. Focusing too narrowly on what is supposed to be special about "the photograph" tends to elicit answers that generalize rashly from a limited set of vernacular or documentary examples that do not exhaust the domain—simply because this is what most people think of when they think of a photograph. The stress on non-agential causality as what distinguishes photography's relation to its objects is a product of this lack of reflectiveness about paradigm cases. Focusing on photography rather than the photograph, by contrast, tends to focus attention on the activity of taking photographs. By advocating this shift of perspective, Maynard, like Weston before him, laid a major foundation stone of the New Theory.

So much for what his approach rules out, what does it rule in? Maynard claims that "[w]hat we call 'photography' is a technology. More accurately, it is a branching family of technologies, with different uses, whose common stem is simply the physical marking of surfaces through the agency of light and similar radiations."[29] What is striking about this description is what it does not say: there is no mention of automatic or mechanical recording, belief-independence, or natural counterfactual dependency—the mainstays of Orthodox accounts. Maynard's focus on process over product can be read as a plea to return to the reflections of photography's earliest pioneers, in order to take the road less travelled in theoretical reflection since. Photography's pioneers also focused on the image-rendering process rather than its products. It was, after all, their competing processes (and not the products of those processes) that were the subject of claim and counterclaim, patents, contracts, and, in Daguerre's case, a state pension. For all their misleading pronouncements about giving nature the capacity to depict itself, photography's inventors were primarily concerned with perfecting that very process. This could not be left to nature, no matter how natural the process was supposed to be.

Maynard's proposal is that we need to think more carefully about what the process they invented involves, rather than taking this on trust. His corrective to any account that reduces photography to its natural dimension is to refocus attention on what photography as a technology enables human beings to do. Under this heading, Maynard characterizes photography, variously, as a tool for marking diverse surfaces with light, a technology for marking surfaces with a variety of diverse functions and uses, and, finally, a family of imaging technologies. Like Wittgenstein's account of games as a family resemblance concept, this family contains complex patterns of similarities and differences, complicated offspring, and hybrid offshoots. Unlike the Wittgensteinian notion, everything called photography shares a common stem: the use of light and other radiations to mark various surfaces. So conceived, photography need no longer be understood primarily as a means of producing pictures; it is a set of tools for amplifying various human capacities, notably our capacities for detecting, imagining, and picturing.

To approach photography as a technology is to ask after the human capacities it amplifies. Most fundamentally, for Maynard, photography amplifies our mark-making capacities, by harnessing the effects of light on various surfaces: it is a complex array of technologies for marking sensitized surfaces through the action of light, not simply for the sake of being seen, but of being recognized as designed for this purpose. Only some such markings are pictures, and only some of those pictures—*pace* Scruton and Currie—are pictures of anything. Here is an account, markedly different to the way of thinking that Scruton and Currie represent, that not only stresses photography's place in human practices, and for achieving human ends, but, highly atypically, builds in no ground-level commitments to realism, resemblance, or even reference. That is, no requirement that a photograph has an object, something that it depicts or even causally refers back to, in order to count as such. Wilson wants to extend Maynard's project of redirecting attention from the product to process, and shares his general concern with photography as an expression of human agency. But in Wilson's case, the animus is on teasing out the implications of no longer treating that process as a black box.

So what is wrong with folk, theoretical, and philosophical conceptions of the photographic process? Simple: they all assume that a photograph comes into existence the moment it has been "taken," which is typically identified with the moment of exposure. But this is not in fact true. In the case of analogue photography, opening the shutter and exposing the film to light only generates a "latent image." The image does not become visible until the film has been processed and, if the film is negative or colour reversal, does not become visible in its final, recognizable form until printed.[30] Open the camera in a misguided attempt to examine the latent image and one will destroy it. In the case of digital photography, exposing the sensor to light causes the capacitors that make up its surface to transmit electrical charges, but the charged or uncharged state of those capacitors not only has to be recorded in binary form, but the resulting code must be output through several stages of digital processing before it generates a visible image. In modern cameras this process is too quick to be humanly detected, but it nonetheless consists of stages that can be distinguished both conceptually and functionally: output the same code (the same strings of 0s and 1s) through a different algorithm and it need not even generate an image file. Processed differently, it could be output as a sound, and that it can shows there is a distinction to be drawn between the information stored and the algorithms required to output that information in visible form. Break the image-rendering process post-exposure, but pre-processing, and one need not emerge with an image at all, and this shows that exposure alone is not sufficient for producing images.

The important point is that in neither the analogue nor the digital case do we have a photograph, if that is taken to imply an image that can be visually appreciated, simply by virtue of exposing a light-sensitive surface to light. More is required to generate a visible image, and this expands the space for further acts and processes to count as "strictly photographic." Given that, without such processes, we have not yet built enough into our account to secure the production of a visible image (and no one denies that photographs are visible), such processes cannot be ruled out of some notional domain of "photography proper." For reasons of this kind, Wilson argues that we need to dispense with the black box treatment of the photographic process that characterizes folk theory and philosophy alike. In place of a default account along these lines:

i. a "pro-filmic" event of some kind takes place before the camera;
ii. the camera takes a photograph of the pro-filmic event;
iii. copies of that photograph (taken to exist at stage [ii.]) are printed;
iv. the appearance of the photograph allows the viewer to learn about the appearance of the pro-filmic event;

Wilson proposes a revised account along the following lines:

i. a changing light image, generated by light sources and objects, forms in real time on the film plane (or CCD sensor);
ii. a "photographic event" occurs when information from that light image is recorded (though no photograph yet exists);
iii. the information stored undergoes a process (or processes) to create a visual image (the "photograph") or multiple copies thereof;
iv. the appearance of this photograph allows the viewer to learn about the nature of the photographic event.[31]

On the new account, we are to understand "photography" to involve an array of practices for creating, storing, and displaying photographs; a "photographic process" to be a multi-stage affair that includes a photographic event and the production of photographic images; and the "photographic event" itself, which now does the heavy lifting, to mean the recording of the light image. So understood, a "photograph" is a visual image, the causal history of which necessarily implicates a photographic event, and photographs will be individuated by means of such events. Photographs that look different, but can be traced to the same photographic event, will be instances of the same photograph, and photographs that look similar, even to the point of indiscernibility, but implicate different photographic events, will be instances of different photographs.

How does this more fine-grained account of the photographic process advance debate? Consider the light image. This comprises light emitted or reflected by objects in the scene and focused by a series of lenses onto the camera's film plane or sensor. Changes in the light image are counterfactually dependent on changes in the scene, and take place in real time. The light image can in principle be visible—as may be seen by stepping inside a camera obscura, or looking at the ground-glass back of an early view camera—even if the design of modern cameras typically hides it from view. Nonetheless, the light image is not to be confused with the photograph because, unlike a light image, a photograph does not remain counterfactually dependent on the scene it depicts. It may be raining on the Eiffel Tower today, misty and overcast tomorrow, but the sun will continue to shine in your holiday snaps regardless. Not so the light image: turn a room facing the Eiffel Tower into a primitive pinhole camera by blacking out the windows and the inverted image projected onto the far wall will continue to track the weather for as long as sufficient light from the scene continues to penetrate the gloom. This is because a light image, but not a photograph, continues to respond in real time to changes in the scene. So far, so obvious: until one realizes that, so described, the light image is a much better embodiment of Scruton's standard analogues for photography (such as mirrors and empty frames) than the latter are for photography itself. The light image, though perhaps not the photograph itself—this remains to be seen—really does stand in a "merely causal" relation to the scene that it resembles. If this is correct, the "ideal photograph," on which Scruton's argument pivots, turns out to be an idealization of the light image rather than the photograph proper, and Scruton's argument hangs on conflating a way-stage in the photographic process with its finished product:

> [I]n Scruton's sense, [the light image] is in broadly the same category as mirror images and the "image" produced by holding up an empty frame. And that is my whole point. A light image may be focused so as to visually resemble the appearance of a scene (to human eyes) and stands in a merely causal relation to that scene. … Scruton's ideal photograph is nothing more than an image of this kind.[32]

On Wilson's account, by contrast, the formation of a light image is necessary but not sufficient for the creation of a photograph, since the latter requires the recording of that image plus further stages of processing to make it visible. Moreover, depending on the time taken to record a light image, a photographic event may, once processed, generate images that could not otherwise have been seen, given the limits of human perception. This would be the case, for example, with images traceable to very long or very short photographic events.[33] So what could have been seen in real time in a light image and what can be seen in the resulting photograph frequently come apart.[34] Nor should the photographic event be confused with a photograph: recording the light image is not a visible event, and its result is not typically visible, absent further processing. That these processes normally take place beneath the threshold of human perception does not change the fact that they are distinct stages in a multi-stage process.

Wilson's reconceptualization of the photographic process opens up a range of interesting possibilities, not least for addressing scepticism regarding the possibility of robust, fictionally competent, photographic art. This is because her more fine-grained conception of the photographic process allows us to reconsider what counts as strictly photographic. If a photographic event is necessary, but not sufficient, for the creation of a photograph, then all those subsequent stages of image processing—without which there could be no visible image—should in principle count as strictly photographic. If one cannot generate a photograph without the use of such means, they can hardly be regarded as incidental to "photography proper." Earlier I characterized representing by *strictly* photographic means, extrapolating from Currie, as the use of standard camera operations to project light onto film (or sensor) in such a way as to represent the source by origin, and *only* so represent it. Should standard darkroom operations be understood as fulfilling this condition? Posing this question flushes out the difficulty: because he assumes, like Scruton, that a photograph exists the moment the film has been exposed, Currie has nothing to say to such questions. On the Orthodox view they simply do not arise. But the point of the revisionist account is to show that Orthodox theorists have offered no principled grounds for maintaining, but merely assumed, that exposing film or sensor to light is sufficient to create a photograph; moreover, there are good reasons to think that it does not.

Consider making prints from negatives: creating prints by non-automated means has always involved selective manipulation of light (over- and under-exposure, partial screening, dodging and burning, etc.), typically to compensate for over- or under-exposure in the original plate or negative. It has also involved combination printing, especially early on, to make up for the insensitivity of early photographic materials, or the limits that various optics continue to place on what can be depicted without loss of focus, distortion or resolution in a single exposure.[35] And it has involved the use of all these methods, singly or in combination, for more inventive purposes.[36] Which, if any, of these operations should be classed as strictly photographic?

I suspect that many would be prepared to allow—albeit at the cost of some patching up of the standard theory—minor adjustments for exposure to go through. There will be questions about the ad hoc nature of such manoeuvres, and the principled basis for ruling in some such corrections and others out, but set aside such fine-grained questions here; the purely inventive use of such methods to generate fictional scenes is sure to be ruled out.[37] But it bears asking why. Composite printing, for example, has been a prominent photographic tradition from the outset, especially when photography sought to establish its artistic credentials by competing with painting.[38] Henry Peach Robinson's *Fading Away* (1858) and *Bringing Home the May* (1862), highpoint or nadir of Victorian pictorialism, depending on your taste and theoretical commitments, make use of five and nine negatives respectively. Oscar Rejlander's *Two Ways of Life* (1857) is stitched together from 32 negatives. And Frank Hurley, in his monumental *An Episode after the Battle of Zonnebeke* (1918), used 12 separate negatives to create a visceral sense of trench warfare not achievable in a single exposure using cumbersome equipment in a war zone. Surrealist intentions aside, Jerry Uelsmann's use of up to a dozen enlargers to superimpose multiple images is, at least technically, a descendant of these ways of working.[39] To be clear: I am making no claims for the artistic value of such work. I simply want to know on what principled grounds it can be excluded, contrary to critical and art historical practice, from the domain of photography.[40]

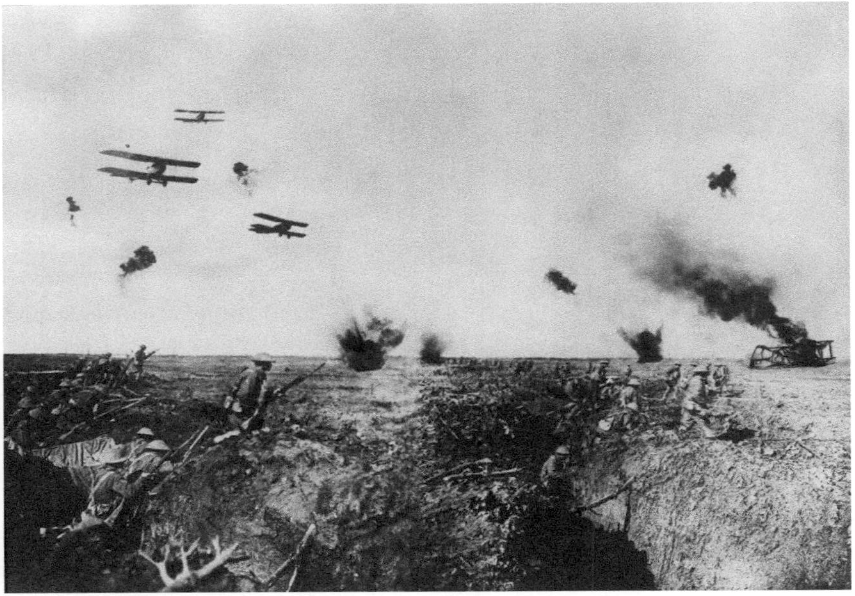

Figure 2.5 Frank Hurley, *An Episode after the Battle of Zonnebeke*, 1918, printed c. 1919. National Gallery of Victoria, Melbourne. Gelatin silver photograph, 14 ⅛ × 19 ⅛ in. (35.8 × 48.5 cm) irreg. (image); 14 ⅛ × 19 ¼ in. (36 × 48.8 cm) irreg. (sheet). Purchased NGV Foundation, 2008 (2008.366).

If it cannot legitimately be excluded, this suggests the starting point for a much stronger response to the sceptic than Currie's, one which aspires to show that photography can be fictionally competent, not merely in the weak (representation by use) sense of representing *y* by recording *x*, but in the strong (representation by origin) sense of representing a fictional source directly. Prima facie, it looks as if this should not be possible, given that fictional entities cannot leave traces in real light-sensitive media. But should this perception turn out to be based on naive assumptions about how photography works, it may be possible to show how photography could represent ficta *by origin* for the first time. This is Paloma Atencia-Linares's strategy, and it is one route to the New Theory.[41] If it goes through, scepticism about photography's fictional competence will be comprehensively defused. By contrast, any account that turns, like Currie's, on representing ficta by recording non-ficta need not trouble Scruton.[42]

Atencia-Linares's chief example, Wanda Wultz's *Io Gatto* (1932), is a photograph of a "cat-woman" that could have been made either by exposing the same piece of film twice in camera or, more likely, by exposing the same sheet of paper to two different negatives in the darkroom. It involves nothing more than the interaction of light and photosensitive surfaces, first in camera and then in the darkroom. Given that this interaction is required for the generation of any (analogue) photograph, Atencia-Linares asks: what principled grounds are there for ruling them out in this instance? The reason such examples are likely to be ruled out, I take it, is that they are not naturally counterfactually dependent on a single spatio-temporally continuous scene. That is, Orthodoxy and folk theory alike tend, implicitly, to assume that photographs document how things stood at a particular place and time and, hence, that any genuine photograph will be a (mind-independent) record of some actual scene's appearance. Atencia-Linares regards this to be ad hoc—something cooked up solely to preserve Orthodox theory in the face of the counter-example. I am not myself persuaded by this, but whether or not it is ad hoc does not ultimately matter. For even if the response can be shown to be principled, Atencia-Linares argues, it does not suffice to rule out the depiction of fictional entities by exploiting photography's capacity for long exposures of single spatio-temporally continuous scenes.[43] Moreover, much like other Orthodox responses to photographs of ficta, it begs the question by implicitly assuming the truth of photography's fictional incompetence, when this is precisely what such examples are intended to put pressure on.

Against any argument that can be reduced to the schema "x is picture of ficta, but photographs cannot depict ficta, so x cannot be a photograph," Atencia-Linares stresses the respects in which even photographs of ficta partake of what is typically held true of photographs: they are traces of the objects that produced them, and we need to grasp this fact in order to appreciate them. Even in such cases, photographers are constrained by the world in ways that painters are not. Granted, such images are no longer naturally counterfactually dependent on how things stand at a particular spatio-temporal location, but the proposal is precisely to give this up as a way of conceiving photography *tout court*. The fact that individual photographs, such as *Io Gatto*, presuppose intentionality is consistent with photographs and paintings generally differing in this regard. So the revisionist proposal, in this weak form, only conflicts with the implausibly strong view that photographs are *always* belief-independent, and not with the weaker, and more reasonable, view that, unlike paintings, they are *typically* belief-independent.

New Theory, restrictive and permissive

This is a point on which proponents of "weak," or what I shall call also "restrictive," versions of the New Theory can agree with recent defenders of a more nuanced, "second-generation" Orthodoxy. For just this reason, however, one might wonder whether this is not a concession too far for resolute New Theorists; for it is not obvious that anyone but the most doctrinaire defender of the Orthodox view need reject the claim in such weak form. Even Scruton could accept it for many (perhaps even all) real-world photographs. Accepting Atencia-Linares's claim does nothing to undermine the distinction between painting and photography that has been the cornerstone of Orthodox accounts from the beginning. We need only accept that making images by harnessing the power of light to mark surfaces is sometimes another way of making intentionally mediated images. In the light of such cases, Atencia-Linares proposes a definition of photographic means according to which photography is fictionally competent:

> Photographic means: any action or technique performed or taking place during the production of an image, including the stages of transduction and storing, that consists solely in the exploitation, manipulation, or control of the incidence of light onto, and its interaction with, a photosensitive material.[44]

By "transduction," Atencia-Linares has in mind the processes through which a latent image has to pass to become a patent (visible) image. By "storing," she means the process or processes required to "fix" (render permanent) the image thereby generated. Only downstream of both do we have a photograph, because without the first we do not have anything to visually appreciate, and absent the second we do not have anything that will not fog on further exposure to light.[45]

I am sympathetic to the animus, if not every detail of this account, as I am sympathetic to the more nuanced understanding of the photographic process that underpins it. Orthodox theorists, by contrast, are likely to find it far too generous. Against this, I believe there is good reason to see it as still too restrictive. Take the constraints it imposes on what may count as strictly photographic. What differentiates photography from non-photography on this account is not natural counterfactual dependency, but the fact that all and only photographs implicate a photographic event. This is necessary but not sufficient for the production of a photograph, however, as no photograph exists solely by virtue of one. For just this reason, any processing required to make the image visible cannot be excluded from the domain of photography proper. But Atencia-Linares's definition arguably only recognizes a subset of such processes as strictly photographic. By singling out control of light's interaction with photosensitive materials it rules in some, but not all, of the things that photographers typically do in the darkroom. This may be intended to head off the charge of drawing the boundaries on what may count as photographic too wide, but it has some arbitrary-looking consequences.

Imagine a photographer who wants to inhibit the exposure of some part of an image while printing. If she does this by cutting a paper mask to occlude that area of the negative, or uses some kind of baffle (including her hands) to shield the relevant area of the unexposed paper ("dodging"), this will count as making an image by strictly photographic means, as both are means of controlling the interaction of light with a photosensitive material. But if a more expedient or accurate way to achieve the same result were to paint an opaque masking agent onto the negative's emulsion, it is not clear that this would also count. The difficulty for proponents of restrictive accounts is that it is hard to distinguish the latter from painterly retouching, which is off-limits to proponents of the strictly photographic. But given that both are ways of controlling the interaction of light with a light-sensitive material, how can one pass but not the other?

Perhaps this example will be deemed inconclusive, so consider a clearer case. Another entirely standard means of achieving the same result that would be ruled out on this account is selectively developing the surface of the print by holding some area of it in (or out) of the developer during development. This will be ruled out because it does not "consist solely in the exploitation, manipulation, or control of the incidence of light onto, and its interaction with, a photosensitive material," despite involving the control of something equally fundamental to photography, the processes through which the chemical reaction of silver halides to light becomes visible. For the same reason, if a photographer allows light to pass through her hands so as to expose a particular area of a print for longer ("burning in") this counts as strictly photographic means. But if a more expedient or accurate way to achieve the same result were to rub that area of the print vigorously with a cotton bud during development, so as to speed up the developer's action (by raising the local temperature of the print's surface), that would not.

Such prohibitions arguably distinguish what is photographic from what is not in arbitrary ways. Photography involves a range of processes including not only the manipulation of light, but control of chemical reactions through use of accelerants, inhibiting agents, and temperature. Is the photographer obliged to take the more circuitous route, should they want their work to count as pure? It is hard to see why they should. From where would such prohibitions or prescriptions derive their normative force? It is not for philosophy, but first-order practice and its criticism, to determine what counts as a photograph. Such prescriptiveness is even reminiscent of Scrutonian strictures it is meant to outflank: "When the photographer sees the photographic plate, he may still wish to assert his control. … He can proceed to paint things out or in, to touch up, alter or *pasticher* as he pleases. But of course he has now become a painter, precisely through taking representation seriously."[46] Granted: Atencia-Linares draws the boundary of what is acceptable considerably further out, thereby allowing more in; but that is ultimately a difference of degree rather than kind.

Lopes takes a very different approach. Like Atencia-Linares, Lopes forgoes natural counterfactual dependency as a necessary condition of an image counting as photographic. Unlike Atencia-Linares, Lopes is not only willing to forgo this for the odd exception that nonetheless proves the more general rule, but believes that natural counterfactual dependency fails to parse between photographs and hand-made images in general.[47] Were this the core difference, Lopes argues, many drawings that involve "belief-independent feature-tracking," including (but not exhausted by) some doodles, rubbings, tracings, and more or less automatic or mechanical drawings, ought to count as photographs. Appealing to the non-conceptual content and sub-personal recognitional capacities mobilized by perception, Lopes maintains that, as a kind of "applied recognition," drawing often involves belief-independent feature-tracking. It requires hand–eye coordination and advanced motor skills, but need not continuously implicate concepts of what is drawn. When it does not, drawing cannot be dependent upon beliefs, since beliefs entail concepts.[48]

Belief-independent feature-tracking does not parse between photography and painting, but between the automatic and non-automatic processes to be found in both. What differentiates photography from painting is not belief-independent feature-tracking, but the fact that some images are made with photographic technologies and others are not. The real question is: what makes an imaging technology photographic? Again, one sees the New Theory's debt to Maynard. According to the New Theory, what renders a process photographic is implicating a photographic event in its causal history. Darkroom techniques such as dodging and burning, double-exposure, or use of multiple enlargers are central to the history of the discipline; just as the manipulation of variables such as hue, contrast, saturation, and other forms of post-production, such as gradient mapping, are already central to that of digital photography. So long as they implicate a photographic event they are photographic—irrespective of whether they preserve belief-independence.

Lopes agrees with Atencia-Linares and Wilson that such imaging processes are necessary. Unlike Atencia-Linares, he holds that none need be specific to photography. This does not mean we need give up talk of traces and testimonies, or natural versus intentional counterfactual dependency altogether; it means that these cut across, rather than parse between, media. Photographic technologies, Maynard maintains, are a family of technologies for marking surfaces with light; what distinguishes photography is the use of light to form the image itself. Wilson's account of the photographic event is essentially a refinement of this: photographs *originate* in events of marking surfaces with light, but are neither reducible to, nor to be identified with, those events. Instead, photography is a process for creating, storing, and displaying images that originate in such events. On Lopes's preferred formulation:

> [A]n item is a photograph if and only if it is an image that is a product of a photographic process, where a photographic process includes (1) a photographic event as well as (2) processes for the production of images.[49]

This definition makes one very elegant move. It consists of two independent clauses and it is their independence that is crucial: the first secures the distinction with non-photographic images by means of reference back to a photographic event; this means that the second, concerning the use of various processes for the production of images, need no longer discharge this burden. This frees up the latter to include all manner of non-photographic imaging technologies, since what marks an image as "photographic" is no longer dependent on such processes. In effect, the first clause acknowledges the irreducibly causal or natural aspect of photography—not its "mechanical" dimension, as Lopes has it, since camera-less images have been part of photography from the outset—but it shrinks this to a point, the recording of a light image.

The resulting account does not require that photography be belief-independent, or counterposed to a class of belief-dependent hand-made images. The key move is to reconceive photography as a multi-stage image-making process that begins, but does not end, in a photographic event: all photographs implicate such an event, but further image-rendering processes are required to make the information recorded available in a form that may be visually appreciated. From the perspective of an Orthodox theorist, this will be way too permissive, and the obvious remedy is to build back in something like belief-independent feature-tracking:

> [A]n item is a photograph if and only if it is an image that is a product of (1) a photographic event and (2) processes for the production of images that (3) ensure belief-independent feature-tracking.

What I later call "second-generation" Orthodox theorists (and perhaps also "restrictive revisionists") will want to qualify this:

> [A]n item is a photograph if and only if it is an image that is a product of (1) a photographic event and (2) processes for the production of images that (3*) *generally* ensure belief-independent feature-tracking.

Lopes might even agree. But from his perspective, the interesting question will be what forces the concession. Whether (3) is true in its more restrictive form will depend on what social institutions and practices a given form of photography serves. Medical, scientific, diagnostic, forensic, and legal practices are all "knowledge-oriented," and that they are imposes additional constraints on the legitimate uses of photography within them: chiefly, that they do not encourage the formation of false beliefs about matters of fact within the relevant domain. But such restrictions are not constitutive or definitional of photography per se. I shall deal with some of the issues this throws up more fully in the next chapter; here I want to focus on several other potential difficulties for Lopes's account: the problem of individuating photographs by means of photographic events; the problem of identifying any particular photograph as a photograph of *x*; and a more general question concerning the account's extensional adequacy. Take these in turn.

According to the New Theory, we individuate photographs by counting photographic events: if you want to know how many different photographs (as opposed to how many different instances of photographs) there are in an exhibition, determine how many different photographic events the prints or other displays in the exhibition derive from.[50] Appearances can be misleading, and it may not always be possible to tell but that only shows that one can be wrong, or lack the required information, not that there is in principle no answer to be had.[51] But what if the image in question is a product of more than one such event? This does not only apply to such obvious cases as combination prints or digital montages. Most analogue photographs are a product of at least two such events: the one (or more) that takes place in camera; and the one (or more) that takes place in the darkroom. Photograms can also be the result of an iterated series of photographic events in the darkroom, and images that blend photographic and non-photographic technologies often involve more than one, at different stages of their creation. Depending on which of these events one individuates a photograph by, one may identify that photograph in question differently.

Why does this matter? Consider the 6,600 rolls of unedited work that Garry Winogrand left on his untimely death from cancer in 1984, totalling some quarter of a million frames. These included some 4,100 rolls of processed but unproofed film that Winogrand had yet to contact print, and 2,500 rolls of unprocessed film the contents of which he had never even seen. Winogrand's influential supporter John Szarkowski, MoMA Director of Photography, oversaw their processing, cataloguing, and proofing, only to dismiss the results as evidence of a lamentable falling off in later life. Only a small sample were included in the posthumous retrospective organized by Szarkowski in 1988. But the late work has since enjoyed something of a renaissance: in 2013, the first retrospective of Winogrand's work in a quarter of a century brought together over 300 images, of which almost half came from this previously unexplored trove; of the 400 images in the catalogue, 164 derive from the 6,600 unproofed and/or unprocessed rolls. None of this late work had been exhibited or published before, and about a third had not previously been printed.[52]

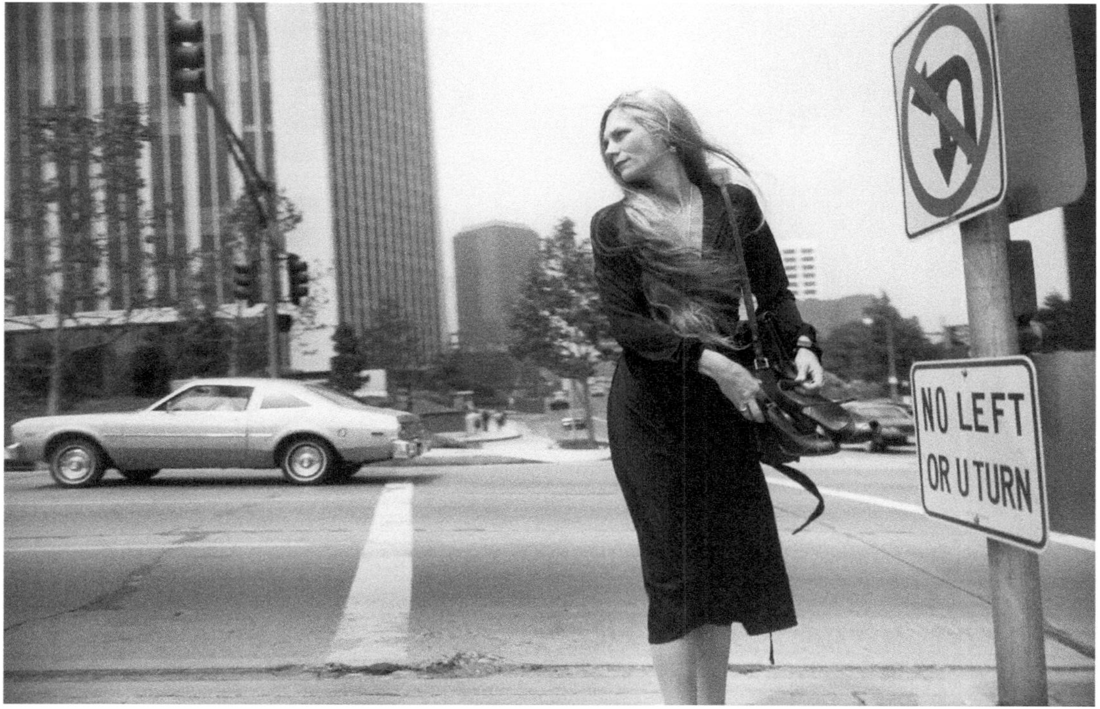

Figure 2.6 Garry Winogrand, *Los Angeles*, c.1980–1983. Gelatin silver print, dimensions unspecified. Garry Winogrand Archive, Center for Creative Photography, University of Arizona. © The Estate of Garry Winogrand, courtesy Fraenkel Gallery, San Francisco.

In both exhibition and catalogue, the works approved by Winogrand during his lifetime and those posthumously selected were clearly distinguished. The question raised by the latter is obvious: to whom should these posthumously selected works be attributed? According to the New Theory, no photographs yet existed in the case of the 2,500 rolls of film left unprocessed at the time of Winogrand's death, and perhaps also in the case of the 4,100 rolls that had been processed but not proofed. But if they did not come into existence until after his death, it is not obvious that they can be attributed (at least solely) to Winogrand. Do they then belong in his catalogues and exhibitions? It seems natural to offer at least a qualified yes: who, if not Winogrand, should they be attributed to? Winogrand took them, and a competent judge should be able to identify them, stylistically, as late Winogrands. But since a photograph has yet to be created prior to processing and printing on the New Theory, and decisions effecting the latter impact on the images that result, this seems to commit us to saying no: it is the final print, rather than the processed filmstrip or contact sheet, that is the correct object of appreciative attention.

Perhaps this is too quick: what if processing and printing are carried out in accordance with those conventions that Winogrand himself adhered to, assuming he adhered to any, and these can be identified? Would we not then want to say that it was Winogrand, rather than some combination of Winogrand and the curators and printers responsible for his 2013 retrospective, who executed these works remotely? This is not unlike the master in Demachy's thought-experiment—even if in this case from beyond the grave.

This depends on whether one individuates photographs by means of their originating event or those subsequent events that generate the final image. If one opts for the former, photographs will be individuated by the initial exposure of the film to light; if one opts for the latter, they will be individuated by, for example, exposure of the photographic paper to light. If the former, photographers turn out to have created all the pictures standardly attributed to them, though this seems incompatible with the New Theory in some cases; if the latter, some turn out to have been created after their supposed author's death, a result that will seem unpalatable to many, but is consistent with the New Theory. As yet, it is unclear how New Theorists intend to resolve this.[53]

Second, consider the problem of identifying a particular photograph as a photograph of *x*. Given that belief-independent feature-tracking no longer places any constraints on how a photograph of *x* must look, what determines when an image still counts as such a photograph? What is to stop the photographer recursively applying one image-rendering process after another to an image that, because it originated in a photographic event, continues to count not only as a photograph, but perhaps also as a photograph of what was before the camera during the recording of information from the scene? If nothing prevents either, then a photograph of the Eiffel Tower could in principle be manipulated to the point of prompting viewers to see the Taj Mahal in its surface, while still counting as a photograph of the Tower nonetheless. But what would it mean, in such circumstances, to claim the image is still a photograph of the Tower?

This opens onto a more general question, concerning the scope or extensional adequacy of New Theory: do permissive versions of the theory in particular correctly sort photographs from other kinds of images in such a way as to rule in all and only photographs? It is consistent with Lopes's take on New Theory, for example, that an image need not be what many would identify as a photograph at all. Take Gerhard Richter's paintings *Lesende* (1994) or *Betty* (1988) (Plates 1 and 2): though they might perhaps be mistaken for colour photographs in reproduction, "paintings that take photographs as subject-matter or source material" seems to be the least contentious description of these works. They are paintings of or from photographs, and they are perhaps also about the photographs that they are paintings of. As is well known, this is not how Richter himself sees them. Richter calls them "photo-paintings," by which he means something stronger than paintings of, from, or about photographs, but a way of *making photographs by painting*:

> I'm not trying to imitate a photograph; I'm trying to make one. And if I disregard the assumption that a photograph is a piece of paper exposed to light, then, I am practicing photography by other means: I'm not producing paintings that remind you of a photograph but producing photographs. And, seen in this way, those of my paintings that have no photographic source (the abstracts, etc.) are also photographs.[54]

Lopes wants to take Richter at his word. This is not possible on the Orthodox theory, but the New Theory provides just what is required. Given the independence of its two conditions, and the fact that both paintings originate in photographic events—both are painted from photographic sources—both count as photographs for Lopes.[55] This will be already enough to make many baulk.[56] But the photographic look of these images arguably obscures just how counter-intuitive a result this is. To see this, it is necessary to look away from images that so obviously resemble their photographic sources.

Imagine the following case. Using an opaque projector, Richter projects a photograph of Kölner Dom onto the surface of a canvas, traces its outlines, then sets about painting in the image. Almost finished, he begins "blurring" the likeness thereby created, by dragging solvent across its wet surface. Applying more and more solvent, but still not happy, he eventually resorts either to scraping away the image entirely or dragging fresh paint across the canvas with an outsized silkscreen blade. The resulting image is a largely monochromatic grey abstract with residual traces of other colours and some facture. How should we understand it: is it as a painting, a photograph, or both? In one obvious sense it is a painting: it is made by applying oils to a stretched linen support, and it can be placed within a lineage of abstraction and the monochrome. But it also implicates a photographic event in its causal history. Like *Betty*, it originates in a photographic event to which further imaging processes have been applied. So described, there is little to distinguish them conceptually. But if it is still a photograph, what is it a photograph of? Can it really be described as a photograph of Kölner Dom?

Lopes talks variously about mark-making being "guided by" or "under the control of" information output from a photographic event, and of photographs being "output by processes where information in light images of pro-photographic scenes inputs into the making of visibly marked or differentiated surfaces."[57] These are vague formulations; it is hard to be sure what they rule in or out. What constitutes sufficient control or guidance for something to count as a photograph of a given subject on this account? Perhaps Lopes takes being "under the control of" information recorded from a photographic event to be a vague notion with fuzzy borders: if so, what counts in one instance need not generalize to others. Be that as it may, one thing is clear: he cannot appeal to belief-independence, to rule an image in or out, without sliding back into the account he wants to outflank. So as yet it seems he has offered no principled basis for saying that this is *not* a photograph of Kölner Dom.

Perhaps this is a bullet that Lopes is prepared to bite. He acknowledges that "nothing in this new theory ... restricts how the light image is formed or how an artifactual image is finally rendered.... Since a photograph might also be rendered through Photo-shopping or drawing ... there is potential for a massive loss of information from the pro-photographic scene."[58] Discussing Wolfgang Tillmans, he grants that "the new theory does not require that photographic processing preserve most, or much, information recorded in the photographic event."[59] Read carefully, such formulations seem to imply that *total* loss information, total absence of control, would rule the resulting image out, even for Lopes. If so, more needs to be said if he wants to stop this slope extending all the way to Richter's grey monochrome. Where would Lopes draw the line, and on what grounds?

One way to go might be to place an experiential or appreciative condition on what suffices to count as a photograph of *x*. Set aside its causal history, and focus for a moment on our imagined monochrome: absent special considerations in its favour, we would not typically entertain a grey monochrome as a picture of Kölner Dom. Were it titled *Kölner Dom*, that would certainly give us pause. That aside, anything we would typically entertain as a picture of that building would either resemble it to the point of facilitating a visual experience as of the Cathedral, or at the very least permit us to see something that could be the Cathedral in its surface. Unless the thinnest recognitional requirement is met, however, we are likely to reject—absent special considerations in its favour—the claim that the monochrome is a picture of the Cathedral. The spirit of Lopes's proposal, I take it, is that there is no reason to treat photography differently in this regard. Perhaps one should say that once its photographic genesis no longer bears on its appreciation in any way, the canvas really is just a monochrome painting.

Asking whether this is true of our imaginary example is an interesting question, and one that seems to generate a dilemma: either the image is a photograph, and a total loss of information is possible after all; or it is not a photograph, and its photographic origins do not matter to its appreciation. The former is unpalatable, for reasons already considered, and the latter will often be false: it can make a difference to appreciating two (even indiscernible) monochromes to know that only one was arrived at by over-painting a prior photo-realist image. One need only imagine another such monochrome derived from a photograph, this time titled *Auschwitz*, to see this quite vividly. In such a case, the artist's refusal to depict its ostensible subject would clearly be relevant to the work's appreciation.[60] But a third possibility appears consistent with Lopes' approach: our imagined monochrome may no longer be a photograph of Kölner Dom, but its photographic origins continue to bear on its appreciation as a painting even so. Were this the case, Lopes's actual position would turn out to be less permissive not only than Richter's and those of his critics who endorse his more extreme pronouncements, but also than Lopes himself is sometimes given to imply.

Notes

1 Roger Scruton, "Photography and Representation," *Critical Inquiry* 7:3 (Spring 1981), p. 589.

2 Lee Friedlander, "An Excess of Fact," in *The Desert Seen* (New York: DAP, 1996), p. 104.

3 Scruton, "Photography and Representation," p. 588 [my insertion].

4 Scruton does not put it in this way, but his understanding of photography ought to rule out talk of photographic subjects. See Dawn M. Phillips, "Photography and Causation: Responding to Scruton's Scepticism," *British Journal of Aesthetics* 49:4 (October 2009).

5 Scruton, "Photography and Representation," p. 578.

6 Dominic McIver Lopes claims, in *The Four Arts of Photography: An Essay in Philosophy* (Oxford: Wiley-Blackwell, 2016), that every premise in the sceptical argument is false. For a summary, see my critical afterword "Doing Justice to the Art in Photography," pp. 135–138.

7 See Wittgenstein on "family resemblance." *Philosophical Investigations*, §67ff.

8 One way to see this is to consider the work of painters, such as Jackson Pollock, Morris Louis, or Ian Davenport, whose work foregrounds the use of natural, causal processes. Another is to consider paintings made by machines. On the latter see Dominic McIver Lopes, *Understanding Pictures* (Oxford: Oxford University Press, 2004), p. 182ff.

9 The classic expression of this thought is G.E.M. Anscombe and Donald Davidson's notion that acts are only "intentional under some description." See

G.E.M. Anscombe, *Intention* (Cambridge, MA: Harvard University Press, 1957) and the essays in Part I of Davidson's *Essays on Actions and Events* (Oxford: Oxford University Press, 2001). For its application to photography, see Dominic McIver Lopes, "Afterword: Photography and the 'Picturesque Agent'," in Diarmuid Costello, Margaret Iversen, and Joel Snyder (eds.) "Agency and Automatism: Photography as Art since the 1960s," *Critical Inquiry* 38:4 (Summer 2012) and Diarmuid Costello, "But I *Am* Killing Them! Reply to Charles Palermo and Jan Baetens on Agency and Automatism," *Critical Inquiry* 41:4 (Autumn 2014).

10 On the impact and ramifications of zero-sum conceptions for Orthodox theory, see Diarmuid Costello and Dawn M. Phillips, "Automatism, Causality and Realism: Foundational Problems in the Philosophy of Photography," *Philosophy Compass* 4:1 (2009), pp. 14–18.

11 Compare Cavell: "You can always ask, of an area photographed, what lies adjacent to that area, beyond the frame. ... When a photograph is cropped, the rest of the world is cut *out*. The implied presence of the rest of the world, and its explicit rejection, are as essential in the experience of a photograph as what it explicitly presents." See *The World Viewed*, pp. 23–24.

12 See Robert Wicks, "Photography as a Representational Art," *British Journal of Aesthetics* 29:1 (January 1989); William King, "Scruton and the Reasons for Looking at Photographs," *British Journal of Aesthetics* 32:3 (July 1992); Nigel Warburton, "Individual Style in Photographic Art," *British Journal of Aesthetics* 36:4 (October 1996).

13 Dominic McIver Lopes, "The Aesthetics of Photographic Transparency," *Mind* 112 (July 2003).

14 "Transparency" is Kendall Walton's term for the distinctive kind of indirect but nonetheless literal seeing that photographs allegedly afford: we (literally) see *x*, by seeing *y*, when *y* is a photograph of *x*. This is the focus of Chapter 3, below. See Kendall Walton, "Transparent Pictures: On the Nature of Photographic Realism," *Critical Inquiry* 11:2 (December 1984).

15 David Davies has since argued that, even taken together, satisfying the style and object arguments does not suffice to undermine Scruton's position. See "Scruton on the Inscrutability of Photographs," *British Journal of Aesthetics* 49:4 (October 2009) and "How Photographs 'Signify': Cartier-Bresson's 'Reply' to Scruton," in Scott Walden (ed.) *Photography and Philosophy: Essays on the Pencil of Nature* (Oxford: Wiley-Blackwell, 2008).

16 This distinction is often phrased in terms of *natural* versus *intentional* counterfactual dependency in discussions of Kendall Walton. See Walton, "Transparent Pictures," pp. 262–265, and Gregory Currie, "Photography, Painting and Perception," *Journal of Aesthetics and Art Criticism* 49:1 (Winter 1991), p. 25.

17 Gregory Currie, "Visible Traces: Documentary and the Contents of Photographs," *Journal of Aesthetics and Art Criticism* 57:3 (Summer 1999), p. 288.

18 On the distinction between "photograph of—" and "photographic picture of—" see Patrick Maynard, "Photography," in Jerrold Levinson (ed.) *The Oxford*

Handbook of Aesthetics (Oxford: Oxford University Press, 2003). On depiction and detection, see his "Talbot's Technologies: Photographic Depiction, Detection and Reproduction," *Journal of Aesthetics and Art Criticism* 47:3 (Summer 1989), and *The Engine of Visualization: Thinking through Photography* (Ithaca, NY: Cornell University Press, 1997).

19 Whether one thinks it depicts Othello will depend in part on how one conceives the role of intention in determining pictorial content.

20 That Currie, despite the greater nuance of his account, does not mean to contest Scruton is signalled by adopting the term "ideal documentary" to characterize the class of narrative films he wishes to isolate. See "Visible Traces," p. 291, pp. 289–290 and pp. 291–293.

21 "Some, but not all," because photographs could do this as often as not without transforming our understanding of photography.

22 Maynard, "Talbot's Technologies," p. 264.

23 Currie, "Visible Traces," p. 289.

24 Gregory Currie, "Pictures of King Arthur: Photography and the Power of Narrative," in Walden, *Photography and Philosophy*.

25 Currie develops this into an account of "representational dissonance" in "Pictures of King Arthur," pp. 273–278. Like photography, cinema is a "source-based representational system": it can only represent its source (typically an actor) by origin and everything else (typically a character) by use. But cinema has the benefit of imaginatively engaging narratives to counteract the tendency of the source to "pop out," thereby making what is represented by use more salient than what is represented by origin. It is hard for photography to compete with this.

26 Note the affinities to Scruton: the image of Durham Cathedral generated by an explosion in a paint shop is not a painting of the Cathedral for the same reason that the line of detritus left by the retreating tide is not a representation of the Kent coast. Both can be explained in non-agential terms. The differences between Currie and Scruton are largely semantic. An accidental photograph, like any photograph, counts as a "representation" for Currie, since it represents by origin whatever it is a trace of. Scruton would not call this a "representation," because it does not express a thought about what it depicts. But Scruton's reasons for withholding the term are consistent with Currie's reasons for granting it.

27 Currie, "Pictures of King Arthur," p. 271. Currie reveals the normative commitments of his account, when he describes it as concerned solely with the "normal" use of photography, "the use we might describe as its proper function."

28 Ibid., pp. 268–269.

29 Maynard, *The Engine of Visualization*, p. 3.

30 This is not true as a general claim, but it is true for all photographic processes that involve the intentional use of chemical solutions, if not chemical reactions per se. The fact that it does not apply to "natural" or "self-generated"

photographs may for some constitute reason to deny that these are photographs. In such cases the image appears over time with exposure to light. Anyone who denies that such cases are photographs would have to explain why Henry Fox-Talbot's contact prints of lace are photographs.

31 Phillips, "Photography and Causation," pp. 336–338.

32 Ibid., p. 337.

33 Think of exceptionally short photographic events, such as those involved in Harold Edgerton's photographs of nuclear explosions, taken with a specially developed camera capable of shutter speeds of 1/4,000,000th of a second, or exceptionally long photographic events such as those required by powerful telescopes that produce photographs of stars by superimposing a series of all-night exposures that track a section of the night sky.

34 See Snyder and Allen, "Photography, Representation and Vision."

35 See Michael Fried's account of Jeff Wall's Morning Cleaning, Mies van der Rohe Foundation, Barcelona (1999) in *Why Photography Matters as Art as Never Before* (New Haven, CT: Yale University Press), pp. 66–76.

36 Initial debates occasioned by digitalization were often based on neglect of this history: oft-expressed worries about "painting with pixels" transforming the "ontology of the photographic image" from the 1990s replay debates occasioned by pictorialism in the later nineteenth century.

37 "Suppose I were to take figures from a photograph of, say, Jane, Phillip, and Paul, and, having cut them out, I were to arrange them in a montage … the final result [may] represent, say, a lovers' quarrel; but it is not a photograph of one. It represents a quarrel because it stands in precisely the same intentional relation to a quarrel that a painting might have exhibited. Indeed, it is, to all intents and purposes, a painting, except that it happens to have employed photographic techniques in the derivation of its figures." Scruton, "Photography and Representation," pp. 592–593.

38 There is no reason to think that this constitutes an illegitimate aspiration for photography unless one has already made various restrictive assumptions about what is proper to a given medium. Such substantive restrictions cannot be made without argument. Noël Carroll argues that all attempts to do so are either vacuous or under motivated. See *Theorizing the Moving Image*, Part I. For my own take on these issues, see "On the Very Idea of a 'Specific' Medium: Michael Fried and Stanley Cavell on Painting and Photography as Arts," *Critical Inquiry* 34:2 (Winter 2008) and "Automat, Automatic, Automatism: Rosalind Krauss and Stanley Cavell on Photography and the Photographically Dependent Arts," *Critical Inquiry* 38:4 (Summer 2012).

39 The widespread use of digital montage by Gregory Crewdson, Andreas Gursky, and Jeff Wall, among others, is in this respect not as novel as is often suggested.

40 For the record: with the exception of Hurley, whose work is interesting in its own right—and whose *An Episode after the Battle of Zonnebeke* (1918) I take to be a source for Jeff Wall's *Dead Troops Talk (A Vision after an Ambush of a Red Army Patrol, near*

Moqor, Afghanistan, Winter 1986) (1992)—I find all this work aesthetically and artistically lamentable. But that is a matter of critical judgement, not a definitional question about what counts as photography.

41 See Paloma Atencia-Linares, "Fiction, Non-Fiction, and Deceptive Photographic Representation," in Diarmuid Costello and Dominic McIver Lopes (eds.) "The Media of Photography," a special issue of *Journal of Aesthetics and Art Criticism* 70:1 (Winter 2012).

42 Since Scruton does not deny that one can take a picture of a draped nude and call it Venus, or a sleeping drunk and call it Silenus, he can redescribe cases of alleged representation by use as recordings of prior representational acts.

43 Atencia-Linares cites several ingenious examples to make this case, including Gjon Mili's famous 1949 photographs of Pablo Picasso drawing various fictional creatures, such as a centaur, with a light pen. See "Fiction, Non-Fiction, and Deceptive Photographic Representation," pp. 24–26.

44 Atencia-Linares, "Fiction, Non-fiction and Deceptive Photographic Representation," p. 22.

45 Ibid., p. 21.

46 Scruton, "Photography and Representation," pp. 592–593.

47 Lopes, *The Four Arts of Photography* and, in summary form, "Jetz sind wir alle Künstler," in Julian Nida-Rümelin and Jakob Steinbrenner (eds.) *Fotographie: zwischen Inszenierung und Dokumentation* (Ostfinden: Hatje Cantz Verlag, 2012), p. 106ff.

48 In "Pictorial Experience," §9.4 of *Understanding Pictures*, Lopes considers the moon-drawings from which Galileo learnt, by replicating the patterns of light and dark visible on the moon's surface, that the moon was not smooth.

49 Lopes, "Jetz sind wir alle Künstler," p. 115. This definition is expanded in *The Four Arts of Photography*: "a photograph is an image output by a mark-making process taking input from an electro-chemical event that records information from a light image of a pro-photographic scene" (p. 81). I prefer the earlier version.

50 In "Jetz sind wir alle Künstler," Lopes recommends counting photographs by counting photographic events.

51 This can give rise to some surprising results. Imagine two photographs that look entirely different but are in fact instances of the same photograph, since both are generated from non-overlapping portions of the same negative or file. One might appear to be a grainy black-and-white film still of King Kong atop the Empire State, while the other shows, in lush colour, a bunch of lilies in a showroom interior. If the former is a blow-up of a postcard propped against the base of the vase seen in the latter, they are instances of the same photograph, since they share the same photographic event, which both represent only partially.

52 *Garry Winogrand*, curated by Leo Rubinfien, Erin O'Toole, and Sarah Greenough (New Haven, CT: San Francisco Museum of Modern Art and Yale University Press, 2013).

53 One way to go from here might be to distinguish between works and their instances along lines familiar from multiply instantiated art forms such as music,

where we standardly distinguish between the work and its performances. Dawn Wilson is working on an account along these lines, but the details remain to be made out.

54 Gerhard Richter, "Interview with Rolf Shön," in Richter, *The Daily Practice of Painting:Writings 1962–1993*, ed. Hans-Ulrich Obrist (London: Thames & Hudson, 1995), p. 73.

55 In fact for Lopes they are both photographs *and* paintings: paintings because Richter uses richly embodied mark-making, hand–eye coordination, and advanced motor skills; photographs because they implicate photographic events.

56 "One might … sever the counterfactual dependence of a photograph's features on its external object—by over-painting it … this would render the photographic mechanism redundant. Consequently, the resultant picture would not be genuinely photographic." See Catharine Abell, "The Epistemic Value of Photographs," in Abell and Katerina Bantinaki (eds.) *Philosophical Perspectives on Depiction* (Oxford: Oxford University Press, 2010), p. 84, p. 101.

57 Lopes, *Four Arts of Photography*, p. 97.

58 Ibid., p. 109.

59 Ibid., pp. 123–124.

60 Compare Alfredo Jaar's *Rwanda Project*, a series of photographically based installations documenting the genocide in Rwanda. In refusing to depict its victims, Jaar pointedly refuses the standard tropes of photojournalism. The unseen presence of what is not depicted nonetheless pervades the works, and means everything to their appreciation.

Three

Transparency and its critics

As I have presented it so far, the New Theory has one notable omission and leaves one obvious question unanswered. The omission is that it is not premised on responding to the strongest version of Orthodoxy. To date, it arises largely from contesting Scruton's scepticism. Kendall Walton's work presents a much stiffer challenge because, unlike Scruton, Walton is not a sceptic about photographic art. Not only does this present no difficulty for his account, but in Walton one finds resources for understanding both photography's aesthetic significance and its epistemic advantages over other forms of depiction. This brings me to the hard question for New Theory. Scruton provides one way of thinking about photography's epistemic advantage: it is because pure photographs have a strictly causal relation to their objects, one that bypasses the intentions and beliefs of the photographer (and, so too, the lapses of human attention), that they are necessarily accurate sources of information about the appearance of what they depict. But for just this reason they cannot be vehicles of significant artistic expression, since the latter depends on the artist's decisions about what to thematize and what to suppress, and how to go about doing so. New Theory will offer no advance over Orthodoxy if it can only show how pure photography can be serious art at the cost of rendering its epistemic capacities mysterious. The hard question for New Theorists is how to account for photography's epistemic advantage.

New Theory is clearly better equipped than Orthodoxy to explain photography's artistic potential: given its more nuanced conception of the photographic process, it has a correspondingly richer conception of photographic agency. Since the photographic process comprises a number of stages, all of which are necessary to the creation of an image that can be visually appreciated, the photographer can exercise his or her agency purely photographically by intervening in any stage of that process. It is whether New Theory can, consistent with this account of what makes photography art, also explain the epistemic advantage many take to distinguish photography that remains to be seen.

Seeing directly and indirectly

Walton's account, by contrast, already speaks to both. It brings a fully fledged theory of depiction, developed largely independently of photography, to bear on what makes photographic depiction distinctive. What makes a photograph a picture is what makes anything a picture: it is a two-dimensional surface in which one can see a three-dimensional scene, without being under any illusion that one is in the presence of the scene itself. Like pictures in general, photographic pictures are "props in games of make-believe" that serve as "mandates to imagine."[1] Pictures prompt us to imagine, of our acts of seeing them, that these are acts of seeing what they depict. This is not some special or obscure ability, and nor is it volitional; it is simply what it is to see a scene in a flat surface for Walton. Walton expresses this by saying that it is fictionally, rather than literally, true that we see what is depicted. This is because it is only true in the game of make-believe in which the picture itself serves as a prop. What makes photographic pictures photographic is, accordingly, something that marks photographs out from pictures in general. Photographs are a special kind of picture through which we literally, if indirectly, see the world itself (as opposed to its depiction) by seeing its photograph. That is, we see the subject S by seeing the photograph P when P is of S. So with photographs, but not other kinds of pictures, it is literally true that I see their depicta indirectly, and fictionally true that I see them directly. The latter is true of all pictures and is what makes photographs a kind of picture. The former is only true of mechanically generated pictures and is what makes photographs (and films comprising photographs) a special category of "transparent" pictures.[2] I see Mont Sainte-Victoire itself, indirectly, by seeing its photograph; but, as with its painted depiction, I only imagine that I see it directly. What makes photographs pictures is responsible for their aesthetic significance, what makes them a special category of transparent picture is responsible for their epistemic advantage.[3]

Because it already speaks to both, it is Walton's account that New Theorists should be cutting their teeth on. Viewed in this light, it is hard not to see the focus on Scruton as something of a distraction. The real challenge for New Theorists is how their account fares against Walton. Is there reason to prefer it? Does it offer any advance over what remains, for all the controversy it has generated, the single most influential statement in the philosophy of photography? Because "Transparent Pictures" addresses both the epistemic and aesthetic capacities of photography, whereas New Theory has to date focused on the latter, Walton's account has a prima facie advantage over the New Theory. Given this, I now turn to Walton, and what New Theorists might offer in reply. Walton's central (and notorious) claim is that we *see through* photographs:

> The invention of the camera gave us not just a new method of making pictures and not just pictures of a new kind: it gave us a new way of seeing.
>
> ... Photography is an aid to vision, and an especially versatile one. With the assistance of the camera, we can see not only around corners and what is distant or small; we can also see into the past. We see long deceased ancestors when we look at the dusty snapshots of them. ... Photographs are *transparent*. We see the world *through* them.[4]

Right away one sees Walton's dual interest in photography's aesthetic and epistemic capacities: "a new method of making pictures" and "an aid to vision," respectively. For Walton what is distinctive about photography is that it is *both*: like painting, drawing, or etching it is a way of making pictures; like telescopes, microscopes, and mirrors it is a way of seeing the world. Acknowledging photographs' prosthetic functions need not entail denying their imaginative functions; rather, photographs constitute a special kind of transparent picture through which we see the world. Here Walton is in agreement with

Patrick Maynard, for whom the interaction between photography's epistemic and aesthetic capacities is central: "'Photography' might be most simply characterized as the site of the most spectacular interaction of depictive and detective functions."[5] Photography is the interaction of a depictive function (in Walton's terms, "a mandate to imagine") with an extension of our natural powers of visual detection:

> Mechanical aids to vision don't necessarily involve *pictures* at all. Eyeglasses, mirrors, and telescopes don't give us pictures. To think of the camera as another tool of vision is to de-emphasize its role in producing pictures. Photographs are pictures, to be sure, but not ordinary ones. They are pictures through which we see the world.[6]

For Walton, describing photographs as "transparent" does not imply, as it would for Scruton, that photographs are invisible. On the contrary, we see *S by seeing P*. In fact, "seeing through" photographs not only does not imply the invisibility of the surface through which we see—unlike windows and eyeglasses—it requires that we see that surface. So it cannot be like seeing face to face, and this creates the conceptual space to take an aesthetic interest in the way objects appear in photographs that we could not take in the same objects seen directly. This, in a nutshell, is Lopes's argument against Scruton's "equivalence thesis," and we can now see how it draws on Walton. Rather than implying invisibility, Walton understands transparency to involve the preservation of "perceptual contact" with the objects thereby seen.

Walton recognizes that the transparency thesis will strike many as counter-intuitive. So he starts with a slippery slope argument intended to soften up his critics' intuitions. Designed to head off the most obvious objections at the outset, it invites critics to spot a difference of kind (rather than degree) that would halt the slide down the slope to the conclusion that we see through photographs. In effect it asks: why *not* call photographs transparent? But it does not offer positive considerations in favour of doing so. Are we willing to say that we see things through eyeglasses, windows, and telescopes? Tick. What about around blind corners with the aid of convex mirrors, or from under water with periscopes? Tick. If you grant seeing around corners and from under water, why not grant that security guards can see occluded buildings on the far side of the complexes they guard via CCTV cameras, or that we can see our favourite teams, from outside the stadium, when their games are broadcast live? And if you are prepared to grant all that, why not also grant that we see through documentary films and pre-recorded TV, even though it is not broadcast live?[7] That being so, why not grant that we see through photographs, which is no more indirect than many of these cases?

The problem is that most of Walton's critics are not prepared to grant all this. All accept the first group as unproblematic. Most will, subject to certain caveats about the number of mirrors involved, accept the second. The problems set in with the third: neither CCTV nor live broadcast convey "egocentric information." That is, information *internal to what is seen* about its spatio-temporal location relative to its perceiver.[8] Because we cannot tell how what is seen in a photograph relates, spatiotemporally, to the photograph through which we are now seeing it, photographs do not communicate how we are positioned relative to the things thereby seen. When a photograph seems to afford such knowledge, this is typically contingent on the circumstances in which we see it—such as viewing it in the room in which it was taken or in the company of its subject—rather than a feature of the photograph itself.

Imagine sitting before a shuttered window that, were it not shuttered, would afford a view of the Eiffel Tower, and flipping through a book of photographs of the Tower taken around Paris. Nothing in those photographs themselves gives you your current position relative to the Tower: to know that, you need to open the shutters. Of course, you may know the location of the room, and you may know the city well, in which case you may be able to *infer* which photograph represents the view from the window, and thereby shows how you are positioned relative to the Tower. But this is not something you learnt from looking at the photograph; on the contrary, your prior knowledge allowed you to understand what you were seeing in it. Contrast this with seeing the Tower through those tourist telescopes dotted around the city. Here there is no difficulty orienting yourself egocentrically to the Tower. Provision of egocentric information is regarded by many of Walton's critics as a condition that all genuine seeing must fulfil. Because photographs fail to provide such information, such critics maintain that while we do see through lenses and mirrors, we do not see through photographs.[9]

Walton responds that mere seeing, as opposed to the cognitively more demanding activity of forming beliefs about what one sees, need not entail knowing the location of what one sees relative to where one sees it from. Even proponents of the egocentric information objection, such as Noël Carroll and Currie, accept that we see through mirrors. But if one extends the chain of mirrors sufficiently, one can no longer tell where an object seen through them is located relative to oneself. This does not prevent us *seeing* the object, however; we merely no longer see *where* it is located. In response, Currie bites the bullet: we normally see through mirrors, but once egocentric information is lost, as it is with a protracted series of mirrors, we no longer do so. From Walton's perspective, Currie is only forced into this concession because he places the bar on seeing much too high: forming beliefs about what one sees, including beliefs about its location, requires the use of concepts; mere seeing does not.

Moreover, Walton points out, many cases of what we take to be egocentric information preserving perception implicitly depend on background information not given in perception itself. Imagine seeing someone reflected in a mirror through a half-open door in your own home. Your home is a space you know intimately. You know, for example, the orientation of that mirror, despite the fact that its edges may not be visible, and that it is not reflecting an image from another mirror occluded by the half-open door. Only because you already know all this—as you know that you are seeing via a mirror rather than directly—do you know where the person reflected is located relative to you. But none of this is given perceptually, although the reflection itself is. Analogously, even should a complex set of calculations be required to work out where a rose reflected in a chain of mirrors is located relative to its viewer given the number, orientation, and nature of the mirrors involved, the viewer is still seeing the rose; she is just not seeing where it is.[10]

Conceptual analysis and theory construction

For all Walton's efforts to defuse the transparency thesis's counterintuitiveness, the majority of commentators continue to find the claim that we see through photographs unconvincing.[11] I am not myself overly exercised by whether or not the thesis is counter-intuitive, or whether Walton's attempts to demonstrate that it is do not succeed. My own view is that appeals to intuition should be treated with caution, since they often mask unacknowledged, culturally or historically parochial, theoretical commitments. Instead I want to focus on a question that goes unasked, irrespective of the verdict one comes to concerning the theory's intuitiveness. Suppose Walton's critics are right to find the thesis counter-intuitive; should Walton even be *trying* to convince them otherwise? If Walton really is "proposing something of a conceptual revision," that the transparency thesis strikes his critics as counter-intuitive is presumably to the point.[12] Walton's later methodological reflections suggest that he may have since come to this realization himself, even if he did not recognize it then. This tends to pass unremarked, as does the fact that, for all the controversy that calling photographs "transparent" has elicited, the mind-independence thesis with which Walton underwrites it is taken as uncontroversial by those same critics.

To see this, consider Walton's positive argument. Apparently anticipating scepticism about the strength of his negative, slippery slope, argument, Walton goes on to propose two necessary, but not jointly sufficient, conditions on seeing. To count as a genuine instance of seeing, an experience must minimally (i) depend causally and counterfactually on what is seen and (ii) preserve real similarity relations. Take these in turn. When one looks at a photograph, the causal chain between scene and seeing of that scene through its photograph is unbroken; the photograph is caused to look the way it does by what was in front of the camera, in conjunction with the laws of optics, chemistry, and electrical reaction—subject to whatever variables of image capture and image processing have been applied—and so too is one's perception of the resulting photograph. One's visual experience remains counterfactually dependent on what was before the camera: had, contrary to fact, what was before the camera been different, the photograph would have differed accordingly. Perception can be understood causally or counterfactually, and there is a rich causal and counterfactual dependence of what is seen in photographs on what was before the camera when they were taken.

Since much the same can be said of many naturalistic paintings—had, contrary to fact, there been an orchard rather than a solitary dead tree behind the farm buildings, the painting of the scene would have differed accordingly—this claim needs tightening up: only photographs are *mind-independently* counterfactually dependent on the scene. Had what was before the camera been different, the resulting photograph would have differed accordingly, irrespective of whether the photographer noticed the difference or intended to record it. By contrast, whether a painting would have differed depends on the painter not only noticing, but intending to depict that difference. What appears in the painting is therefore dependent on the mental states of the artist, and what appears in the photograph is not.

In Currie's terms, paintings are a kind of visual testimony; they record the painter's beliefs about the scene. Photographs are a kind of a visual trace; they record the scene independently of the photographer's beliefs about it. If a painter hallucinates pink elephants while painting monkeys, he will produce pink elephant pictures; should the photographer hallucinate pink elephants while photographing monkeys, she will produce monkey photographs—assuming both retain control over their equipment. Because photographs show us how things actually were, whereas paintings show us how painters believed they were, seeing through a painting depends on the intervening mental states of another agent, whereas seeing through a photograph does not. Seeing through a photograph is thus "naturally dependent" on the scene, seeing through a painting "intentionally dependent."

But natural counterfactual dependence is only a necessary, not a sufficient, condition of seeing. Imagine a machine that records optical input from a scene, and outputs it in the form of verbal description; the latter would not facilitate seeing the scene. Why not? Because, unlike pictorial representations, verbal descriptions fail to preserve what Walton calls "real similarity relations." There are similarities between seeing scenes directly and seeing the same scenes through pictures that do not hold between seeing scenes directly and reading (however exhaustive) a description. For example, seeing scenes face to face or through pictures will be determinate in all manner of ways that verbal descriptions are not. Walton focuses on the discriminatory errors we make with respect to each: in looking at a picture, as in looking at the scene directly, we might mistake a house for a barn because these look similar. In reading or hearing a verbal description, we are more likely to mistake the word "house" for the words "horse" or "hearse," because these words look and sound similar. Similarly, when looking at a scene or a picture, but not when reading or listening to a description, we might mistake a hearse for an ambulance or old Volvo, because these look similar, but we are unlikely to mistake the words "old Volvo" for the word "hearse" in a verbal description. In depiction, as in perception, we confuse what is perceptually, rather than graphically (or acoustically), similar. Because seeing through pictures preserves such "real similarities" and reading descriptions does not, our contact with the world through pictures is like that through perception, and unlike contact with the world through descriptions.

At this point, Walton's critics will point out that the errors to which viewing things through photographs are prone have only a minor overlap with those to which seeing directly is prone. Because photographs do not provide egocentric information, we can make neither spatial nor temporal errors about how the objects seen through them are located relative to ourselves. So photographs do not put us in a position to make many of the perceptual errors we make about objects seen directly. And this is not surprising; in this, photographs are like any other kind of picture.

What goes unremarked in such exchanges are the respects in which Walton's negative and positive arguments (the slippery slope and two conditions on seeing, respectively) pull in opposite directions. The slippery slope is essentially an intuition pump: it tests our intuitions about a variety of cases. Testing our intuitions in this way will flush out whatever folk theory of perception we implicitly subscribe to. But why bother consulting our intuitions, if the theory at stake is revisionist? One of his earliest respondents, Edwin Martin, pointed out that on Walton's account it makes sense to say we see earthquakes through seismograms, feet through footprints, and meteors through craters. In reply, Walton acknowledged that footprints and death masks are transparent, given their rich causal and counterfactual dependence on what caused them: we see particular feet or faces through both.[13] At this point it should have been apparent that Walton's conception of seeing was revisionist: very few would say, *on consulting their intuitions*, that we see feet through footprints. If this counts as "seeing," why appeal to ordinary language or everyday intuitions about mirrors and telescopes?[14]

This impression has only deepened since. Currie, for example, objected that what Walton calls seeing through photographs does not count as such.[15] Imagine two clocks, A and B, such that B is remotely controlled by radio signals from A; had A been different so too would B, and so would my perception of B. Do I therefore see A by seeing B? Am I "seeing through" B to A? Most people (if my students are in any way representative) want to say no, but it is hard to see how they can on Walton's account. Both his conditions on seeing are fulfilled. Walton's response is to point out that if only the position of one clock's hands is determined by that of the other's, then there is not a rich enough causal and counterfactual dependence to claim that we see through one to the other. At best we see through the arms. Suppose a combination of cheap materials and exposure to direct sunlight causes the face of A to fade to the point that its numbers can no longer be made out, while that of B, kept in the shade, remains pristine. If I look at B at 2.10 I see both hands pointing to the number two. Since that is no longer on A to be seen, we cannot be seeing A by seeing B; we are only seeing B.

Were the example tweaked to take account of this reply, as Berys Gaut has done, by giving us a version that has robotic safari park gorillas whose movements are controlled by radio signals from their live counterparts some miles away, Walton is willing to bite the bullet and concede that we see A by seeing B.[16] But, again, very few would find it *intuitive* to say that we see real but absent gorillas by seeing their robotic doppelgängers. Contrary to what his appeal to the slippery slope implies, the clarifications Walton has since offered only deepen the sense of counter-intuitiveness surrounding the transparency thesis. And rightly so, if Walton really is proposing a revision of how we conceptualize seeing. If seeing one clock counts, certain conditions being met, as seeing another, if seeing a footprint counts as seeing a foot, and seeing a robot counts as seeing a real gorilla whose movements it replicates, why appeal to ordinary-language considerations about "what we would say when" about mirrors and the like?

Walton's 2007 Presidential Address to the American Society of Aesthetics tackles such questions head-on by taking conceptual analysis and theory construction as its theme. Initially Walton appears to endorse a project of conceptual analysis that he associates with Wittgenstein: philosophy aims at the clarification of thoughts, it does not advance theses, but leaves everything as it is. He includes the transparency thesis under this head, but grants: "[h]ow things are and what it is to leave them that way is not an obvious or straightforward matter."[17] Getting clear about this requires getting clear about the role that intuitions should (and should not) play in philosophy. Intuitions reflect sedimented folk theories and, to the extent that these have stood the test of time, they deserve respect. But given the frequent lack of consensus as to what is intuitive—as debate about transparency itself attests—and the likelihood that appeals to intuition mask unthematized theoretical commitments, Walton comes out in favour of theory construction rather than conceptual analysis.

Theory building, as Walton conceives it, is akin to what scientists do once the data is in; organizing it in a perspicuous manner so as to provide an elegant, systematic, and maximally explanatory account of how things stand in a given domain. Conceptual analysis, by contrast, clarifies the concepts that folk wisdom provides. Philosophers in search of a theory to explain a particular problem are advised to start by examining the concepts and theories that folk wisdom supplies. So construed, appeals to our intuitions about "what we would say when," are a way of clarifying our implicit folk theories. By evaluating folk theory, conceptual analysis serves as a *propaedeutic* to philosophical theorizing proper. This is the role of the slippery slope in "Transparent Pictures": it is a piece of conceptual analysis designed to flush out our intuitions about seeing through mirrors, telescopes, and the like. And rightly so, according to Walton's account of how we should go about constructing theories in philosophy, beginning with an analysis of everyday folk wisdom.

The problem, seen in the light of these later methodological reflections, is that Walton attempts to use the slippery slope argument to motivate the conclusion that we see through photographs *directly*. That is, he tries to use the slippery slope as a direct route to the transparency thesis. But this is not something that—according to his own methodological claims—such an argument could achieve.

Walton complains that when his critics object that it is counter-intuitive to say that we see through photographs, they are implicitly relying on a folk conception of seeing. In doing so, they misconstrue the argument of "Transparent Pictures" as an attempt to capture that conception. But the transparency thesis cannot be confirmed or refuted by consulting our intuitions; it is a theoretical claim motivated by the two conditions that Walton sets out in the latter half of his essay. For just this reason, Walton's own attempts to use the slippery slope to rebut claims that his notion of "seeing through" photographs is counter-intuitive were misplaced. Not only is Walton's thesis counter-intuitive to most of his respondents, but *that it is* is to the point. Testing his account against their intuitions, as most of Walton's critics insist on doing, need not trouble Walton, if his project is to foster a revision of those very intuitions. But if that is what is at stake, why try to motivate it by appealing to everyday intuitions about telescopes and the like? This only muddies the waters: our intuitions, what we would say when, are precisely what the account is designed to put pressure on.

Transparency and mind-independence

I have suggested that Walton's negative and positive arguments pull in opposite directions and that, faced with a choice between them, his own methodological reflections suggest we should opt for the latter. Even taken on their own, however, both face difficulties. Take these in turn. Though most of Walton's critics find the transparency thesis counter-intuitive, I depart from both his critics and (at least early) Walton in thinking that he should not be trying to disabuse them of this impression. But just what is it that makes the transparency thesis seem so counter-intuitive?

Perhaps Walton equivocates between photographs and photographic apparatus. As two-dimensional surfaces in which we see three-dimensional scenes, the former are a kind of picture; as series of lenses and mirrors through which we see the world, the latter are a type of visual prosthesis. Cameras are not unlike periscopes or telescopes, with the added functionality of being able to record the images that they provide. The claim that we see through cameras and other lens systems is uncontroversial; the claim that we see through photographs is not. Prima facie, it looks as though only lenses of various kinds (cameras, telescopes, microscopes, eyeglasses, windows, windscreens, etc.) are "transparent" in an everyday sense of the term. We literally see through such lenses to what is physically behind or beyond them: if I place my glasses on my desk, I still see my desk through them; if I place a photograph of my glasses on the desk, I no longer see that portion of its surface that the photograph occludes. In seeing directly we see through things that are transparent to what is beyond them, but in "seeing through" photographs we do not. And, unlike photographs, we do *not* see through media that are literally transparent when we focus on their surfaces: if I focus on the surface of my glasses or a window pane in order to clean them, I no longer see through them to what is beyond them; by contrast, I have to focus on the surface of a photograph in order to "see through" it in Walton's sense. This is why transparency not only does not entail invisibility for Walton but precludes it: we have to focus on the surface of the picture to see through it. For just this reason, however, Walton's use of "transparency" is highly idiosyncratic: media that are literally transparent *are* invisible in use. We have to make a conscious effort to focus on their surfaces, and when we do, we no longer see through them. With photographs the opposite is true.

That photographic apparatuses, such as cameras, are aids to vision need not entail that their products also are. Cameras may be a technology in Maynard's sense of amplifying certain innate human capacities, while photographs are often just a kind of picture. Some may think this depends on the kind of photograph at issue: intuitions will likely vary between, say, microphotography of skin or hair that generates seemingly abstract images, defamiliarizing close-ups of body fragments, clearly legible X-rays, and straightforward nudes. With some, but not others, it may seem natural to say that we see a body through its depiction, and with some we may be genuinely unsure what to say. Or consider astrophotography of invisible gases condensing in distant nebulae: should we think of this as allowing us to see what cannot otherwise be seen, hence an aid to vision, or as strictly speaking incomprehensible in these terms—since invisible gases do not reflect the visible spectrum? Walton cuts through such difficulties by claiming that photographs as such are aids to vision;

through them we indirectly see the world itself, and not merely its depiction.

Most commentators who do not grant that we see through photographs do grant that we see through the viewfinders of our SLR cameras, even though what we thereby see is mediated by a series of lenses and mirrors. Though the reasons for this difference in intuitions are not often spelt out, I take this to be because, in the latter case, it is the reflected or emitted light from the objects seen through the camera that is focused by the lens and reflected by a mirror before it reaches our eyes, just as it is in natural vision. This is also true in cases of "seeing back in time," such as seeing the light from distant stars. When we look at the resulting photograph, by contrast, it is the print's or screen's reflected or emitted light, rather than that of the objects "seen through" it, that reaches our eyes. Seeing through cameras, though mediated by a series of mirrors and lenses, is in this sense direct, and so no different to seeing through eyeglasses, around corners with the aid of convex mirrors, or from under water with periscopes. Seeing through photographs, by contrast, is indirect.[18]

At this point one might wonder whether this is not to agree, in a roundabout way, with Walton himself—after all, Walton insists that seeing through photographs is indirect. Not really. Walton asks us to accept that seeing through photographs is of a piece—"a single natural kind"—with seeing through periscopes and convex mirrors. In doing so, he seems to conflate seeing through photographs and seeing through cameras and other visual prostheses. Seeing via the standard through-the-lens viewfinder of a traditional SLR camera just *is* seeing through a combination of mirrors and inverted periscope; add a telephoto lens and it just is seeing through a telescope of sorts. In all such cases seeing is direct. Seeing through photographs, by contrast, is indirect for the reasons that Walton gives; one sees S by seeing—which is to say *looking at*, rather than "through"—P, when P is a photograph of S. But while one may see distant stars by looking at their photographs, one cannot see distant stars by looking at a telescope, or from underwater by looking at a periscope. There is a clear difference between the two cases.[19]

What of Walton's positive argument? For all the controversy that claiming photographs are transparent has elicited, the "mind-independent thesis" underwriting that claim has been widely accepted. The mind-independence thesis claims that it is a necessary condition of seeing that one's perceptual experience depend causally and counterfactually on what is seen: we "see through" photographs because had, contrary to fact, what was before the camera at the moment of exposure been different, what one sees in the resulting photograph would have differed accordingly—irrespective of whether the photographer noticed the difference or intended to record it. What we see in a painting, by contrast, would only have differed had the painter not only noticed the change but decided to depict it. This shows that painting is, and photography is not, dependent on the mental states of the artist. This distinction is widely accepted by philosophers. Should it be?

It is notable that the mind-independence thesis strikes philosophers as much more plausible than it does photographers, critics, and historians of photography. Is this because the latter do not appreciate the philosophical point at issue, or because philosophers are poorly informed about how photography works, or both? Here I think it worth stressing the importance of what one takes as a paradigm case, since this will have significant, though often unwitting, repercussions for the philosophical theory one goes on to elaborate off its back. Walton acknowledges that the paradigm case for his own account is the snapshot, rather than photographic art. A more apposite case still might be time-lapse nature photography or speed cameras, of which it is literally true that the mechanism fires off automatically, irrespective of what anyone believes is in front of the camera at the moment of exposure. Were one to base one's account on the kind of authorial control exercised by photographic artists, by contrast, one would expect the account that emerges to be correspondingly different.

But is this just to beg the philosophical question at issue? The fact that photographers have it in their gift to set all manner of variables, as critics of mechanical conceptions of photography such as Joel Snyder stress, is typically thought to beg the question in this way.[20] Such commentators (to take only the analogue case) draw attention to the innumerable decisions about set-up, point of view, lighting, framing, camera hardware and settings, film and paper stock, darkroom, and other variables that photographers routinely make.[21] In so doing, they are part of a tradition that stretches back to Emerson and Evans. All this may be granted, the standard philosophical response runs, and it still hold that from the moment of exposure to the resulting print—at least in any fully automated process—the information channel from input to output is impermeable to the photographer's mental states.[22] Granted, such "encapsulation" is weakened when the full range of darkroom techniques is employed but, setting this aside, what was before the camera at the moment of exposure, as opposed to what the photographer *believed* was before the camera, should be retrievable from the resulting photograph, assuming one knows enough about how the variables were set.

Is this true of significant photographic art? Take Lee Friedlander's *Stems*, a series of late flower photographs made between 1994 and 1999, as a test case. What they show, the standard argument runs, can only be what was there to be seen.[23] But what about how they show it? Here one finds a narrow set of parameters persistently mined for their aesthetic potential: the works are all black and white, domestic in scale, photographed on 35 mm or square medium format film, from close enough so that the vases fill the frame. Each image depicts the stems of cut flowers in clear glass vases of various shapes filled with water. There is little background detail, pointedly shallow depth of field, and the subject is framed in such a way that either the top or the bottom of the vase, and sometimes both, are cropped out. In none are the flowers as a bunch visible, though in one or two images the odd tulip head curves back into shot. At first glance the subject appears to be the stems, but on closer inspection it is as much the effects of glass and water on refracting and focusing light as the stems themselves that are thematized. It will be apparent to anyone familiar with Friedlander's oeuvre that photography itself is being playfully allegorized here.

This is not some bare recording of flowers in water, then, but the making present, through the medium of photography, of a limited, but persistently mined, set of features within a tight set of constraints. Some of these features, such as the play of light and shadow, or the minute oxygen bubbles that cling to the stems in several of the images, would not be visible to everyday human attention, or at least not salient, absent the photographs that thrust them into relief. The photographs clearly depend on *what* was there, but *how* what was

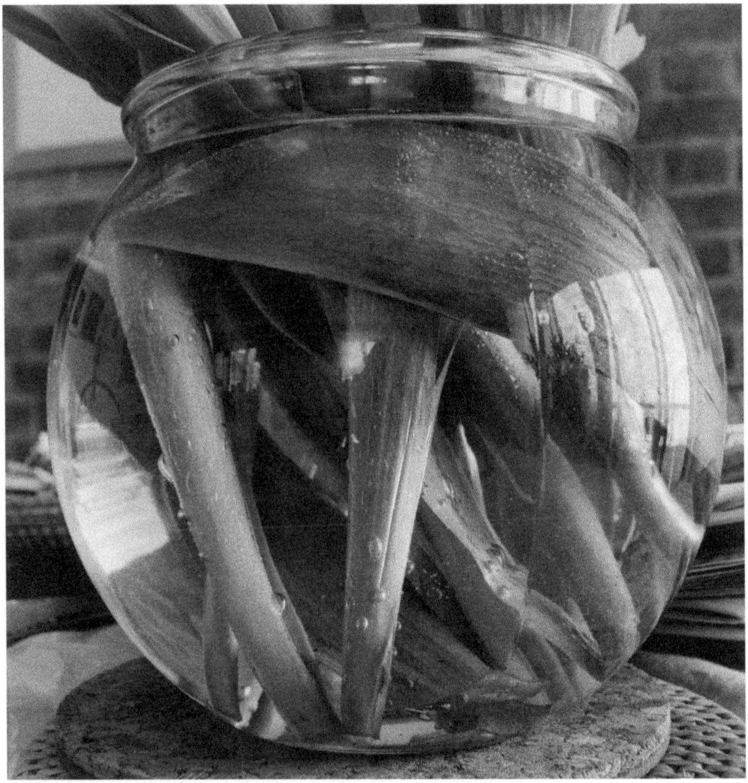

Figure 3.1 Lee Friedlander, *Stems* 1, 1999. Gelatin silver print, paper dimensions 20 × 16 in. (50.8 × 40.64 cm). Collection of the artist. © Lee Friedlander, courtesy Fraenkel Gallery, San Francisco.

there appears to depend, equally clearly, on this particular photographer's exploitation of precision optics and the capacities of various films, papers, filters, and developing agents to enhance tonal contrast and the like. One need only compare Friedlander's images to Karl Blossfeldt's taxonomic plant photography or Robert Mapplethorpe's erotic images of orchids and calla lilies to be struck by this fact.

So what? Walton acknowledges that photographs can show us the world from a particular photographer's point of view, without this denying the fact that they show us the world itself from that point

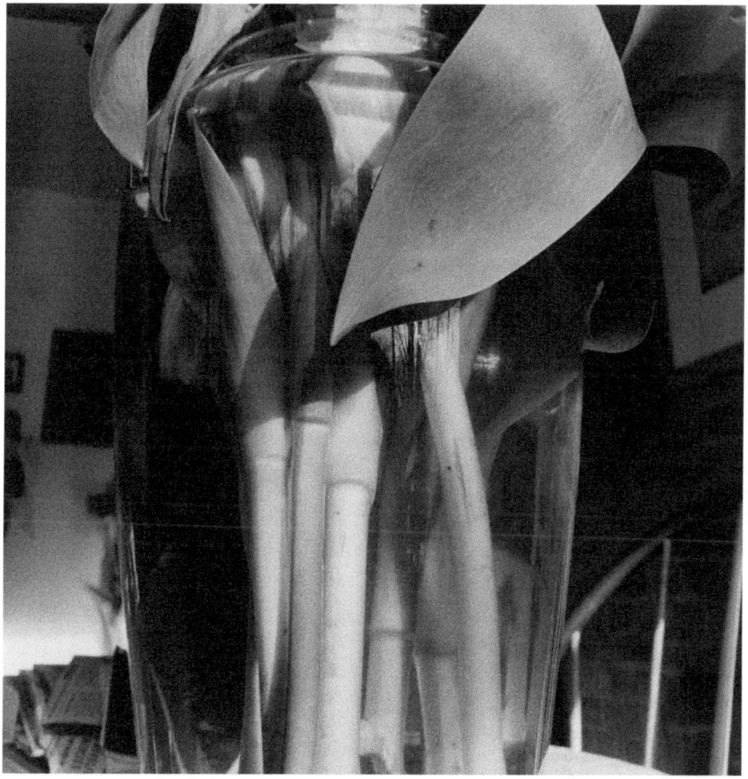

Figure 3.2 Lee Friedlander, *Stems* 2, 1999. Gelatin silver print, paper dimensions 20 × 16 in. (50.8 × 40.64 cm). Collection of the artist. © Lee Friedlander, courtesy Fraenkel Gallery, San Francisco.

of view, and not merely its depiction. So Walton could grant all this while insisting that the distinction between natural and intentional counterfactual dependence parses between photography and painting nonetheless. To see whether this is true, take Édouard Manet's equally late series of flower paintings, made between 1881 and 1883, as a comparison case. Are there differences of the kind that Walton's account requires?

Consider the counterfactuals. Suppose that, contrary to fact, Manet breaks for lunch while painting *Roses mousseuses dans un vase* and unknown to him several small but visible petals towards the rear of his still life fall away (Plate 3). Suppose further that Manet's housekeeper disposes of them before he resumes work. Should Manet fail to attend to this aspect of the scene again, the change will pass unmarked in the painting. Walton's account goes through: what we see in the finished painting is intentionally, rather than naturally, dependent on the mental states of the artist; whatever the painter fails to notice (or notices, but decides not to depict) does not make it into the finished work. Does this differ in the required way from Friedlander?

Again, consider the counterfactuals. Suppose that, contrary to fact, having set up a particular still life, placed the camera on a tripod, and opened his lens's diaphragm to its maximum in order to reduce depth of field to a minimum (thereby pushing what is in focus into sharp, but very shallow, relief), Friedlander leaves the room to take a call. Returning to his camera, and being careful not to jolt the tripod, Friedlander takes one last look through his viewfinder and finding everything to his satisfaction trips the shutter, having failed to notice that an in-shot, non-occluded but out-of-focus stem toward the rear of the vase has been removed by an irresponsible guest with a weakness for impulsive romantic gestures. Does Walton's account go through?

Contrary to philosophical expectations, the answer is no. Unless the photographer notices the difference and intends to record it, by adjusting his camera settings accordingly, it will not show up in the final image. What one sees in the final image will be the same—half a dozen or so stems pressed up against the near side of the vase in sharp relief against an indistinct, out-of-focus background—irrespective of whether that particular stem is present or not. Understood technically, this is a product of how camera optics (specifically, the inverse relation between aperture and depth of field) function. Understood aesthetically, it is a product of Friedlander's intentions, as embodied by the way he deploys such technical constraints and camera capabilities in the service of his art. Because the missing stem makes no difference to realizing his intentions, it plays no role in the decisions determining the final image.

Friedlander's camera, free from outside interference and functioning as it should, fails to record a perceptible change in the world—the removal of an in-shot, non-occluded stem. Friedlander's images fail to track this perceptible change because he fails to notice it; and he fails to notice it because it makes no difference to realizing his intentions. So *what* appears in the photograph—and not just *how* what appears appears—turns out to be intentionally dependent on the photographer, at least in some cases. Call such photographs, determined by Friedlander's use of his medium to realize his goals, relevantly mind-dependent. The same is no doubt true of much photographic art. Where is the difference from Manet?

What Walton misses is the depth of decision that pervades every aspect of a convincing work of art, photographic or otherwise. The Orthodox account may work for snapshots, but it does not capture large swathes of photography beyond this. Like Orthodox theory more generally, Walton's account takes folk theories of photography, themselves premised on point-and-shoot technology, too much on trust. As a result his account is insufficiently sensitive to the ways in which photographs may be relevantly dependent on the mental states of the photographer in such a way as to undermine any hard and fast difference between photographs and other forms of depictive art.[24]

Photography and epistemic value

Of course, the mere fact that objections to Walton's account can be raised hardly shows the New Theory to be in better shape. Walton's dual focus on photography's epistemic and aesthetic capabilities, brought together in the idea of a "transparent picture" certainly seems better placed to account for photography's epistemic capacities. One might worry that the New Theory, by contrast, only does justice to photographic art at the cost of making a mystery of many everyday photographic practices. This is the hard question for New Theorists.

Walton's account has generated a substantial literature about the nature of photography's epistemic advantage over forms of depiction. Photographs in general, but not paintings in general, the resulting accounts tend to run, support counterfactuals about the appearance of whatever they depict. Had this looked different, their photographs would have differed accordingly. This makes photographs more reliable as sources of evidence and this explains why they are used in a wide variety of diagnostic, medical, scientific, legal, and forensic contexts. Scott Walden, for example, solicits our intuitions on cases of the following kind: imagine we are shown a drawing and a photograph of the lawn in front of a ground-floor window believed to have been used as access for a burglary.[25] The former shows a well-kept lawn, the latter shows the same lawn with the residue of what might be footprints. Do we not have good reason to believe, given what we know about cameras as recording machines, that the latter records something that the former misses? Perhaps the draughtsman focused his efforts on rendering the dirt on the windowsill, or was having an off day and failed to notice the depressions. Walden calls the intuition that we have greater warrant for beliefs formed on the basis of looking at the photograph the "objectivity thesis," and explains it along Waltonian lines. Note that this intuition being well founded depends on what we believe we know about the camera as a recording apparatus being correct.[26]

Jonathan Cohen and Aaron Meskin concur that photographs have a special epistemic status, but deny, like others who deny that we see through photographs, that this has anything to do with photographs being transparent. Despite this, they endorse Walton's claim that we see via complex arrangements of mirrors, even if we are unable to form beliefs about where the object thereby seen is located.[27] Because they agree with Walton that undermining of belief does not suffice to undermine seeing, but with Walton's critics that we do not see through photographs because photographs fail to preserve egocentric information, they need to reformulate the latter point in such a way that it is not undermined simply by pointing out that we continue to see in the absence of beliefs about location. "Doxastic" versions of the objection make beliefs about the object's egocentric location a necessary condition of seeing, "non-doxastic" versions do not. This is because doxastic versions of the objection confuse the conditions required for seeing with the more demanding conditions for *knowing that* one sees. The latter requires beliefs about location; since we can see in their absence, the former does not. Photography's failure to provide egocentric information is independent of the viewer's knowledge or beliefs about what is seen.

Cohen and Meskin conceive visual experience, following Fred Dretske, as a non-doxastic process that carries egocentric spatial information, where "information carrying" is as "a kind of (objective) probabilistic, counterfactual supporting relation between independent variables."[28] This is less forbidding than it sounds. Take their own example: a thermometer carries information about body temperature if and only if there is a probabilistic correlation between the two. That is, the probability of a body's temperature being 37 °C conditional upon the thermometer reading 37 °C must be much higher than the probability of that body's temperature being 37 °C conditional upon the thermometer not reading 37 °C, assuming the thermometer is well calibrated, free from outside interference, etc. For such a correlation to count as information carrying rather than merely adventitious, however, it must support the relevant counterfactuals.[29] A thermometer stuck on 37 °C applied to a body that, it so happens, is also 37 °C does not carry information about that body, since it would continue to read 37 °C irrespective of the temperature of what it is held up to.

Such objective, probabilistic correlations hold irrespective of anyone's beliefs about the matter; analogously, whether photographs carry egocentric information will depend on whether a photographic depiction sustains objective, probabilistic relations to what it depicts, not on anything we may take ourselves to be justified in believing about what it depicts on its basis. We do not see through photographs (photographs are not transparent) because there is no such relation between what we see in them and our egocentric relation to what is so seen. There may be a de facto correlation, as would be the case were one to superimpose, à la René Magritte, a photograph of exactly the right scale, over the window through which it was taken, and view it (with one eye closed) from the exact position of the camera when taking it; but that is like holding a broken thermometer up to a body that is the temperature it would read anyway. Move the photograph, or shift one's viewing position slightly, and either the photograph's, or one's own, relation to what it depicts will change, without its depiction changing accordingly. Because it fails to support the relevant counterfactuals, seeing the photograph does not count as seeing what it depicts. Crucially, because such probabilistic relations (or lack thereof) hold independently of anyone's beliefs about the matter, Cohen and Meskin's account is not undermined by pointing out that we can see independently of knowledge or beliefs about egocentric spatial location. They agree.

But why, if photographs are not transparent, are they nonetheless epistemically privileged? The fact that photographs carry information about the visual properties of the objects they depict without carrying information about their egocentric location is the source of this epistemic advantage: as "spatially agnostic informants," they are able to carry information about an object's or scene's visual properties even when egocentric information is unavailable. Ordinary vision and genuine visual prostheses, by contrast, only carry the former in virtue of carrying the latter. Photographs are thus "undemanding" sources of visual information. This is also true of some, perhaps even many, drawings and paintings for Cohen and Meskin: it is true of most veridical still lifes, landscapes, and portraits, for example, that had what they depict looked different, their depiction would have differed accordingly. Despite this, viewers' divergent background beliefs about paintings and photographs as kinds or types of images make photographs (as a type of image) "salient" vehicles of such information in a way that paintings (as a type of image) are not. For it is often true that had, contrary to fact, the subject of a painting looked different, the painting would *not* have differed accordingly, and this impacts viewers' background beliefs about paintings and photographs as kinds of images. This is especially true if the token at stake is typed generically as a "painting" or "landscape painting," rather than, more specifically, as a "veridical landscape painting."

So understood, the epistemic advantage of photographs over manugraphs is not an *intrinsic* feature of photography or painting, but contingent upon the history of their uses, and the divergent beliefs about paintings and photographs as kinds of images that result from those uses.[30] Were those background beliefs to change (as they may once consumer access to digital editing software like Photoshop becomes more widespread) one could expect perception of photography's epistemic advantage over manugraphs to change accordingly. Cohen and Meskin's acknowledgement that photography's special epistemic status is not a product of intrinsic features of photographs and paintings, but the upshot of a combination of facts about the relations that (often) hold between token photographs and paintings and what they depict, and our background beliefs about photographs and paintings as kinds of images, makes their account of the difference between photographs and manugraphs markedly weaker than Walton's or Walden's. For it relies as heavily on psychological facts about viewers as it does on any objective facts about the images in question.[31]

Nonetheless, Cohen and Meskin's account continues to trade on a contrast between what is taken to be *generally* true of photographs and paintings as image kinds. And this is something that New Theorists need to address. For even if such differences are ultimately contingent, to the extent that they rely on beliefs about image kinds that might have been different and might yet change depending upon the ongoing uses of diverse image kinds, there are presumably good reasons—the most important grounded in what is distinctive about photography as an imaging technology—why photographs have had the kind of uses that they have. And once one specifies what these are (speed, accuracy, reliability, potentially limitless reproduction without degradation, the need for little specialist skill or training), we seem to be thrown back into the arms of Orthodoxy.

It bears remarking, however, that the Orthodox account has moved on since Walton. Catharine Abell, for example, has developed a more nuanced conception of the epistemic value of photography to underwrite the kind of intuitions that typically underpin Orthodox accounts of photography's epistemic privilege. On this view, a picture can only provide compelling evidence concerning the features of what it depicts if it is a product of a reliable picture-making process. A process is "more reliable the more likely it is to produce pictures whose depictive content is accurate; whose internal objects have only features possessed by their external objects."[32] So conceived, reliability is a measure of the accuracy of a picture-making process. Abell understands accuracy, following Cohen and Meskin, in terms of information carrying, though she departs from them by unpacking this in terms of the likelihood of pictures produced by such a process fostering true beliefs about the objects depicted.[33]

On its own this will not suffice, as my Friedlander example (in which the removal of a visible, non-occluded stem makes no difference to the resulting picture) shows. Such a picture fails to carry information, and hence is not accurate, concerning a crucial feature of its external object, the number of stems present and discriminable to normal human perception. Perhaps to deal with cases of this sort, Abell adds a rider concerning the amount of detail (essentially, fineness of grain) that a reliable picture needs to encode: "even if it is the result of a reliable process, a picture will not reveal features of an object that are easily overlooked unless it carries a reasonable amount of information about that object."[34] The more information such a picture "depictively encodes" (the more features of its external object about which it carries information in pictorial form), the richer it will be.[35] Seen in terms of this dual requirement, the Friedlander is informationally less rich than (an otherwise similar) photograph of the same scene in which all the non-occluded stems in the vase can be individuated. Qua photograph, the Friedlander is a product of a reliable process, but with respect to the number of stems present it is not as rich as it might be. The same would be true of ill-focused photographs—though there is nothing ill-focused about the Friedlander. As such, the Friedlander has little epistemic value with respect to the number of stems present. So the epistemic value of photographs cannot be an all or nothing affair:

> A picture is richer relative to features of type F, the more information about F features it carries. We thus need to distinguish between a picture's EV [epistemic value] *simpliciter*, and its EV relative to features of a certain type. A picture's EV *simpliciter* is a measure of its richness and of the reliability of the process by which it was produced, while its EV relative to features of a certain type is a measure of its richness relative to features of that type, and the reliability of its production process relative to features of that type.[36]

That is, we see the world more fully through some photographs than others, and we see through many (perhaps even all) photographs more fully with respect to some features than others. Because the Friedlander is the result of a reliable picture-making process it has epistemic value, but that value is richer with respect to some features (the presence of oxygen bubbles clinging to the stems) than others (the number of stems present). Because reliability and richness are independent they need not co-vary: a picture can be reliable but not rich (a poorly focused photograph) or rich but not reliable (a good treasure map).

It is Rob Hopkins, however, who has made the most ambitious claims for photography's epistemic advantage over other forms of depiction. Alongside Currie, Hopkins is arguably Orthodoxy's leading contemporary proponent and, like Currie, he is working out of a more Scrutonian than Waltonian tradition. Hopkins's key claim is that while photographs, like other pictures, sustain pictorial experience (we see things in their surfaces), unlike other pictures, they afford a special kind of "factive pictorial experience."[37] When the photographic process works *as it should*, the resulting images necessarily show how things were when they were taken. So looking at these images affords factive mental states, states that are guaranteed to represent how things actually were: "for any token state of that kind, if that token state represents it as the case that *p*, then it is the case that *p*." What is unique about photography is not that we see through photographs—Hopkins denies that photographs are transparent—but that, assuming everything is working as it should, if subject *S* sees in a photograph *P* that *p*, then *p*.[38]

For this to be true, every stage in the intervening causal process, from initial exposure to visual processing, must exhibit something like factivity. Hopkins accepts that information may be lost along the way, but not that it may be added, on pain of undermining factivity. Thus, some of the things photographers typically do in the darkroom (dodging, burning, and so on) may determine what information gets preserved in the final print, but they do not determine whether that information is there to be preserved in the first place. At least this is true of what Hopkins calls, without further ado, "traditional photography," and this explains both its special epistemic status and what is special about the experience of looking at "traditional" photographs.

The ideas of design and proper functioning are central to Hopkins's account. Cameras are designed to produce images that sustain factive pictorial experience, understood as "seeing-in" that necessarily represents how things were when those images were taken. But to prevent the idea of sustaining such experience becoming trivial, we need to be able to pick out those experiences independently of their getting things right. If we can only identify those experiences in terms of their getting things right, the account becomes circular, by building accuracy into our way of identifying the experiences in question. Hopkins proposes a two-stage method to avoid this. First, grant that photography is designed to sustain accurate seeing-in. Then—rather than identifying factive pictorial experiences directly in terms of that goal—take the idea of affording accurate seeing-in as placing a general constraint on how every element in the process must function. Each stage (exposure, focusing, processing, printing, and the like) can then be specified in terms of a more specific set of norms governing its proper functioning.[39] Though such norms gain their rationale from the overarching aim of securing accurate seeing-in, and thereby sustaining factive pictorial experience, they may be characterized independently of that goal. Because they can, Hopkins's account avoids the charge of circularity.

Because Hopkins's account aspires to explain what is epistemically special, not only about photographs, but also the experience of looking at photographs, the idea of everything functioning as it should extends all the way out to the norms governing what it is to see in photographs, namely, to "see in them only what is consistent with the way that, in general, you know the world to be."[40] At this point, the account really does court the risk of circularity, since this seems to presuppose just what the account itself ought to establish, namely, that photographs do indeed show us how the world is. This may be because, in back of Hopkins's account, is a set of default assumptions about the differences between manugraphs and photographs. Though he grants the existence of mechanical or quasi-mechanical ways of rendering images by hand (rubbings, tracings, and gridded-up transfer processes of various kinds), such that these may also, other conditions being met, sustain factive pictorial experience, he does not grant that this damages the general contrast. Why not? Because, in one way or another, these are all non-standard examples. But that they *are* non-standard is something the account ought to establish; it cannot simply be assumed. Hopkins does accept—unlike Scruton et al.—that this is ultimately contingent. What is marginal *might* have been central, but as a matter of fact it is not: "as things are we treat handmades differently from photographs because only the latter support factive pictorial experience. And, as things are, we are right to so treat these two groups, at least by and large."[41] Presumably, Hopkins takes this to be so obvious as to require no demonstration.

Note that what is special about the phenomenology of looking at photographs depends in Hopkins's account, as in others', at least in part on viewers' background beliefs about photography as a process for making pictures. This is not a problem, according to Hopkins, because our everyday folk theory of photography provides just what is required. The folk know that photography aims to produce pictures in which we see things as they were when those pictures were taken—pictures that, in Hopkins's terms, support accurate seeing-in. And they know, because photography has this overarching aim, that its various parts and mechanisms (cameras, enlargers, films and developers; more recently sensors, software algorithms, and screen displays) will be designed and calibrated so as to secure it. Finally, they know that, when everything works as it should, this will be precisely what is achieved. Given this, if they take themselves to be looking at a photograph of which all this is true, they will take their pictorial experience to be accurate as a matter of necessity. Hopkins grants that how demanding a claim is being made for photography on this account depends ultimately on how strong we take the notion of factivity in question to be. At the very least, he takes the weakest reading of it as a material conditional to be justified: there are no actual cases in which every element of the process works as it should but the resulting image fails to sustain factive seeing-in.

Is this true? Hopkins's approach is meant to provide a method for neutralizing counter-examples: in each case, what might seem to be a counter-example to the claim that photography sustains factive pictorial experience turns out not to be such, because it flouts one or more norms of proper functioning. There is more than an echo of Scruton's use of the "ideal photograph" in Hopkins's understanding of "traditional photography": all real-world examples that might seem in danger of shipwrecking the theory turn out not to be such, because they depart from the posited ideal of sustaining factive pictorial experience. But consider my Friedlander example in this light.

No norm of proper focusing—the most obvious candidate—has been flouted. The stems in the foreground are pin-sharp, as on Hopkins's account they presumably should be qua photographic subject. Grant, for the sake of argument, that Friedlander has not compromised the photograph's information-carrying capacity by darkroom trickery of any kind, and hence that what we see in the final image is purely a product of skill in manipulating standard camera variables (aperture, shutter speed, and the like) in the service of his ends. Where does this leave us? What is supposed to be in focus is in focus, no camera malfunction is involved, and no norm-flouting of any kind has been engaged in; Friedlander has simply exploited the capacity of precision optics to afford dramatically shallow depth of field.

Despite this, the resulting image fails to sustain factive seeing-in. Seeing the photograph and seeing the scene come apart since changes to the scene need not show up as changes in the resulting photograph. Whether this is a genuine counter-example to Hopkins depends on whether everything in the photographic process was working as it should. Have we seen anything to suggest that it was not? Contrast this case to Bill Brandt's repurposing of an antique brass and mahogany Kodak camera with an extremely wide-angle lens and minute aperture focused on infinity, designed to enable untrained police photographers to document entire crime scenes with maximum depth of field. Brandt used this camera, contrary to the purposes for which it was designed, to achieve the startlingly distorted close-ups of nudes for which he is perhaps still best known. But there is no equivalent use of technology against the grain here.

Recent Orthodox theory is, not unsurprisingly, more nuanced than its first-generation ancestors: note, for example, the ineliminable role that the background beliefs of one stripe or another play in all the more recent accounts just canvassed. Acknowledgement of this dimension—together with retreat to what is *generally* (if not exceptionlessly) true of painting and photography—is what unifies recent Orthodox theorists and distinguishes them from their forebears. All appeal in one way or another to the saliency of various kinds (or sub-kinds) of images and image-rendering processes for viewers, or to what we know (or think we know) about the camera as a recording mechanism, or to folk theories of photography in explaining what we understand ourselves to be seeing when we see a photograph. For just this reason, all will suffer accordingly if what we know (or think we know) under any of these heads turns out to be false. And it is: for all such theories rely on a conception of when photographs come into existence that does not withstand scrutiny.

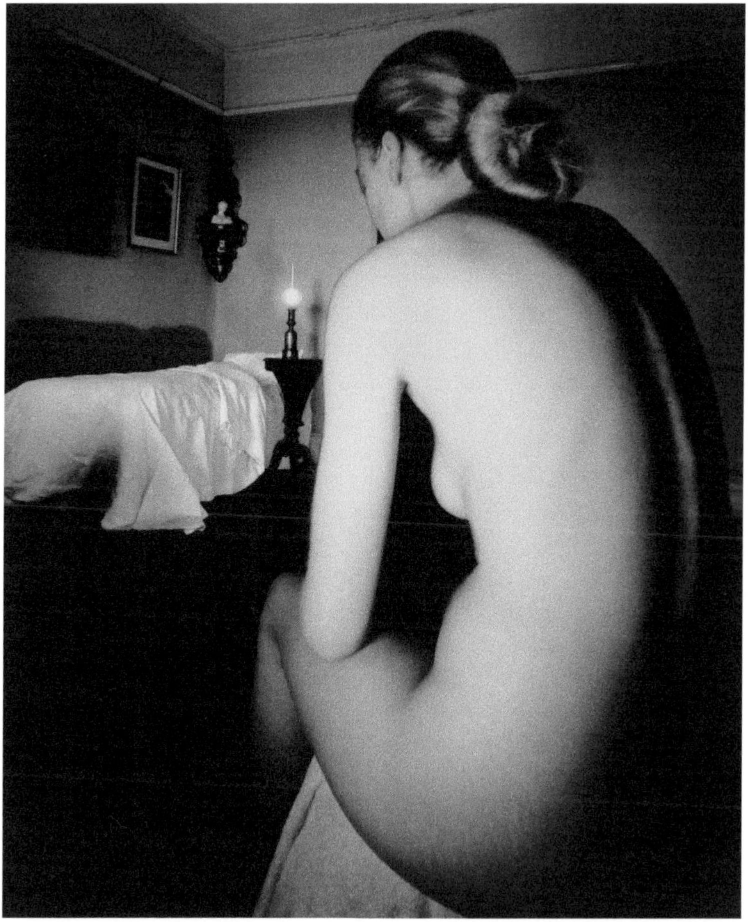

Figure 3.3 Bill Brandt, *Nude, Campden Hill, London*, 1949. Gelatin silver print, 9½ × 7¾ in. (24.1 × 19.7 cm). © Bill Brandt Archive.

What alternative account can New Theorists give of photography's epistemic privilege, if it is not explained by Orthodoxy being true? To date Lopes offers the most developed answer. Lopes refuses to endorse the view that photography has a monopoly over belief-independent feature-tracking.[42] This alone does distinguish Lopes: Cohen and Meskin, Abell, and Hopkins all grant that the distinction between photographs and manugraphs cannot be exhaustively captured in terms of the contrast between belief-independent and belief-dependent feature-tracking. Cohen and Meskin acknowledge ornithological drawings, Abell cites botanical drawings, and Hopkins accepts various kinds of mechanical or quasi-mechanical rendering may bypass belief. These are not mutually exclusive kinds, even for recent Orthodox commentators. With the exception of Cohen and Meskin, however, each tends to present these as exceptions that prove the more general rule.

Lopes draws a more radical conclusion, proposing that we abandon the tendency to align the distinction between belief-independent and belief-dependent feature-tracking with that between photography and manography altogether. This is to repudiate one of the most foundational distinctions in the philosophy of photography. In support of this proposal, Lopes points to a wide variety of drawings, including architects' blueprints and plans, archaeological drawings, and technical drawings of various kinds that routinely carry more information about what is drawn, by adhering to strict professional norms of both execution and interpretation, than any photograph could achieve.[43] In the opposite direction, he draws attention to a similarly wide variety of contemporary photographic practices—that Orthodoxy would have to regard as impure or not "strictly photographic" in one way or another, but which New Theory has no difficulty accommodating—to show that photography often fails to track features independently of belief. Lopes himself singles out various artistic practices centred on the material processes and procedures of photography itself, which he dubs "lyrical," to just this end (Plate 4).[44]

Orthodox and New Theorists concur that photographs are widely regarded as epistemically privileged. But that may just be a psychological fact about us, and how we are inclined to treat photographs. Lopes asks whether photographs really warrant such treatment. That they warrant such treatment is best explained by Orthodoxy being true. So, if they do warrant it, the New Theory is in trouble. Indeed, merely granting the psychological claim, as Lopes does readily, would already seem to put the New Theory in difficulty: for it is hard to understand *why* we would treat photography as we do if photographs are not epistemically privileged in some relevant way.

What form of collective irrationality might explain that? Is it simply tradition and path dependence: the canonization and institutionalization of certain widespread uses of photography?

The answer is surprisingly simple. Orthodoxy, which underpins the normative thesis, conflates what Lopes calls "standard" (and what Hopkins calls "traditional") photography with photography per se. That is, it reduces the latter to the former. Set aside the dissatisfying vagueness of these terms here: though "standard"/"traditional" photography comprise an important, central, and very large subset of photographic practices, and one that continues to exert considerable sway over our understanding of photography's nature, they do not exhaust the domain. Photography is a remarkably diverse body of practices, as indeed is "painting" when actually examined—cast your eye back over the lists earlier (p. ix–xiii)—and diverse practices are governed by diverse norms. "Standard photography," as Lopes conceives it, comprises a wide variety of photographic practices governed by knowledge-oriented norms. Practices of these kinds are responsive to just the kind of norms governing how photographic equipment is designed, manufactured, and used that Hopkins's understanding of factive pictorial experience requires. But such norms are not *intrinsic* to the nature of photographic technologies per se; rather they are imposed on how those technologies are used by the various social functions (notably furnishing information and evidence) that such knowledge-oriented practices typically serve.

Consider the various diagnostic, medical, scientific, and forensic uses of photography to which Orthodox theorists typically appeal: all are paradigmatically knowledge-oriented. Most have professional associations that either rule out certain actions or explicitly codify (in some cases in minute detail) how photographs in the relevant domain are to be taken. Thus in 1989—presumably in the teeth of pressure generated by the new digital technologies—the Associated Press adopted the policy that "the content of a [press] photograph will never be changed or manipulated in any way."[45] And the National Institute of Justice in the US lays down detailed guidelines that the relevant photographs must follow.[46] These norms are strictly policed, and the sanctions for breaking them can be severe; press photographers found to have done so may never work again.[47] That the sanctions are severe shows that fidelity to the facts is of paramount importance in these domains. Should the photographer cross-process her film in the wrong chemicals, or otherwise depart from standard uses of equipment and film stocks, the unpredictable effects on colour tracking and the like would conflict with the social functions that such photographic practices are meant to serve (Plate 6).[48] That such norms *need* to be enforced shows as well as anything might that nothing intrinsic to photographic technology precludes their being broken. And that no norms prevent their being broken in practices such as art shows as well as anything might that such practices are typically governed by altogether different norms.

Lopes's goal is to show that knowledge-oriented practices, widespread though they may be, do not exhaust photography in general, and so should cease to dominate our thinking about it; conversely, aesthetically oriented practices, widespread though they may be, are not coextensive with manography per se, so should cease to dominate our thinking about hand-rendered images. The spirit of this proposal runs counter to Orthodoxy, which tends to over-identify photography with, even if it no longer reduces it to, its epistemically oriented practices, just as it over-identifies manography with, even if it no longer reduces it to, its aesthetically oriented practices. The normative (as opposed to merely psychological) thesis concerning photography's epistemic privilege is not a thesis about photography per se; it is a thesis about those kinds of photography that serve a variety of knowledge-oriented functions pressed into dubious service for the whole domain. Though the restrictions it requires may hold of images produced for a variety of documentary or investigative purposes, they do not hold for other kinds of photographs. For this reason, they cannot constitute the general requirements against which all candidate photographs are to be judged before being granted admission to the domain of the strictly photographic. Most obviously, they offer a terrible starting point for considering photographic art. What has led many philosophers to think otherwise is a narrow diet of examples that misrepresents the scope of the domain. This shows what a distorting effect folk wisdom ("the camera never lies!") or appeal to supposedly "pre-theoretical" intuitions—as reflected in insufficiently self-reflective choices of paradigm cases—can have on debate.

Lopes's proposal for a revised normative thesis, consistent with these facts, is that "images made by belief-independent feature-tracking have an epistemic virtue not possessed by other images."[49] "Traditional" or "standard" photography secures such virtue by using photography in ways that preserve belief-independent feature-tracking, but it is the latter that does the heavy lifting, not the fact that the images are made photographically. For it is fully consistent with the latter, on the New Theory, that such images need not track features independently of belief. Just as it is consistent with the theory that manugraphs can track features independently of belief.

This answer directs our attention to the diverse social practices that various kinds of photography subtend, but may not take the implications of its own recommendations sufficiently seriously. For once the knowledge-oriented norms governing the uses of photography within a given social practice are sufficiently well established and robust, belief-independent feature-tracking itself may, if not fall away altogether, then at least no longer dominate to the exclusion of other, belief-dependent forms of imaging. Take, for example, the digital manipulation of colour and other values in diagnostic, medical, and astronomical photography (Plate 7). This flouts belief-independent feature-tracking but, in doing so, often aids extraction of the sought-after information, by making the presence of particular gases, kinds of cell tissue, and the like easier to identify. This is possible in such fields because the channel conditions of the equipment used (how it is set up and calibrated for a given observation) can be closely monitored and controlled by highly skilled lab technicians in a way that they cannot be out in the field. The requirement to generate diagnoses that are effective or predictions that are testable ensures that the photographic processes in question do not, despite manipulation of discrete variables, misrepresent the facts (as to the presence of gases or cell types) in the relevant domain. That crime scene and press photography, by contrast, are often conducted under far from ideal conditions out in the field, in which channel conditions cannot be closely monitored and controlled, explains why these practices must adhere to quite different norms and such manipulation is not tolerated. In this way, what is typically thought to undermine objectivity—human interference in image generation and rendering—may actually support and even enhance objectivity, given institutional contexts of a certain kind.

Notes

1 Kendall Walton, "Representation and Make-Believe," in *Mimesis as Make-Believe: On the Foundations of the Representational Arts* (Cambridge, MA: Harvard University Press, 1990). For a summary, see "Meditations on a Hobby Horse," in *Marvelous Images: On Values and the Arts* (Oxford: Oxford University Press, 2008).

2 Walton accepts that some hand-made pictures may fulfil this account, but only if their execution is close to being mechanical.

3 This is to one side of Walton's own concerns in "Transparent Pictures." The fact that we literally, if indirectly, see the subjects of mechanically generated pictures underwrites the distinctive sense of "perceptual contact" with their subjects that such pictures—especially when they are subjects who matter to us personally—afford, which Walton himself is seeking to characterize. In this his account has certain affinities with Bazin's, albeit without the latter's more enthusiastic psychological and ontological claims. Nonetheless, it is the way in which Walton's distinctive combination of imaginative and literal seeing provides the resources to ground—from within an Orthodox perspective—photography's oft-noted epistemic advantage, but without thereby compromising its aesthetic claims, that should cause New Theorists to pay attention.

4 Walton, "Transparent Pictures," p. 251.

5 Maynard, *The Engine of Visualization*, p. 120. Neither depiction nor detection distinguishes photography for Maynard; it is the extent to which they interact that does this.

6 Walton, "Transparent Pictures," p. 252.

7 Walton accepts that this requires seeing into the past. But so does seeing stars through telescopes, and we do not typically deny that this constitutes seeing the stars. This response glosses over a difference that I return to below: seeing stars through telescopes is a kind of direct seeing, whereas seeing stars through photographs is a kind of indirect seeing.

8 On photography and egocentric information, see: Nigel Warburton, "Seeing through 'Seeing through Photographs'," *Ratio* 1 (June 1988); Currie, *Image and Mind*, pp. 48–78; Carroll, *Theorizing the Moving Image*, pp. 49–74 and Noël Carroll, "Toward an Ontology of the Moving Image," in Cynthia Freeland and Thomas Wartenberg (eds.) *Philosophy and Film* (New York: Routledge, 1995); and Jonathan Friday, "Transparency and the Photographic Image," *British Journal of Aesthetics* 36:1 (January 1996).

9 Or imagine the following case. As I walk around a chair I see different aspects of that chair; what I see is relative to where I see it from. If I walk around a photograph of a chair, no new aspects of the chair are revealed. At a certain

point I may cease to see the chair, but that is because I can no longer see the face of the photograph, as an object in my space, not because the chair is no longer visible in the photograph. Now imagine I were to walk around the chair with a photograph of it in my left hand, and a lens or a mirror trained upon it in my right hand: the image in my left hand remains constant throughout; what can be seen in my right changes as my relation to the chair changes. Compare Bence Nanay, "Transparency and Sensorimotor Contingencies: Do We See through Photographs?" *Pacific Philosophical Quarterly* 91:4 (2010).

10 How one understands the relation between perception and cognition depends in part on whether one thinks perception has "non-conceptual contents" that outstrip the concepts through which we seek to represent it. See José Bermúdez and Arnon Cahen, "Non-Conceptual Mental Content," in *The Stanford Encyclopedia of Philosophy*, Fall 2015 edn., Edward N. Zalta (ed.), especially §4: http://plato.stanford.edu/entries/content-nonconceptual/.

11 Lopes is a notable exception: but since he thinks *all* pictures are transparent, he concurs with Walton's more Orthodox critics in thinking how one answers this question generalizes. For Lopes all pictures are transparent; for most they are all opaque.

12 Kendall Walton, "Looking Again through Photographs: A Response to Edwin Martin," *Critical Inquiry* 12:4 (Summer 1986), p. 805.

13 Edwin Martin, "On Seeing Walton's Great-Grandfather," *Critical Inquiry* 12:4 (Summer 1986) and Walton "Looking Again through Photographs," p. 805.

14 As early as 1986, Walton acknowledged that he was proposing "something of a conceptual revision" ("Looking Again through Photographs," p. 805). And he insists on this point in his (2008) "Postscripts to 'Transparent Pictures'": "My project is theory construction, not conceptual or linguistic analysis" (Walton, *Marvelous Images*, p. 111).

15 Currie, "Photography, Painting and Perception," pp. 23–29.

16 Berys Gaut, "Cinematic Art," *Journal of Aesthetics and Art Criticism* 60:4 (2002). Had Walton wished to be scholastic, he could have pointed out that unless the gorillas are identically oriented to the wind in both locations, we will not see the hairs on the real gorillas by seeing those of their doppelgängers. Indeed, were the environments not also identical, a real gorilla climbing a tree might cause its doppelgänger to topple over on the flat, and so on. As these requirements are filled in, the claim that we see one by seeing the other may come to seem increasingly trivial.

17 Kendall Walton, "Aesthetics—What? Why? and Wherefore?" *Journal of Aesthetics and Art Criticism* 65:2 (Spring 2007), p. 150.

18 Compare Berys Gaut, *A Philosophy of Cinematic Art* (Cambridge: Cambridge University Press, 2010), pp. 91–92 and pp. 95–97. This needs finessing. EVF cameras, mobile phones, and VR set-ups that track your environment as you move around in it present a challenge to this view. In such cases it is not the

light from the scene that reaches the viewer's eyes, yet it seems strained to say that we do not therefore see the scene.

19 Compare Dretske: "You don't have to see what is going on *in* or *on* the lenses of the binoculars to see what is happening on the field." Fred Dretske, "Abstract of Comments: Seeing through Pictures," *Noûs* 18:1 (1984), p. 74.

20 See Scott Walden, "Objectivity in Photography," *British Journal of Aesthetics* 45:3 (July 2005).

21 Neil Walsh Allen and Joel Snyder, "Photography, Vision and Representation," *Critical Inquiry* 2:1 (Autumn 1975) and Joel Snyder, "Picturing Vision," *Critical Inquiry* 6:3 (Spring 1980).

22 The case is typically made by appeal to Fred Dretske, *Knowledge and the Flow of Information* (Cambridge, MA: MIT Press, 1981). See Jonathan Cohen and Aaron Meskin, "On the Epistemic Value of Photographs," *Journal of Aesthetics and Art Criticism* 62:2 (Spring 2004), p. 200ff.; Walden, "Objectivity in Photography," p. 263ff.; and Abell, "The Epistemic Value of Photographs."

23 Walden, "Objectivity in Photography," p. 268.

24 This is not an isolated example. Imagine the following: one takes a lengthy (30-minute-plus) time exposure of an unlit harbour on a dead calm night using a tripod-mounted camera, with its lens stopped right down for maximum depth of field, and a slow film for maximum resolution. Various boats come and go, but none of this makes it into the resulting picture, processed and printed without trickery, which is a richly detailed image that shows only those boats that remained static throughout. One can imagine analogous images of dance performances that show only stages or military drills that show only parade grounds. These are not mere thought experiments; real examples punctuate the history of photography, from Daguerre's *Boulevard du Temple* (1838), stripped of all passing traffic by the 15-minute exposure to Hiroshi Sugimoto's 90-minute-plus exposures of movie theatres illuminated by dazzling white screens, documenting the showing of an entire movie. Shallow depth of field is just another way to blur out non-occluded objects within the camera's field of view. For more examples, see Allen and Snyder, "Photography, Vision and Representation."

25 Walden, "Objectivity in Photography," p. 261.

26 It bears remarking that Walden has a dual career as a philosopher and a photographer; so one might think that if anyone was well placed to know, it would be him.

27 "Belief is fragile with respect to perturbations that leave seeing intact, so no doxastic state can be necessary for seeing." Cohen and Meskin, "On the Epistemic Value of Photographs," p.199.

28 Ibid., p. 200.

29 For the foundations of this view, see Jonathan Cohen and Aaron Meskin, "An Objective Counterfactual Theory of Information," *Australasian Journal of Philosophy* 84:3 (2006).

30 Thus they grant ornithological illustrations an equivalent salience to photographs for those who use them to identify birds. Cohen and Meskin, "On the Epistemic Value of Photographs," p. 206. Abell grants a similar value to botanical drawings: "The Epistemic Value of Photographs," p. 83. The same can be said of archaeological drawings, architects' blueprints, and technical drawings in general.

31 Compare Cohen and Meskin, "Photographs as Evidence," in Walden, *The Pencil of Nature*, pp. 76–77.

32 Abell cashes this out by appeal to David Lewis's possible-world semantics for counterfactuals: a process for making pictures is more reliable the greater the distance between the nearest possible world in which a non-actual picture produced by that process depicts its object as it was when the picture was taken and the closest possible world in which that picture exists but depicts its object as other than it was when the picture was taken.

33 Abell, "The Epistemic Value of Photographs," pp. 85–86.

34 Ibid., p. 87.

35 Ibid., p. 87ff.

36 Ibid., p. 88.

37 Robert Hopkins, "Factive Pictorial Experience: What's Special about Photographs?" *Noûs* 46:4 (2012).

38 "For any token experience of that kind, if what is seen in the picture is that *p* then *p*." Ibid., pp. 711–714.

39 Ibid., p. 717.

40 Ibid., p. 718. I am simplifying here for the sake of brevity. Ultimately "every viewer should see in a photograph only facts consistent with *perfect* general knowledge of how things are. For only appeal to perfect general knowledge allows pictorial experience to meet its wider goal of tracking the facts."

41 Ibid., p. 729.

42 See Lopes's account of Galileo's moon drawings in *Understanding Pictures*, ch. 9.

43 Dominic McIver Lopes, "The Knowing Eye," in *The Four Arts of Photography*, especially pp. 111–113.

44 Dominic McIver Lopes, "Lyricism: The Third Art," in *The Four Arts of Photography*.

45 William J. Mitchell, *The Reconfigured Eye: Visual Truth in the Post-Photographic Era* (Cambridge, MA: MIT Press, 1994), p. 18.

46 Lopes, "The Knowing Eye," pp. 109–110.

47 Brian Walski was summarily dismissed from the *Los Angeles Times* when it was realized that he had created a composite from two images of a British soldier directing civilians near Basra during the Iraq War taken moments apart. The image had been published on the front cover of the 31 March 2003 edition. See Walden, "Truth in Photography," in Walden, *Photography and Philosophy*. By contrast, Wall was in no danger of being struck from Marian Goodman's roster when it was realized that *Dead Troops Talk* shows the same model more than once (Plate 5).

Since the norms governing photojournalism have no automatic purchase on practices serving non-epistemic ends.

48 This would be one reason that Richard Mosse's hot-pink images of war-torn Congo, made by shooting infrared film in daylight, cannot be confused with war photography. Just as the ways in which Walid Raad and the (fictional) Atlas Group subvert standard conventions of reporting and archival documentation would be one reason their research into the Lebanese conflict could not be confused with photojournalism. Similarly, flouting norms of legibility would be one reason that Thomas Ruff's pixelated screen grabs would make for very poor pornography.

49 Lopes, "The Knowing Eye," p. 112.

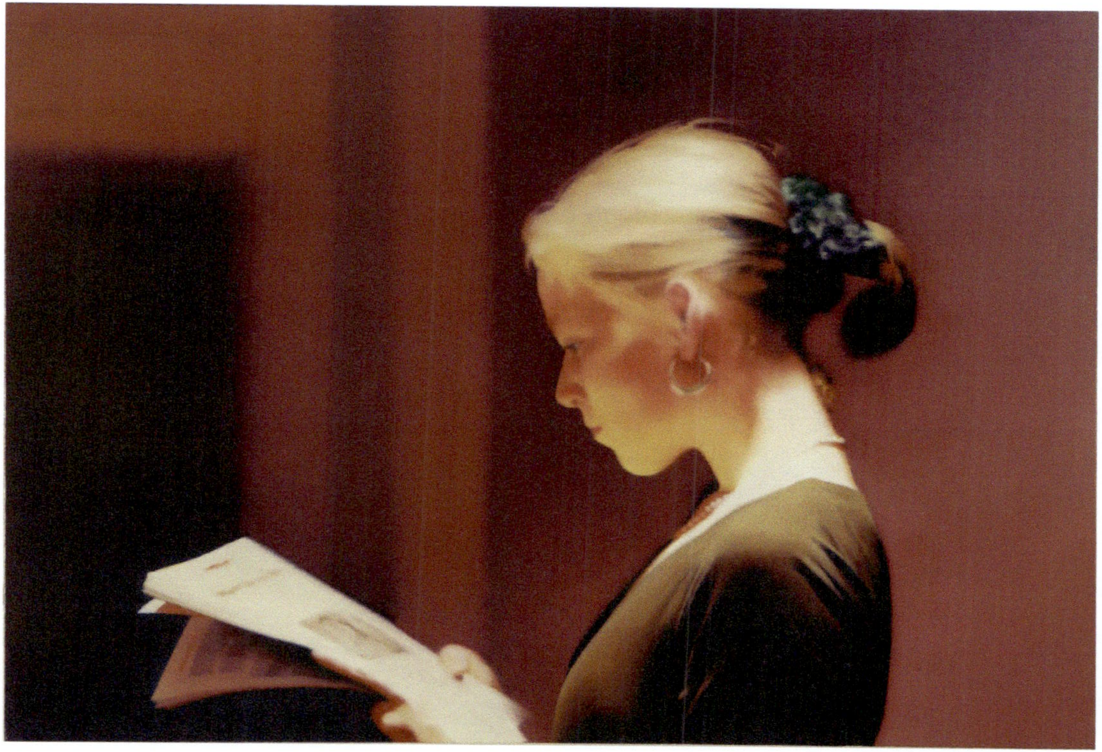

Plate 1 Gerhard Richter, *Lesende*, 1994. Oil on canvas, 20 ⅛ × 28 in. (72 × 102 cm). Image © Gerhard Richter. Reproduced with permission of the artist.

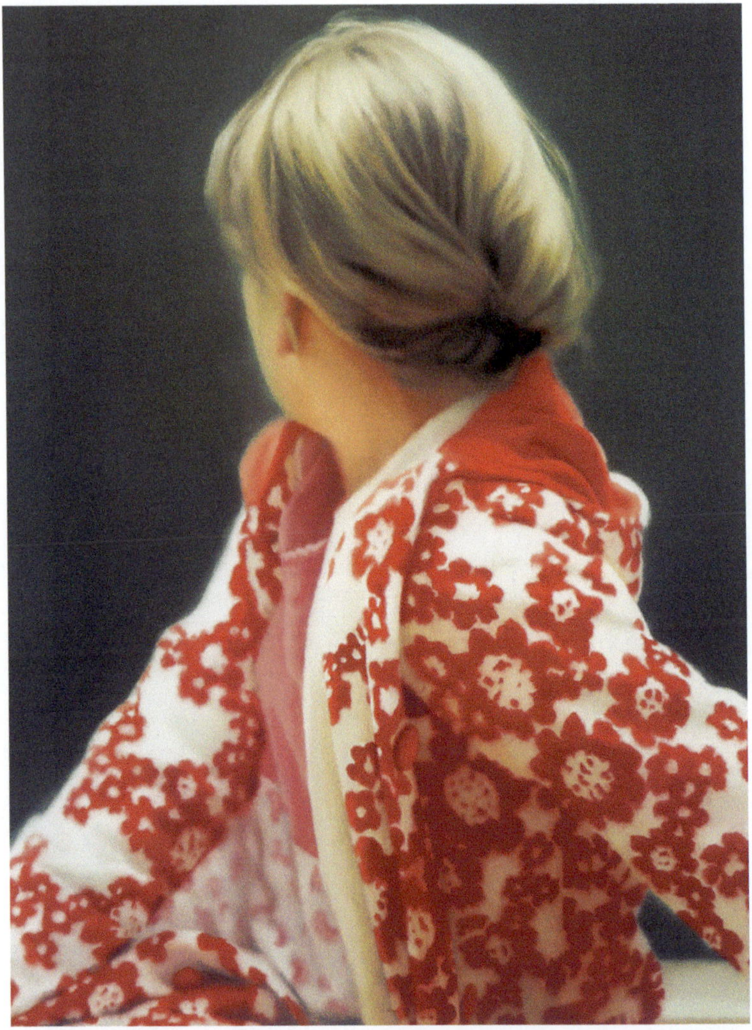

Plate 2 Gerhard Richter, *Betty*, 1988. Oil on canvas, $40\frac{1}{8} \times 28\frac{3}{8}$ in. (102 × 72 cm). Image © Gerhard Richter. Reproduced with permission of the artist.

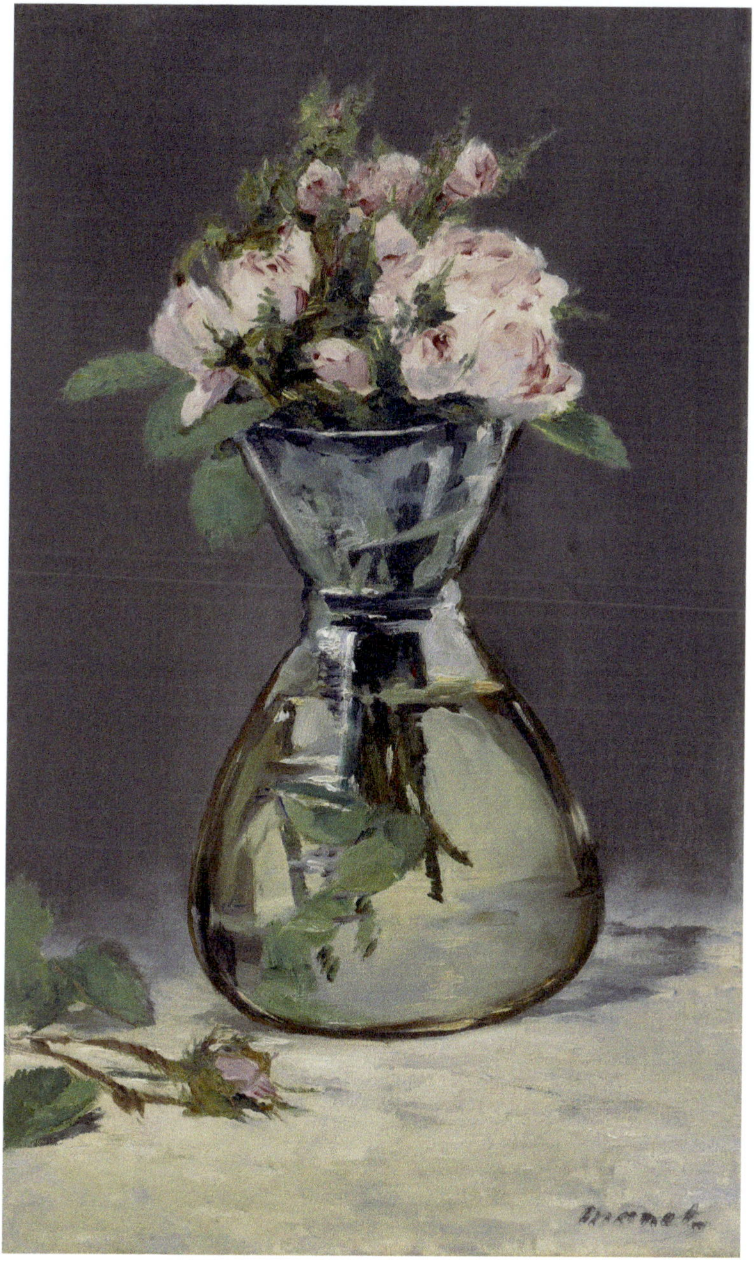

Plate 3 Édouard Manet, *Roses mousseuses dans un vase* [Moss roses in a vase], 1882. Oil on canvas, 22 × 13⅝ in. (55.9 × 34.6 cm). Credit: Sterling and Francine Clark Art Institute, Williamstown, Massachusetts, USA/Bridgeman Images.

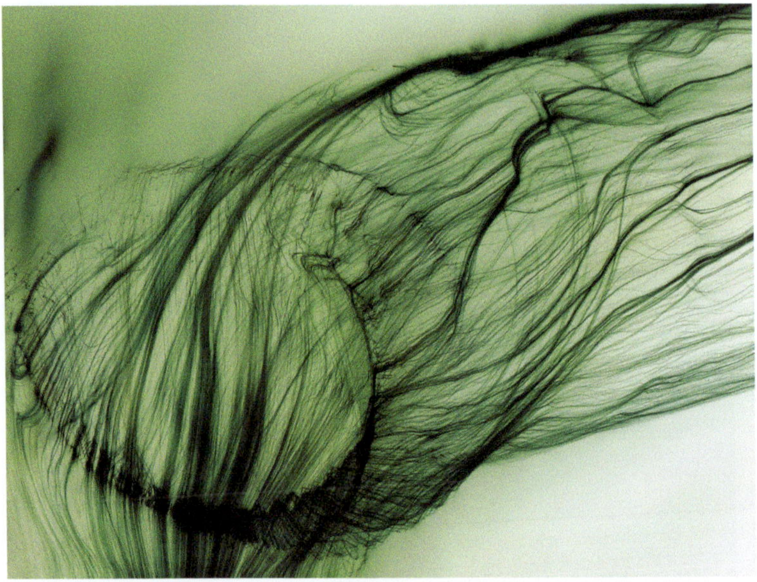

Plate 4 Wolfgang Tillmans, *Freischwimmer* 16, 2003. Chromogenic print, on paper on board, 943 × 707 ½ in. (2,395 × 1,797 cm). © Wolfgang Tillmanns. Image courtesy the artist and Maureen Paley, London.

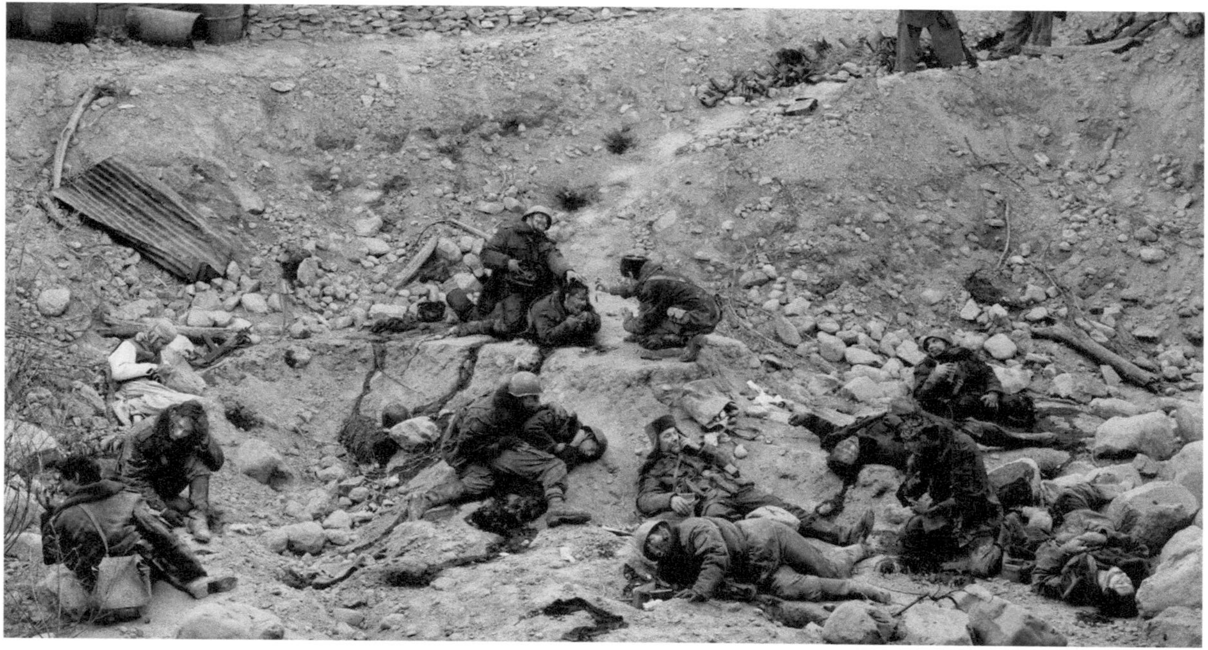

Plate 5 Jeff Wall, *Dead Troops Talk* (*A Vision after an Ambush of a Red Army Patrol, near Moqor, Afghanistan, Winter 1986*), 1992. Transparency in lightbox, 90 1/8 × 164 1/8 in. (228.92 × 416.88 cm). The Broad Art Foundation.

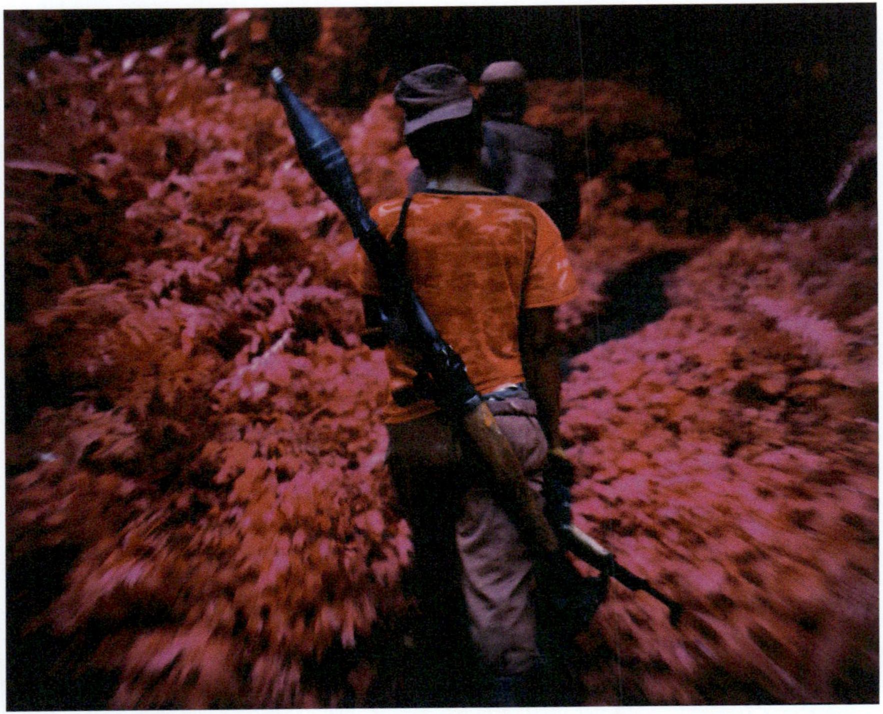

Plate 6 Richard Mosse, *Ruby Tuesday*, 2011. Digital c-print, dimensions variable (48 × 60 in.; 121.9 × 152.4 cm). © Richard Mosse. Courtesy the artist and Jack Shainman Gallery, New York.

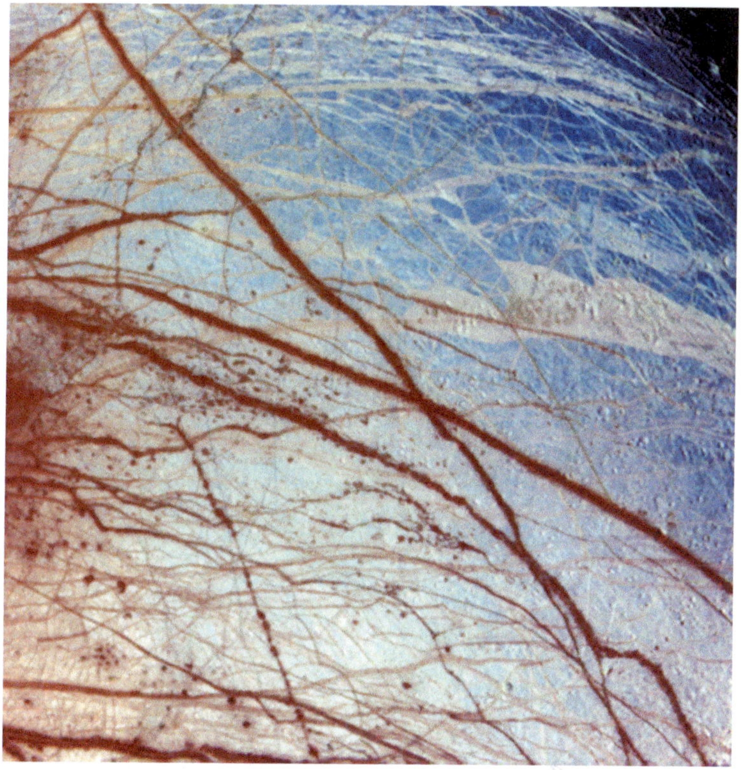

Plate 7 Minos Linea, Jupiter's moon Europa from the Galileo spacecraft. Image courtesy of NASA/Jet Propulsion Laboratory-Caltech.

Note: False colour has been used to enhance the visibility of various features in this composite of three images of the Minos Linea region on Jupiter's moon Europa taken by the solid-state imaging camera on NASA's Galileo spacecraft. Triple bands, lineae, and mottled terrains appear in brown and reddish hues, indicating the presence of contaminants in the ice. The icy plains, shown here in bluish hues, subdivide into units with different albedos at infrared wavelengths probably because of differences in the grain size of the ice. The composite was produced using images with effective wavelengths at 989, 757, and 559 nm. The spatial resolution in the individual images ranges from 1.6 to 3.3 km (1 to 2 miles) per pixel. The area covered, centred at 45N, 221W, is about 1,260 km (about 780 miles) across.

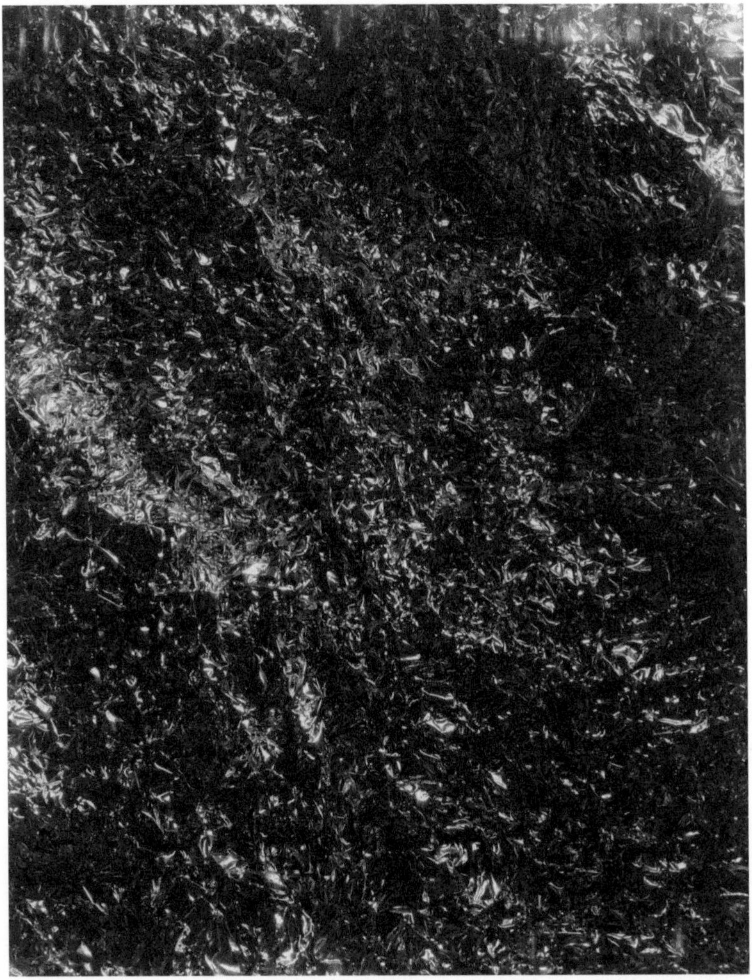

Plate 8 James Welling, *Cascade*, 1980. Gelatin silver contact print, $4\frac{3}{4} \times 3\frac{3}{4}$ in. (12×9.5 cm). Courtesy the artist and David Zwirner, New York/London.

Plate 9 James Welling, 9818, 2009. Inkjet print on rag paper, $33\frac{2}{3} \times 50\frac{1}{2}$ in. (85.5 × 128.3 cm). Courtesy the artist and David Zwirner, New York/London. Philip Johnson Glass House is a site of the National Trust for Historic Preservation.

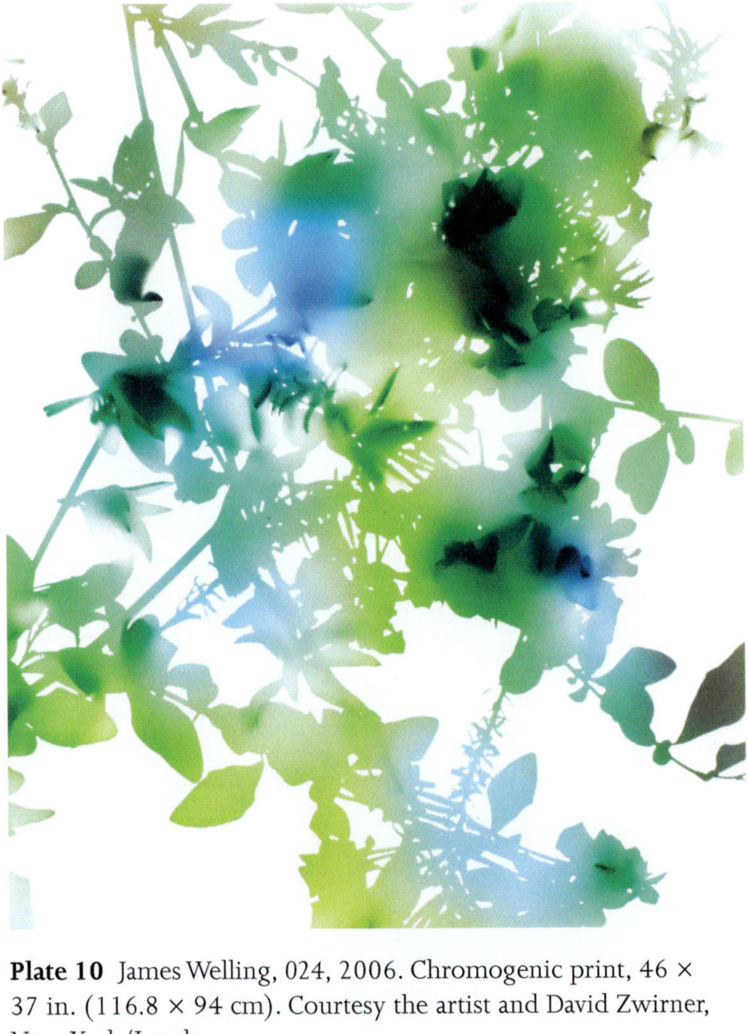

Plate 10 James Welling, 024, 2006. Chromogenic print, 46 × 37 in. (116.8 × 94 cm). Courtesy the artist and David Zwirner, New York/London.

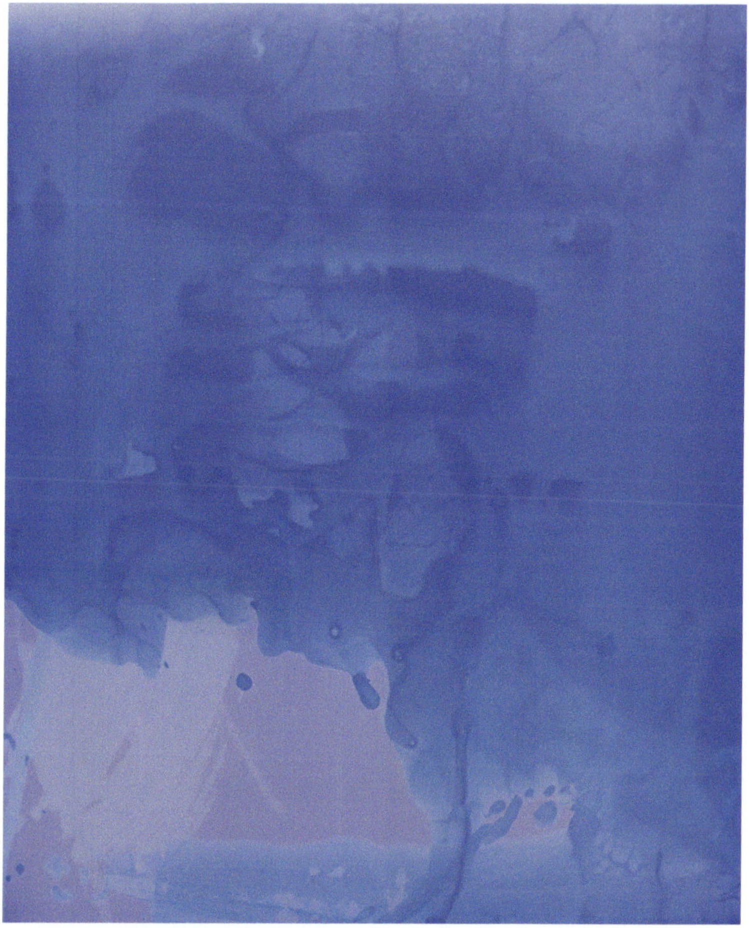

Plate 11 James Welling, *FDB9*, 2009–2012. Inkjet print on rag paper, 48 × 40 in. (101.5 × 122 cm). Courtesy the artist and David Zwirner, New York/London.

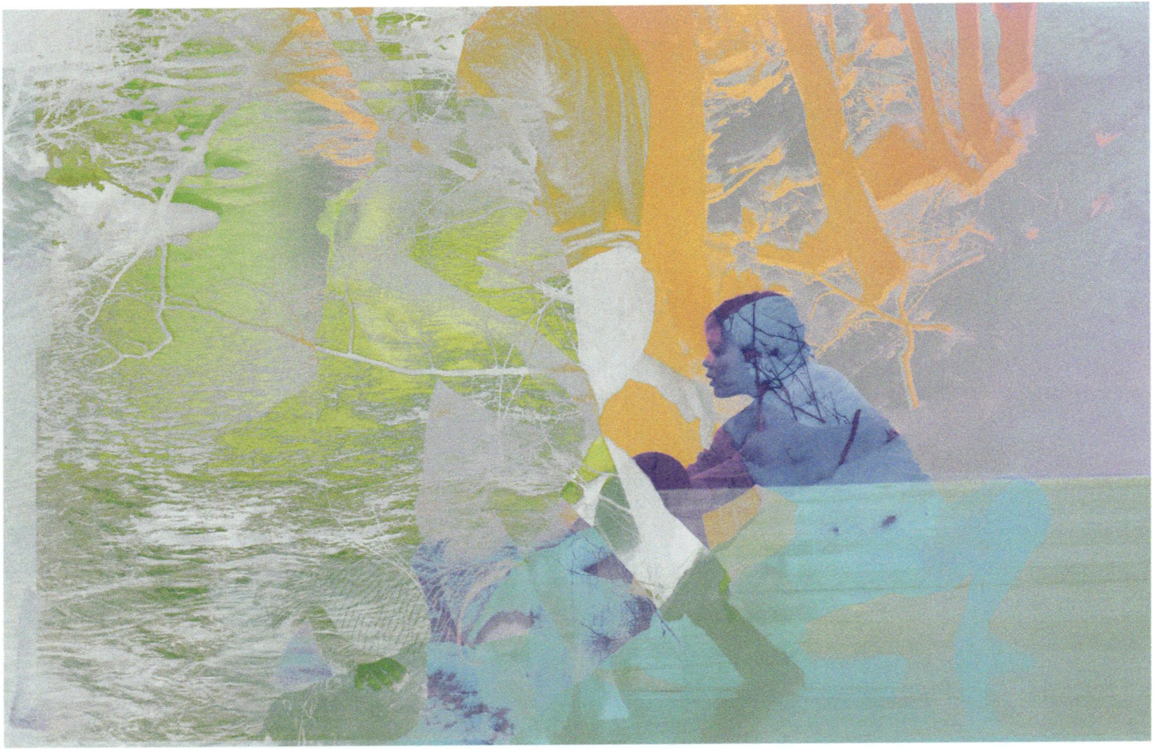

Plate 12 James Welling, 0371, 2015. Inkjet print on rag paper, 42 × 63 in. (106.7 × 160 cm). Courtesy the artist, David Zwirner, New York/London, and Peter Freeman Inc., Paris.

Conclusion

The unity of photography

One obvious test of a theory's adequacy is how it copes with various challenges. We've seen how Orthodox and New Theory cope with the challenge presented by the other's strong suit. For New Theorists, the epistemic value of photography is not an intrinsic feature of photography; it characterizes photography only in so far as it conforms to the knowledge-oriented norms imposed by various social practices that certain kinds of photography subtend. Conversely, for Orthodox theorists, intrinsic possession of aesthetic value is not what makes some photography art; instead, when photography is art, this is always in virtue of respects in which it departs from the strictly photographic, rather than in virtue of being a photograph. It will be clear by now where I stand on these questions and, having set out their respective merits, I am happy to step back and leave the reader to decide. In conclusion I want to consider how Orthodoxy and New Theory alike might respond, not to one another but to a shared test case, and what this says in turn about their respective conceptions of photographic agency.

Autographic and allographic

Recall the curious mixture of enthusiasm and millennialism that greeted the integration of new digital technologies into photography some quarter of a century ago—all that talk about "painting with pixels" and "photography after photography" respectively.[1] Depending on where you looked, either photography was finally a fully fledged art, or the end was truly nigh. For New Theorists, digital capture and processing seem unlikely to raise substantive issues: CCD sensors are just another way of recording information from a light image; the resulting images implicate a photographic event in their causal history; and digital processing is just a way of converting that information into a form that may be visually appreciated. Unless the New Theorist holds an untenably restrictive view of photographic means, the fact that such image processing is digital rather than chemical is immaterial. New Theory, like photography itself, seems able to accommodate the challenge seamlessly.

What about Orthodoxy? The reason digital technologies were greeted with delight or consternation is precisely because they were viewed through an Orthodox optic. It is *because* theorists implicitly conceived photography in terms of something like natural counterfactual dependency or belief-independent feature-tracking that digital capture's expansion of photography's capacity for manipulation presented, depending on your sympathies, such an opportunity or threat: for better or worse photography was finally no longer exhausted by recording! That this should be perceived as a break shows that photography was being conceived in terms of mechanism, automatism, and the like.[2]

At this point, Orthodox theorists face a choice. Either digital photography is merely different in degree to analogue photography in these respects: it may make manipulation easier, faster and harder to detect, but it does not generate entirely new imaging possibilities; or it constitutes a definitive break with the analogue, by virtue of doing just that. The latter is a substantive philosophical claim. If one retreats to the former, not only does digital turn out to be the latest in a long line of technological refinements, enhancements, and extensions of existing capabilities, but Orthodoxy's account of analogue photography as a mechanical or automatic mentation-free zone is in jeopardy: for if digital is indeed only different in degree to analogue photography, then various kinds of manipulation must have been standing possibilities throughout, irrespective of whether they were recognized as such. So it turns out that Orthodoxy, but not the New Theory, *requires* there to be a difference of kind between analogue and digital.

Does this still seem credible? One promising strategy might be to appeal to Nelson Goodman's influential distinction between "autographic" and "allographic" arts.[3] Autographic arts, as the name implies, are "autographed" in an important sense. In a slogan: causal history matters. Because it does, autographic arts can be forged. If a work issued from the brush of Van Meegeren rather than Vermeer, it cannot be a work by Vermeer, no matter how much it may resemble genuine instances of his works. If a multiple is pulled from a plate or mould other than those authorized by Edgar Degas or Auguste Rodin, it cannot be a bona fide instance of their works. As it happens, Rodin willed his entire estate to the French state, including the right to make (within limits) posthumous casts of his sculptures from original plasters and moulds, some of which remained uncast in his own lifetime. The Musée Rodin exercises this right on behalf of the French state.[4] But suppose that none of this were true and the French state simply arrogated to itself the right, after a major work was damaged in a fire, to retro-engineer a new mould from a surviving cast so as to replace the lost work. The result might be qualitatively identical to those produced from the original mould—perhaps even better, given advances in modern casting techniques—but it would not be a genuine Rodin. It is because causal history matters that the autographic arts, singular or multiple, admit of forgery; for only if a work can have the wrong causal history to count as a genuine instance is forgery even possible.

Analogue photography is clearly autographic in Goodman's sense. An instance of Ansel Adams's *Moonrise, Hernandez, New Mexico* (October, 1941) must be one of the (many) prints that Adams printed from the correct negative during his lifetime to count as a genuine instance. If a gallery markets a print as a genuine Adams that was in fact made by some kind of high-quality copy process, then it is peddling a forgery; they are misrepresenting a copy as an original.

Allographic arts, by contrast, cannot be forged. What matters here is not causal history but compliance with a notation. Works of literature and at least non-improvised or "scored" music, and perhaps also architecture and some forms of notated dance, are allographic in Goodman's sense. An art is notational in Goodman's sense if and only if whether or not *x* is an authentic instance of the work can be fully determined by conformity to a notation. So long as the work in question meets all the compliance conditions set by the manuscript or score, it just *is* an instance of that work—no matter how generated.[5] Because the score or notation tells you which features of the work are constitutive and which are contingent, it tells you everything you need to know to identify instances of the work correctly. Causal history falls away as redundant. For works of fiction such as novels this might (standardly) comprise the right words in the right order, spelt in the same way and punctuated correctly. But in the case of concrete (and other forms of) poetry, it might also include spacing, line leading, font size, and so on. By contrast, whether the work is printed on cheap or high-grade stock, bound in paper or by hand, a first edition or cheap Xerox does not generally matter—unless any are indicated as non-standard compliance conditions by the manuscript.[6] Similarly, at least in scored music, the right notes, played on the correct instruments, in the right order and at an acceptable tempo, are typically determined by the score, while other aspects (including ritardando, cadenza, and feel) are left open to conductor or performer interpretation.

This leads naturally to the thought that digital photography, since it appears amenable to a notation, and comprises discrete informational bits that can be cleanly parsed, is allographic. Digital images are comprised of binary code (values of 0s and 1s) and that code gives the information that constitutes them in discrete, parsible chunks. If the instance in question is composed of the right "bits" (the right strings of zeros and ones in the right order), this way of thinking would run, it just is a genuine instance. How it was generated does not matter; all that matters is whether or not it respects the notation.

By contrast, an autographic art such as painting cannot be notated: because paintings consist of a syntactically and semantically dense continuum of information, any deviation, no matter how small, will be significant. Unlike works in allographic art forms, they cannot be parsed between those features that must and those features that need not be respected; every feature is constitutive. Analogue photographs similarly consist of a dense continuum of information. Because the information of which they are comprised does not come in discrete chunks, they cannot be parsed between essential and non-essential features.

Set aside questions about the merits of the distinction, and focus instead on its implications for photography.[7] If plausible, the autographic–allographic distinction seems to offer just what Orthodox theorists need—a principled basis for distinguishing between analogue and the digital cases. But there is reason to be cautious. Suppose one has a way of "coding up from scratch" a putative instance of some photograph: has one thereby created a genuine instance?[8] The compliance conditions have been met; it is the right bits in the right order. On Goodman's theory, if photograph A is constituted by the same code as photograph B they must be tokens of the same type.

But the New Theory shows why this is beside the point: if the instance in question does not implicate a photographic event in its causal history it is not even a photograph, so it can hardly be an instance of the right photograph. It may be a digital *image*, but it is not a digital *photograph*, since light played no role in the formation of the image itself. This may seem to beg the question by presupposing the truth of the New Theory. But all that is thereby presupposed is the irreducible role of light in the photographic process, nothing more—it would take a thick-skinned Orthodox theorist to quibble with that![9] If such a theorist still exists, this may be one point at which the New Theorist simply digs in her heels: "photography" just *means* writing or drawing with light. If what one is talking about no longer involves that, then one is no longer talking about photography, however much an image might resemble a photograph. After all, the New Theory is a theory about how the photographic image comes into being, not a theory about how it looks: works that are photographic may look anything but, and works that are not in fact photographic (such as the hypothetical digital image coded up from scratch) can be indistinguishable from genuine photographs right down to the code of which they are constituted.

Photographic art, agency, and exemplarity

Finally, consider the implications of the two theories for photographic agency. Because Orthodoxy reduces photography to the event of image-transcription (mapping of a pro-photographic scene onto a light-sensitive surface), together with the recording of information from the image thereby created, it is forced to conceive photography as mind-independent: if not ultimately of the camera designers, chemists, and software engineers responsible for determining how scenes will be mapped, processed, and preserved, then at least of those constrained to use what they provide. What may look like photographic agency—all those decisions photographers routinely make prior to exposure concerning lighting, framing, point of view, choice of camera hardware and settings, film stocks and the like and, after exposure, concerning image-processing and rendering, whether chemical or electronic—are strictly speaking either pre- or post-photographic, and so cannot impact on the *formation* of the image itself. I have already offered some reasons for being sceptical about this claim, but suppose for the sake of argument that it were true. The implications for photographic agency would be clear: photographers may control the production of their images in all manner of ways, what they cannot do is intervene in the only way that really matters. Indeed it is the fact that image-formation remains mind-independent that types the activity as photographic.

Contrast this to how things stand on the New Theory. Only those forms of photography that are constrained by *extra*-photographic, knowledge-oriented norms—norms grounded not in any intrinsic, material or technological features of the process, equipment or medium, but in how these can be used in a particular domain—preclude intervening in ways that undermine the counterfactual dependency of image on scene. Outside such photographic practices, according to the New Theory, the photographer can intervene, *strictly photographically*, in any of the stages that are necessary for the production of an image that can be visually appreciated. Since the mere recording of information in a photographic event, together with the mapping process that generates the image so recorded, does not suffice to produce the latter.

To see what this might amount to in practice, consider the work of James Welling as just one example. On the Orthodox account, much of what Welling does will not count as photography; on the New Theory it does. What makes Welling's work an exemplary test case for competing theories of photography is that, across different series, he intervenes in different stages of the photographic process. Taken as a whole, his practice is a sustained exploration of the space of photographic possibility, a space that turns out to be much more capacious than Orthodoxy imagines.[10]

In early series, such as those depicting what turn out to be crumpled foil, velour, pastry, gelatin, and tiles, Welling constructs the pro-photographic scene from the ground up.[11] Aluminum Foil (1980) is exemplary (Plate 8). The camera records what was before it at the moment of exposure, just as Orthodoxy would have it. New Theorists concur, but insist that we conceive the pro-photographic scene as an essential stage *internal* to the photographic process itself. For absent some such scene, there cannot be a photograph. This means that whenever a photographer constructs such a scene he is acting within the domain of photography proper. Ditto if he over-exposes in camera to preserve detail in the shadows, and then has to over-expose again in the darkroom to compensate for density in the resulting negatives. Though the camera may record what was before it at the moment of exposure, as Orthodoxy maintains, this seriously under-describes what is taking place. Given that the pro-photographic scene is downstream of the photographer's intervention, the results can only be understood as "recordings" of a highly mediated kind: they document *what the photographer has done*, off camera, with an eye to the camera that will record it. Orthodoxy's dream of a pristine extra-photographic reality recedes; it fails to capture how the camera can be a means not only of recording a scene, but a condition of the scene thereby recorded. Had there been no camera to record them, these scenes would never have existed.

Contrast these works with Welling's later Glass House series (2006–2009). The pro-photographic scene is now Philip Johnson's Glass House set in the Connecticut landscape. Welling no longer constructs the pro-photographic scene from scratch; he focuses instead on disrupting the formation of the light image that this scene projects onto his camera's sensor, by interposing an array of plastic and glass filters, gels, mirrors, and defraction gratings before the camera during exposure. Whereas digital post-production permits precise control, filters interrupt the optics of the camera in ways that are hard to predict. Reflecting materials held before the camera layer and rearrange the landscape in ways that are all but impossible to resolve. In 9818 (2009), for example, the sun on the photographer's back reappears in shot above the house, thereby transforming the entire landscape, and not just that bit of it that falls within his camera's field of view (Plate 9). By flaunting his own interventions in the creation of these images so ostentatiously, Glass House focuses attention on the improvised, hands-on process of creating the work. Like Aluminum Foil, this work also draws attention to what the photographer has done, albeit quite differently.

Aluminum Foil and Glass House already give us a flavour of Welling's interventions in the first two stages of the photographic process. In several series comprising images constructed from scratch in the darkroom, Welling effectively steps inside the camera to work on the photographic event directly. Take Flowers (2004–2007). At first blush, what these images show may seem obvious: though their colour effects may be difficult to resolve, they appear to depict some kind of foliage, irradiated towards the edges by a strong sun. In fact the series poses an even greater challenge to Orthodox theory. For in this case no worldly scene is recorded, if that is taken to mean something prior to and independent of the camera. Instead, the pro-photographic scene has been created from scratch inside Welling's darkroom, enabling him to act directly on the photographic event itself.

To appreciate what one is seeing, one must understand something of how Flowers are made. This begins with making a photogram, a camera-less contact print generated by selectively occluding a light-sensitive surface exposed to light. Take 024 (2006). Here, plumbago blossoms are laid directly onto the light-sensitive surface: occluded areas remain unaffected, and those exposed to light blacken on being developed (Plate 10). In Flowers, that surface is 400 ASA Tri-X film rather than photographic paper. This allows the resulting photograms to be used as negatives to make prints in the standard way. It also means Welling is obliged to arrange his photograms by touch, in the dark, as the film's sensitivity to all visible light rules out use of a red safety light; in effect, Welling is creating negatives from scratch, without the aid of a camera, and he is doing so blind.[12] The film negatives (the original photograms) are black and white. Colour is added later, during a second print stage, by sandwiching coloured gels in his enlarger's mixing box. Light, filtered first by the opacity of the flowers relative to the film, is filtered for a second time by the gels so that semi-transparent tones of grey register as colours. Where the blossoms touch the film directly during the initial exposure, no light penetrates (assuming that they are opaque), leaving the film clear. Where they were merely close to the film, some light penetrates, producing delicate, gauzy greys; the same is true of anything less than fully opaque, such as translucent petals. Filtering light through coloured gels transforms these greys into hues. Because the original film images are negatives, solid shapes are rendered negatively in clear, unexposed film; when used as negatives in an enlarger, these areas allow light to pass freely, resulting in positive images of flowers in the form of coloured light. A complex, iterated process of photographic labour is being clearly foregrounded here.

Welling has thematized the chemical side of traditional photographic films, papers, developing and fixing agents in similar ways, by producing "wet photograms" from scratch in the darkroom. Take Fluid Dynamics (2009–2012) (Plate 11). For this series, Welling immerses sheets of chromogenic paper in water and exposes them to light prior to development. Prolonged soaking frees up the water-soluble blue dye in the surface of the paper. By exposing the still-wet paper to light, Welling causes the paper to record an image of its own surface at the moment of exposure. In seeing the resulting picture, one is seeing a prior, semi-liquid state of the very surface one is looking at. It is hard to imagine a more insistent reminder of the labour of photography. Like Flowers, though perhaps even more insistently these images direct attention to what has taken place—that is, to what the photographer has done—in order to generate the surface that one is now looking at. We are reminded how much photography involves the handling of various physical materials and stuffs in addition to the screening and control of light.

As Aluminum Foil, Glass House, Flowers and Water demonstrate, Welling draws on resources at every stage of the photographic process. We see the staging and construction of the pro-photographic scene in Aluminum Foil. The landscape in Glass House is fashioned by redirecting the flow of light with mirrors and filters before it reaches the camera, impacting the formation of the light image. In Flowers and Water, the camera is left behind altogether to direct the photographic event in the darkroom. The idea that photographic images are a product of how a particular photographer handles light, chemicals (and digital processes), and not the product of a mechanistic recording process, is brought out in numerous ways. Welling is well aware that his practice implies a broad conception of the medium: "I'm interested in finding new ways of applying materials to a surface. ... Photography is just a different way of applying material and some of my works draw out this process."[13]

The series considered so far involve acting on, or prior to, the photographic event; they are upstream of that event. In several more recent series, Welling explores various forms of image rendering downstream of this event, thereby extending his range of activity across the entire photographic process.[14] What unifies these series is superimposing several images in an image-editing application to generate a new, more visually complex, image. In Flowers (2014), Welling takes three black-and-white film photograms originally made for his earlier series of the same name, and assigns one each to the red, green, and blue colour channels of Photoshop, before adjusting local colour values by selectively altering the saturation and hue. Choreograph (2014–2016) (Plate 12) follows the same process and method, but instead inputs images of dance, landscape, and architecture taken for this purpose.

Why Welling does what he does is not something I can dwell on here.[15] But at least the richness of his practice should be apparent. Welling's practice suggests that if photography is indeed a relation between two terms, these are not—*pace* Orthodoxy—*photograph* and world, but *photographer* and world. Light serves as the basic medium of that relation for Welling as for other photographers, but different photographers and different photographic practices harness the image-forming capacities of light in very different ways. Orthodoxy makes room for none of this: by shrinking photography to mechanized transcription and recording, it ensures that whatever photographic artists do, they do to one side of photography proper. For the same reason, whatever thematic, emotional, or intellectual concerns Welling is addressing through his interventions in pro-photographic scene, light image, and image-rendering processes reside of necessity outside that domain. So long as photography is reduced to the non-agential registration of a light image, much of what a photographer like Welling does cannot be understood. Conceived along the lines of New Theory, it comes into focus as a persistent exploration of an expanded domain of photographic possibility grounded in the event of recording a light image.

* * * * *

At the outset I suggested that one way to locate one's own intuitions in terms of recent thought about photography is to ask oneself two deceptively simple questions, "What is a photograph?" and "What is photography?" before reflecting on the relation of priority or grounding between them. You've made it this far; ask yourself again. Perhaps something has changed.

Notes

1 See the essays gathered in Hubertus von Amelunxen, Stefan Iglhaut, and Florian Rötzer (eds.) *Photography after Photography: Memory and Representation in the Digital Age* (Amsterdam: G+B Arts, 1996). These debates followed a common pattern: proponents of a difference of kind were met with the claim that the difference had been over-stated. See William Mitchell, "Intention and Artifice," in *The Reconfigured Eye* and Lev Manovich, "Paradoxes of Digital Photography," in von Amelunxen, Iglhaut, and Rötzer, *Photography after Photography*, and Jonathan Friday, "Digital Imaging, Photographic Representation and Aesthetics," *Ends and Means* 1:2 (1997) and Nigel Warburton, "Pixels and Pictorialism: A Reply to Jonathan Friday," *Ends and Means* 2:2 (1998).

2 See Barbara Savedoff, *Transforming Images: How Photography Complicates the Picture* (Ithaca, NY: Cornell University Press, 2000), ch. 5.

3 Nelson Goodman, *Languages of Art* (Indianapolis: Hackett, 1976), chs. 3–5.

4 "Laws that Govern the Casting of Rodin's Work," www.cantorfoundation.org/resources/laws-that-govern-the-casting-of-rodins-work/.

5 This has some peculiar metaphysical implications, if all instances and score go out of existence and the work is recreated from scratch at a later date, but set those aside here.

6 There are reasons to be doubtful. Imagine a copy of James Joyce's *Ulysses* printed in the largest font that permits one word per page. Readers need to mount a special platform to turn its pages in a double-height room. But I set such worries aside here.

7 For an overview see John Kulvicki, *On Images: Their Structure and Content* (Oxford: Oxford University Press, 2006).

8 I owe this thought to conversations with Aaron Meskin. See also John Zeimbekis, "Digital Pictures, Sampling, and Vagueness: The Ontology of Digital Pictures," in Costello and Lopes, "The Media of Photography."

9 Or imagine two digital photographs comprising the same code that derive from different photographic events. As notationally identical, they would be instances of the same photograph on this account.

10 The material that follows derives from Diarmuid Costello and Dominic McIver Lopes, "Spontaneity and Materiality: What Photography Is in the Photography of James Welling," unpublished manuscript.

11 The works can be accessed at: http://jameswelling.net/works.

12 I take this to be crucial to the work. See Costello and Lopes, "Spontaneity and Materiality."

13 James Crump, "Ventriloquisms: The Art of James Welling," in *James Welling: Monograph*, ed. James Crump (New York: Aperture, 2013), p. 78.

14 Part of what makes Welling's work interesting is that it straddles traditions typically taken to be incompatible. On the one hand, a recognizably modernist strain stretching back, via Strand and Weston, to Emerson and Evans, which

emphasizes those decisions *in advance of exposure* that determine the finished result. On the other, an interest in intervening in *exposure and post-exposure* image-rendering that can be traced from Moholy-Nagy's darkroom experiments via Stieglitz back to aspects of nineteenth-century pictorialism.

15 See Costello and Lopes, "Spontaneity and Materiality."

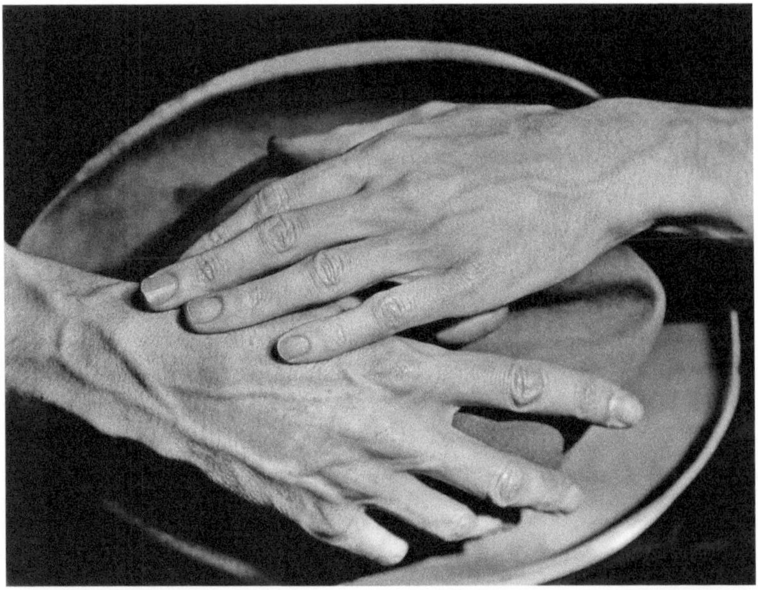

Endpiece Berenice Abbott, *Hands of Jean Cocteau*, 1927. Gelatin silver print, 6⅞ × 9¼ in. (17.5 × 23.5 cm).

Bibliography

Abell, Catharine, "The Epistemic Value of Photographs," in Abell and Katerina Bantinaki, *Philosophical Perspectives on Depiction* (Oxford: Oxford University Press, 2010)

Adams, Ansel, "A Personal Credo," in Newhall, *Photography: Essays and Images*

Allen, Neil Walsh and Joel Snyder, "Photography, Representation and Vision," *Critical Inquiry* 2:1 (Autumn 1975)

Amelunxen, Hubertus von, Stefan Iglhaut, and Florian Rötzer (eds.), *Photography after Photography: Memory and Representation in the Digital Age* (Amsterdam: G+B Arts, 1996)

Anonymous, "Is Photography a New Art?" *Camera Work* 21 (1908), in Trachtenberg, *Classic Essays*

Anscombe, G.E.M., *Intention* (Cambridge, MA: Harvard University Press, 1957)

Arago, Dominique-François Jean, "Report," in Trachtenberg, *Classic Essays*

Atencia-Linares, Paloma, "Fiction, Non-Fiction, and Deceptive Photographic Representation," in Diarmuid Costello and Dominic McIver Lopes (eds.) "The Media of Photography," *Journal of Aesthetics and Art Criticism* 70:1 (Winter 2012)

Bazin, André, "Ontology of the Photographic Image," in *What is Cinema?*, vol. 1 (Berkeley: University of California Press, 1967)

Benjamin, Andrew (ed.), *Walter Benjamin and Art* (London: Continuum, 2005)

Benjamin, Walter, "A Little History of Photography," in Michael W. Jennings, Howard Eiland, and Gary Smith (eds.) *Walter Benjamin*

Selected Writings, vol. 2.ii, 1931–1934 (Cambridge, MA: Harvard University Press, 1999)
——, *On Photography*, ed. and trans. Esther Leslie (London: Reaktion Books, 2015)
——, "The Work of Art in the Age of its Technical Reproducibility," in Michael W. Jennings and Howard Eiland (eds.) *Walter Benjamin Selected Writings*, vol. 3, 1935–1938 (Cambridge, MA: Harvard University Press, 2002)
Bermúdez, José and Arnon Cahen, "Non-Conceptual Mental Content," in *The Stanford Encyclopedia of Philosophy*, Fall 2015 edn., Edward N. Zalta (ed.), especially §4: http://plato.stanford.edu/entries/content-nonconceptual/
Blocher, H. Gene, "Pictures and Photographs," *Journal of Aesthetics and Art Criticism* 36:2 (Winter 1977)
Carroll, Noël, *Engaging the Moving Image* (New Haven, CT: Yale University Press, 2003)
——, "Medium Specificity Arguments and the Self-Consciously Invented Arts: Film, Video and Photography," in Carroll, *Theorizing the Moving Image*
——, *Philosophical Problems of Classical Film Theory* (Princeton: Princeton University Press, 1988)
——, *Theorizing the Moving Image* (Cambridge: Cambridge University Press, 1996)
——, "Toward an Ontology of the Moving Image," in Freeland and Wartenberg, *Philosophy and Film*
Cavell, Stanley, "What Photography Calls Thinking," in William Rothman (ed.) *Cavell on Film* (Albany: State University of New York Press, 2005)
——, *The World Viewed*, Enlarged Edition (Cambridge, MA: Harvard University Press, 1979)
Cohen, Jonathan and Aaron Meskin, "An Objective Counterfactual Theory of Information," *Australasian Journal of Philosophy* 84:3 (2006)
——, "On the Epistemic Value of Photographs," *Journal of Aesthetics and Art Criticism* 62:2 (Spring 2004)
——, "Photographs as Evidence," in Walden, *The Pencil of Nature*
Costello, Diarmuid, "Aura, Face, Photography: Re-reading Benjamin Today," in A. Benjamin, *Walter Benjamin and Art*

——, "Automat, Automatic, Automatism: Rosalind Krauss and Stanley Cavell on Photography and the Photographically Dependent Arts," *Critical Inquiry* 38:4 (Summer 2012)

——, "But I *Am* Killing Them! Reply to Charles Palermo and Jan Baetens on Agency and Automatism," *Critical Inquiry* 41:4 (Autumn 2014)

——, "Doing Justice to the Art in Photography," in Lopes, *The Four Arts of Photography*

——, "On the Very Idea of a 'Specific' Medium: Michael Fried and Stanley Cavell on Painting and Photography as Arts," *Critical Inquiry* 34:2 (Winter 2008)

——, "What's So New about the 'New' Theory of Photography?" *Journal of Aesthetics and Art Criticism* 75:4 (Fall 2017)

——, "What is Abstraction in Photography?", manuscript.

Costello, Diarmuid and Dominic McIver Lopes, "Spontaneity and Materiality: What Photography Is in the Photography of James Welling," unpublished manuscript

Costello, Diarmuid and Dawn M. Phillips, "Automatism, Causality and Realism: Foundational Problems in the Philosophy of Photography," *Philosophy Compass* 4:1 (2009)

Crump, James, "Ventriloquisms: The Art of James Welling," in Welling, *James Welling: Monograph*

Currie, Gregory, *Image and Mind: Film, Philosophy and Cognitive Science* (Cambridge: Cambridge University Press, 1995)

——, "Photography, Painting and Perception," *Journal of Aesthetics and Art Criticism* 49:1 (Winter 1991)

——, "Pictures of King Arthur: Photography and the Power of Narrative," in Walden, *Photography and Philosophy*

——, "Visible Traces: Documentary and the Contents of Photographs," *Journal of Aesthetics and Art Criticism* 57:3 (Summer 1999)

Daguerre, Louis-Jacques Mandé, "Daguerreotype," in Trachtenberg, *Classic Essays*

Davidson, Donald, *Essays on Actions and Events* (Oxford: Oxford University Press, 2001)

Davies, David, "How Photographs 'Signify': Cartier-Bresson's 'Reply' to Scruton," in Walden, *Photography and Philosophy*

——, "Scruton on the Inscrutability of Photographs," *British Journal of Aesthetics* 49:4 (October 2009)

Demachy, Robert, "On the Straight Print," in Hershberger, *Photographic Theory*

Dretske, Fred, "Abstract of Comments: Seeing through Pictures," *Noûs* 18:1 (1984)

——, *Knowledge and the Flow of Information* (Cambridge, MA: MIT Press, 1981)

Eastlake, Lady Elizabeth, "Photography," in Trachtenberg, *Classic Essays*

Emerson, Peter Henry, "The Death of Naturalistic Photography," in Hershberger, *Photographic Theory*

——, *Naturalistic Photography for Students of the Art*, 2nd, rev. edn. (London: Samson Low, Marston, Searle and Rivington, 1890)

——, "Photography, a Pictorial Art," in Newhall, *Photography: Essays and Images*

Evans, Frederick H. "On Pure Photography," in Newhall, *Photography: Essays and Images*

——, "What is a 'Straight' Print?" in Hershberger, *Photographic Theory*

Evans, Walker, "The Reappearance of Photography," in Trachtenberg, *Classic Essays*

Fox-Talbot, Henry, *The Pencil of Nature* (London: Longman, Brown, Green & Longmans, 1844)

——, "Some Account of the Art of Photogenic Drawing," in Newhall, *Photography: Essays and Images*

Freeland, Cynthia and Thomas Wartenberg (eds.), *Philosophy and Film* (New York: Routledge, 1995)

Friday, Jonathan, *Aesthetics and Photography* (Aldershot: Ashgate, 2002)

——, "André Bazin's Ontology of Photographic and Film Imagery," *Journal of Aesthetics and Art Criticism* 63:4 (Autumn 2005)

——, "Digital Imaging, Photographic Representation and Aesthetics," *Ends and Means* 1:2 (1997)

——, "Transparency and the Photographic Image," *British Journal of Aesthetics* 36:1 (January 1996)

Fried, Michael, *Why Photography Matters as Art as Never Before* (New Haven, CT: Yale University Press, 2008)

Friedlander, Lee, "An Excess of Fact," in *The Desert Seen* (New York: DAP, 1996)

Gaut, Berys, "Cinematic Art," *Journal of Aesthetics and Art Criticism* 60:4 (Autumn 2002)

——, *A Philosophy of Cinematic Art* (Cambridge: Cambridge University Press, 2010)

Goodman, Nelson, *Languages of Art* (Indianapolis: Hackett, 1976)

Hartmann, Carl Sadakichi, "A Plea for Straight Photography," in Newhall, *Photography: Essays and Images*

Hershberger, Andrew (ed.), *Photographic Theory: An Historical Anthology* (Oxford: Wiley-Blackwell, 2014)

Holmes, Oliver Wendell, "The Stereoscope and the Stereograph," in Trachtenberg, *Classic Essays*

Hopkins, Robert, "Factive Pictorial Experience: What's Special about Photographs?" *Noûs* 46:4 (2012)

——, "The Real Challenge of Photography (as a Communicative Representational Art)," *Journal of the American Philosophical Association* 1:2 (Summer 2015)

King, William, "Scruton and the Reasons for Looking at Photographs," *British Journal of Aesthetics* 32:3 (July 1992)

Kogan, Terry S., "The Enigma of Photography, Depiction and Copyright Originality," *Fordham Intellectual Property, Media and Entertainment Law Journal* 25:4 (2015)

Kracauer, Siegfried, "Photography," in *Theory of Film: The Redemption of Reality* (Oxford: Oxford University Press, 1960)

Kulvicki, John, *On Images: Their Structure and Content* (Oxford: Oxford University Press, 2006)

Lackey, Douglas P., "Reflections on Cavell's Ontology of Film," *Journal of Aesthetics and Art Criticism* 32:2 (Winter 1973)

Levinson, Jerrold (ed.), *The Oxford Handbook of Aesthetics* (Oxford: Oxford University Press, 2003)

Lopes, Dominic McIver, "The Aesthetics of Photographic Transparency," *Mind* 112 (July 2003)

——, "Afterword: Photography and the 'Picturesque Agent'," in Diarmuid Costello, Margaret Iversen, and Joel Snyder (eds.) "Agency and Automatism: Photography as Art since the 1960s," *Critical Inquiry* 38:4 (Summer 2012)

——, *The Four Arts of Photography: An Essay in Philosophy* (Oxford: Wiley-Blackwell, 2016)

——, "Jetz sind wir alle Künstler," in Julian Nida-Rümelin and Jakob Steinbrenner (eds.) *Fotographie: zwischen Inszenierung und Dokumentation* (Ostfinden: Hatje Cantz Verlag, 2012)

——, *Understanding Pictures* (Oxford: Oxford University Press, 2004)

Manovich, Lev, "Paradoxes of Digital Photography," in von Amelunxen, Iglhaut, and Rötzer, *Photography after Photography*

Marien, Mary Warner, *Photography: A Cultural History* (London: Lawrence King, 2002)

Martin, Edwin, "On Seeing Walton's Great-Grandfather," *Critical Inquiry* 12:4 (Summer 1986)

Maynard, Patrick, *The Engine of Visualization: Thinking through Photography* (Ithaca, NY: Cornell University Press, 1997)

——, "Photography," in Levinson, *The Oxford Handbook of Aesthetics*

——, "Talbot's Technologies: Photographic Depiction, Detection and Reproduction," *Journal of Aesthetics and Art Criticism* 47:3 (Summer 1989)

Mitchell, William J., *The Reconfigured Eye: Visual Truth in the Post-Photographic Era* (Cambridge, MA: MIT Press, 1994)

Moholy-Nagy, László, "Light: A Medium of Plastic Expression," *Broom: An International Magazine of the Arts* 4:4 (March 1923)

Mulhall, Stephen, *Stanley Cavell: Philosophy's Recounting of the Ordinary* (Oxford: Oxford University Press)

Nanay, Bence, "Transparency and Sensorimotor Contingencies: Do We See through Photographs?" *Pacific Philosophical Quarterly* 91:4 (2010)

Newhall, Beaumont (ed.), *Photography: Essays and Images* (London: Secker & Warburg, 1981)

Niépce, Joseph Nicéphore, "Memoire on the Heliograph," in Trachtenberg, *Classic Essays*

Phillips, Dawn M., "Photography and Causation: Responding to Scruton's Scepticism," *British Journal of Aesthetics* 49:4 (October 2009)

Richter, Gerhard, *The Daily Practice of Painting: Writings 1962–1993*, ed. Hans-Ulrich Obrist (London: Thames & Hudson, 1995)

Robinson, Henry Peach, *Elements of a Pictorial Photograph* (London: Percy Lund & Co., 1896)

——, *Pictorial Effect in Photography: Being Hints on Composition and Chiaroscuro for Photographers. To Which is Added a Chapter on Combination Printing* (London: Piper & Carter; Marion & Co., 1869)

Rubinfien, Leo, Erin O'Toole, and Sarah Greenough, *Garry Winogrand* (New Haven, CT: San Francisco Museum of Modern Art and Yale University Press, 2013)

Savedoff, Barbara, *Transforming Images: How Photography Complicates the Picture* (Ithaca, NY: Cornell University Press, 2000)

Scruton, Roger, "Photography and Representation," *Critical Inquiry* 7:3 (Spring 1981)

Snyder, Joel, "Picturing Vision," *Critical Inquiry* 6:3 (Spring 1980)

——, "What Happens by Itself in Photography," in Ted Cohen, Paul Guyer, and Hilary Putnam (eds.) *Pursuits of Reason: Essays in Honour of Stanley Cavell* (Lubbock: Texas Tech University Press, 1993)

Sontag, Susan, *On Photography* (New York: Farrar, Straus and Giroux, 1977)

Stieglitz, Alfred, "Pictorial Photography," in Newhall, *Photography: Essays and Images*

Strand, Paul, "Photography," in Trachtenberg, *Classic Essays*

——, "Photography and the New God," in Trachtenberg, *Classic Essays*

Szarkowski, John, *The Photographer's Eye* (New York: Museum of Modern Art, 2007)

Trachtenberg, Alan (ed.), *Classic Essays on Photography* (New Haven, CT: Leete's Island Books, 1980)

Walden, Scott, "Objectivity in Photography," *British Journal of Aesthetics* 45:3 (July 2005)

——, "Truth in Photography," in Walden, *Photography and Philosophy*

Walden, Scott (ed.), *Photography and Philosophy: Essays on the Pencil of Nature* (Oxford: Wiley-Blackwell, 2008)

Walton, Kendall, "Aesthetics—What? Why? and Wherefore?" *Journal of Aesthetics and Art Criticism* 65:2 (Spring 2007)

——, "Looking Again through Photographs: A Response to Edwin Martin," *Critical Inquiry* 12:4 (Summer 1986)

——, *Marvelous Images: On Values and the Arts* (Oxford: Oxford University Press, 2008)

——, "Meditations on a Hobby Horse," in *Marvelous Images*

——, *Mimesis as Make-Believe: On the Foundations of the Representational Arts* (Cambridge, MA: Harvard University Press, 1990)

——, "Postscripts to 'Transparent Pictures'," in *Marvelous Images*

——, "Transparent Pictures: On the Nature of Photographic Realism," *Critical Inquiry* 11:2 (December 1984)

Warburton, Nigel, "Individual Style in Photographic Art," *British Journal of Aesthetics* 36:4 (October 1996)

——, "Pixels and Pictorialism: A Reply to Jonathan Friday," *Ends and Means* 2:2 (1998)

——, "Seeing through 'Seeing through Photographs'," *Ratio* 1 (June 1988)

Welling, James, *James Welling: Monograph*, ed. James Crump (New York: Aperture, 2013)

Weston, Edward, "Random Notes on Photography," in Newhall, *Photography: Essays and Images*

——, "Seeing Photographically," in Trachtenberg, *Classic Essays*

Wicks, Robert, "Photography as a Representational Art," *British Journal of Aesthetics* 29:1 (January 1989)

Wiertz, Antoine-Joseph, "La Photographie," in Hershberger, *Photographic Theory*

Willis, Nathaniel Parker and Timothy O. Porter, "The Pencil of Nature: A New Discovery," in Hershberger, *Photographic Theory*

Wittgenstein, Ludwig, *Philosophical Investigations*, trans. G.E.M. Anscombe (Oxford: Blackwell, 1953)

Zeimbekis, John, "Digital Pictures, Sampling, and Vagueness: The Ontology of Digital Pictures," in Costello and Lopes, "The Media of Photography"

Index

Note: Page references in *italic* refer to Figures. Page references such as P1 refer to the Plates Section (e.g. P1 refers to Plate 1)

Abell, Catharine 125–126, 131–132
accidental photographs 60, 72
accuracy 14, 125, 127–128
Adams, Ansel 27, 31, 143
aesthetic interest 33, 53–54, 55, 56, 57, 66, 67, 68, 105
aesthetic principle, basic 31, 33, 36
aesthetic scepticism 31, 52–53, 66–67, 68
aesthetic value 2, 105, 121, 134, 141
allographic arts 142, 143–144
Aluminum Foil (Welling, 1980) 146–147, 149
America by Car series (Friedlander, 1995–2009) 62, 63
analogue photography 77, 90, 142, 143, 144
Arbus, Diane 61, 64
Archer, Frederick Scott 11
Atencia-Linares, Paloma 83, 84–85, 87
autographic arts 142–143, 144
automaticity 6, 9, 11, 38, 45–46
automatism 40, 41–42, 43–45, 46

basic aesthetic principle 31, 33, 36
Bazin, André 1, 13, 37–39, 40, 41, 42, 43, 44
belief-independent feature-tracking 87, 89, 93, 131, 132, 135, 142
belief-independent photographs 68, 84
Benjamin, Walter 1, 32
Brandt, Bill 130, *131*
burning 18, 31, 86

calotypes 11
camera obscura 10, 11, 79
cameras 21, 22, 27, 42, 77, 79, 113–114, 115, 127, 147
Cameron, Juliet Margaret 72
causal history 78, 87, 94, 142, 143–145
causality 55, 56–57, 59–60, 61, 75, 87
Cavell, Stanley 1, 42–43, 44
Choreograph (Welling, 2014–2016) 150
Cohen, Jonathan 122–123, 124–125, 131–132
combination prints 15, 17, 81, 83, 90; Minos Linea P7
composite prints 81
conceptual analysis 112
contact sheets 62, 63–64, 92
counterfactual dependence 108–109, 110, 119; natural 75, 85, 87, 142

Currie, Gregory 68, 69, 71, 72, 73, 74, 80, 107, 111

Daguerre, Louis-Jacques Mandé 11, 12
daguerreotypes 11, 13, 40
death masks 39, 41, 68, 110
Demachy, Robert 18, 19, 21–22, 23–24
digital images 88, 133, 144, 145, P5, P6
digital photography 19, 77, 88, 141–142, 143, 145
digital processing 77, 133, 142
direct seeing 66, 103, 114, 115
dodging 17, 18, 19, 27, 31, 86
Durham Cathedral 72–73

Eastlake, Elizabeth 12–13, 14–15, 17, 19, 27
egocentric information 106–107, 110, 122–123, 124
Eiffel Tower 79, 93, 106
Emerson, Peter Henry 15, 16, 17, 18, 19, 24
epistemic advantage 6–7, 102, 103, 104, 121–122, 124, 127
epistemic privilege 125, 131–132, 134
epistemic value 5, 105, 125, 132, 141; New Theory 104, 121, 132, 141; Orthodox Theory 125, 132
Evans, Frederick H. 19, 22, 23, 24
Evans, Walker 3
everyday wisdom *see* folk theory
experimental photographers 36–37
extensional adequacy 89, 93

factive pictorial experience 127, 128, 129, 130, 133
fairies photographs 56, 71
fictional competence 67–68, 69, 71, 74, 83–84, 85
fictional representation 53, 54, 56, 69, 73–74, 83–84
film 1, 32, 70, 71–72, 77, 80–81
fingerprints 39, 41, 68
Flowers (Welling, 2004–2007) 148–149
Flowers (Welling, 2014) 150
Fluid Dynamics (Welling, 2009–2012) 149
folk theory (everyday wisdom) 5, 7, 9, 39, 78, 83, 112, 121
footprints 41, 68, 110
Fox-Talbot, William Henry 11, 12
Frank, Robert 65
Friedlander, Lee 56, 61–62, 120–121, 125, 126, 129–130; *America by Car* series 62, 63; *Stems* series 117–118, *118*, *119*

Glass House series (Welling, 2006–2009) 147, 149
Goodman, Nelson 142, 143, 145
Griffith, Frances 71
gum prints 18

Hartmann, Sadakichi 24
Hopkins, Rob 127, 128, 129, 130, 131–132
Hurley, Frank 81, 82

ideal photographs 52–53, 55–56, 57, 60, 67–68, 79
image processes 75, 77–78, 87–89, 93; photographic processes 45, 74, 75–76, 79–80, 87–89, 135–136
images 2, 4, 6, 10, 11–14, 38, 64, 85–87, 124–125; *see also* digital images; photographs
imprinting 39–40, 41, 42
indirect seeing 66, 68, 103, 115
individuating photographs 89, 90, 92
intentionality 55, 59–64, 72–73, 84

King Kong 70
Kölner Dom 94, 95, 96
Kracauer, Siegfried 1, 32–33, 36–37

light images 10, 78, 79–80, 88–89, 94, 142
literature 143–144
Lopes, Dominic McIver 88, 89, 94–95, 96, 132, 133, 134; aesthetic interest 67; belief-independent feature-tracking 87, 131, 135; photographic style 64; seeing 66

Manet, Édouard 119–120, P3
Man Ray 32
manugraphs 124–125, 128, 132, 134, 135
Maynard, Patrick 6, 7, 69, 71, 75, 76–77, 88, 105
Meskin, Aaron 122–123, 124–125, 131–132
mind-independence 37, 38, 109, 116, 145, 146
Minos Linea, Jupiter's moon Europa P7
modernism 24–26, 33
Moholy-Nagy, László 32, 33, 34, 35
Mosse, Richard P6

narrative film 71–72
natural counterfactual dependency 75, 85, 87, 142
natural processes 41, 42, 46, 54–55
New Theory 6, 7, 31, 52, 68, 75, 83, 84, 92, 93, 150; belief-independent feature-tracking 132, 135; digital photography 141–142; epistemic value 104, 121, 132, 141; photographic agency 102–103, 146; photographic events 87, 90, 94, 145
Niépce, Joseph Nicéphore 11, 12

objectivity 6, 19, 25–26, 38, 135–136
Orthodox Theory (Orthodoxy) 5–7, 8, 9–10, 12, 30, 37, 44, 46, 52, 84, 130, 133, 150; aesthetic value 141; belief-independent feature-tracking 89, 132; digital photography 142; epistemic value 125, 132; photographic agency 145–146; photographic events 80–81, 83, 94, 121

paintings 4, 13, 60, 63, 64, 72–73, 84, 109, 116, 124, 144; aesthetic interest 53, 54; photographic events 94; and photographs 40, 57–59, 124, 125; and photography 19, 43, 45, 57–59, 87; photo-paintings 93; testimonies 68; transparency 55
perception 53, 67, 87, 107, 108–109
photogenic drawing 12
photograms 34, 35, 92, 148, 149, 150
photographers 22, 26, 36–37, 41, 45, 145–146
photographic agency 4, 7, 102–103, 141, 145–146
photographic art 4–5, 7, 23, 52, 102, 117, 121, 134, 141, 150; combination prints 16, 18, 81, 83, 90; fictional competence 67, 80; photographic depiction 103, 116; photographic representation 14
photographic depiction 6–7, 66, 67, 68–69, 71, 103, 121–122, 123, 124–127
photographic equipment 133; cameras 21, 22–23, 27, 42, 77, 79, 113–114, 115, 127, 147
photographic events 78, 80, 85, 87, 88, 89, 90; causal history 78, 87, 94, 145; digital photography 142; New Theory 87, 90, 94, 145; Orthodox Theory 80–81, 83, 94, 121; paintings 94
photographic expression 24
photographic pictures 103–104, 105

photographic practices 133–134, 135–136, 145–146
photographic processes 7, 8, 18–19, 21, 24, 30–32, 77–79, 85, 102–103, 127; history of 11–13; image processes 45, 74, 75–76, 79–80, 87–89, 135–136; mind-independence 6
photographic representation 14–15, 73, 94–96, 109–110, 127–128; by origin 71, 72, 73, 74, 80, 83; by use 71, 72, 73–74, 83
photographic style 64, 66
photographic technologies 6, 76, 87, 88, 133, 134
photographs 27, 30–31, 38–40, 41, 42, 45–46, 55–56, 69, 103, 145; aesthetic interest 67; history of 11–14; image processes 75, 77–78; and paintings 40, 57–59, 124, 125; photographic event 78, 85; seeing through 105, 108, 109, 110–111, 112–114, 116, 122; traces 68; transparency 66; *see also* images
photography 1–2, 4–8, 10, 25, 37–38, 145; history of 11–14; nature of 1, 5, 7, 8, 75, 121; and paintings 19, 43, 45, 57–59, 87; philosophy of 1, 2, 6, 8, 78, 116–117
photo-paintings 93
pictorial experience, factive 127, 128, 129, 130, 133
plastic arts 13, 37–38, 40
posthumous photographs 90, 92
pre-visualization 26–27, 30–31
prints 16, 18, 19, 81, 83, 90; straight 21, 22–23, 24, 52–53; *see also* ideal photographs
probabilistic correlations 123
pro-photographic scenes 95, 145, 146–147, 148
pure photography 4, 5, 10, 15, 18, 19, 23–24, 25, 52–53, 102; *see also* ideal photographs

realism 15, 32, 37, 40–42
real similarity relations 109–110
reliability 125, 126
representational art 43, 53, 54, 55, 57, 58, 66, 67
retouching 19
Richter, Gerhard 93, 94, P1, P2
Robinson, Henry Peach 15, 17, 81
Rodin, Auguste 143

scepticism 43, 44, 83
scored music 143, 144
Scruton, Roger 5, 6, 13, 57, 58, 64, 71, 74, 102; aesthetic interest 54, 56, 67, 68; ideal photographs 52–53, 55, 60, 79; intentionality 59–60, 61
seeing 42, 104, 107, 108–111, 113; directly 66, 103, 114, 115; indirectly 66, 68, 103, 115; through photographs 105, 108, 109, 110–111, 112–114, 116, 122
self-generated photographs 44, 59, 60
Snyder, Joel 44–45, 116
Sontag, Susan 1
standard photography *see* traditional photography
Steichen, Edward 18, 19
Stems series (Friedlander, 1994–1999) 117–118, 118, 119
Stieglitz, Alfred 6, 19, 20, 26
straight prints 21, 22–23, 24, 52–53; *see also* ideal photographs
Strand, Paul 25, 26–27, 28, 29
strictly photographic 77, 80, 85, 132, 134
studio construction 15
subjectivity 4, 21, 38, 43, 44

testimonies 68, 71, 109
Tillmans, Wolfgang 95, P4
traces 68, 71, 74, 109
traditional photography 127, 129, 133, 135
transparency 55, 66, 105, 110, 112–113, 114
"Transparent Pictures" (Walton, 1984) 103, 104, 105–106, 112, 113, 121

verbal descriptions 109, 110

Walden, Scott 122
Wall, Jeff P5
Walton, Kendall 5, 6, 52, 102, 104–105, 118–119, 121; seeing 103, 104, 107, 108, 110–111; seeing through photographs 105, 108, 112–113, 115; transparency 112–113, 114; "Transparent Pictures" 103, 104, 105–106, 112, 113, 121
Welling, James 146–150, P8, P9, P10, P11, P12; Aluminum Foil 146–147, 149; Choreograph 150; Flowers 148–149, 150; Fluid Dynamics 149; Glass House series 147, 149
Weston, Edward 25–27, 30–31
Wilson, Dawn 74, 75, 76–77, 78, 80, 88
Winogrand, Garry 90, 91, 92
Wright, Elsie 71